Advance Praise for *Performance Enablement* Book Endorsements

"*Performance Enablement* brilliantly evolves performance management with a research-driven model that goes beyond traditional approaches. These scientist-practitioners show how goals plus continuous development help employees thrive in today's dynamic workplace. Essential reading for HR professionals, managers, and scholars."

Gary P. Latham,
Fellow Royal Society of Canada

"Shifting from management to enablement changes the assumptions, actions, and impact of delivering performance. The eight Performance Enablement Principles and four key Performance Enablement practices that Edie and Alan identify and make user-friendly come from both experience and research and lead to a valuable paradigm shift."

Dave Ulrich, Rensis Likert Professor Emeritus,
University of Michigan; Partner, the RBL Group

"*Performance Enablement* explains why employers continue to struggle with managing employee performance and shows us how to rethink our simplistic mental models. The new path they plot is based on how employees actually think and behave and what our business goals actually are. It's the best model yet for fixing employee performance."

Peter Cappelli, George W. Taylor Professor of Management,
Director - Center for Human Resources,
The Wharton School, and Professor of Education,
University of Pennsylvania

"Traditional Performance Management approaches are sorely misaligned with the future of work. The traditional assumptions—that roles are static, that work equals full-time jobs, and that performance is easily quantifiable—have been rendered obsolete. Drs. Goldberg and Colquitt use their decades of experience to reimagine employee performance—from something to be "managed" or "evaluated," to something to be "enabled." They transform performance from a transactional compliance exercise into a dynamic process that builds direction, alignment, support, and progress."

Dr. John Boudreau, Emeritus Professor and
Senior Research Scientist, Center for Effective Organizations,
Marshall School of Business, University of Southern California

"In this important book, Colquitt and Goldberg challenge us to move beyond cosmetic reform and confront the mental models that have long kept organizations trapped in cycles of coercion and disengagement. Drawing on decades of research and hands-on experience, they offer a deeply human alternative: 'enabling control' rooted in purpose, autonomy, and genuine belonging. This is essential reading for anyone ready to leave behind the empty rituals of forced rankings and 'pay for performance,' and reimagine performance management as a source of meaning, growth, and shared accomplishment."

Otti Vogt, Founder,
Global Society for Good Leadership,
Former Chief Transformation Officer in ING

"As a former CHRO, I've witnessed firsthand how traditional performance management can sometimes destroy more value than it creates. This brilliant work exposes why our current systems fail and presents a compelling new model. Goldberg and Colquitt don't just critique—they provide practical solutions for the performance enablement transformation every organization needs."

Libby Sartain
Former CHRO (Yahoo, Southwest Airlines),
and Independent Director

"Finally, a book that makes sense of performance management. By reframing it as performance enablement, the authors provide a smarter, more humane, and more effective way to manage people and organizations."

Tomas Chamorro-Premuzic,
Professor of Business Psychology at UCL and
Former Chief Innovation Officer at ManpowerGroup

"Colquitt and Goldberg reimagine how organizations think about performance. Their concept of performance enablement replaces outdated systems with a practical, human-centered approach that helps people grow, contribute, and succeed together. A smart, timely guide for today's leaders."

Eva Sage-Gavin,
Board Director and former CHRO,
Gap Inc., Sun Microsystems

Performance Enablement

Performance Enablement

A New Model for Driving Organizational Performance

Edie Goldberg
Alan Colquitt

OXFORD
UNIVERSITY PRESS

OXFORD
UNIVERSITY PRESS

Oxford University Press is a department of the University of Oxford.
It furthers the University's objective of excellence in research, scholarship,
and education by publishing worldwide. Oxford is a registered trade mark of
Oxford University Press in the UK and in certain other countries.

Published in the United States of America by Oxford University Press
198 Madison Avenue, New York, NY 10016, United States of America.

CIP data is on file at the Library of Congress

ISBN 9780197830611

DOI: 10.1093/9780197830642.001.0001

Printed by Marquis Book Printing, Canada

The manufacturer's authorized representative in the EU for product safety is
Oxford University Press España S.A. of Parque Empresarial San Fernando de Henares,
Avenida de Castilla, 2 – 28830 Madrid (www.oup.es/en or product.safety@oup.com).
OUP España S.A. also acts as importer into Spain of products made by the manufacturer.

FSC www.fsc.org MIX Paper | Supporting responsible forestry FSC® C103567

Contents

Acknowledgements ix

1. **Introduction** 1
2. **Current State of Performance Management** 12
3. **The Purpose of Performance Management** 23

SECTION I. THE BUSINESS CASE FOR CHANGE

4. **The Changing Nature of Work** 35
5. **Implications of the Business Context for Performance Management Practice** 46
6. **Performance Enablement: The Right Model for Today's Business Needs** 57

SECTION II. PERFORMANCE ENABLEMENT PRINCIPLES

7. **Aligning to How Work Gets Done** 69
8. **A Focus on Being Supportive and Positive** 79
9. **Making It Simple and Continuous** 90

SECTION III. PERFORMANCE ENABLEMENT PRACTICES

10. **Make Goals Central** 107
11. **Create a Feedback Culture and Coaching for Future Performance** 121
12. **Focus on Development** 137

SECTION IV. EVALUATION, REWARDS, TECHNOLOGY, AND IMPLEMENTATION

13. **Performance Evaluation** 153
14. **The Performance Management–Reward Connection** 167

15. Technology and Innovations in Performance Enablement **180**

16. Effective Practices in Designing and Implementing Performance Enablement **190**

17. Flipping the Script from Performance Management to Performance Enablement **201**

Notes 213

Index 239

Acknowledgements

We want to begin by thanking Dana Bliss at Oxford University Press for believing in the importance of this book and supporting us through the process. We also want to thank Phoebe Aldridge-Turner, our Oxford Project Editor, for shepherding us through the process and for her flexibility as we worked through the inevitable issues that arise with a project like this.

This book would not exist if it were not for the critique and support of Gary Latham, Ph.D., Mark Sokol, and an anonymous reviewer who reviewed our book proposal. Our book is better because of their feedback, and we are deeply grateful to them for sharing their time and wisdom with us. But a special thanks goes to Gary for reviewing the entire final manuscript and making suggestions that fundamentally changed our book for the better.

A special thanks also goes to Suzan McDaniel, Ph.D., CHRO at Edward Jones; Shonna Waters at Fractional Insights; Lauren Doyle, Director of Talent Management at Adobe; Bhavya Gopalakrishnan, former Head of Human Capital at Arcesium; Gerry Ledford, Ph.D., Research Scientist at the Center for Effective Organizations; Dean Carter, former CHRO and Advisory Board member to multiple companies; David Futrell, Ph.D., former Senior Director of Organization Performance at Walmart; and Amy Steadman, CHRO at MidPen Housing for sharing their stories of research, innovation, and leadership with us.

But most of all, we would like to thank our spouses, John Carter and Dianne Colquitt, for their understanding when our days, evenings, and weekends of writing got in the way of important family time. Without their love, support, and encouragement, we could never have done this.

1 Introduction

Imagine a world where managers and employees are energized by performance conversations, not depleted by them. Imagine a performance management (PM) process that enables performance, instead of judging performance. Imagine a world where PM is seen as a tailwind in organizations, instead of a headwind. John Lennon and the Beatles imagined a world that was different in the 1971 song "Imagine." It wasn't easy then, and it's not easy now.

In this book, we will discuss where organizations, leaders, and HR professionals took a wrong turn with PM, and it's not where most people think. It's not about our practices, but our philosophy, principles, and paradigms. We will argue employee performance shouldn't be "managed" or "evaluated," it should be "enabled."

Modern Performance Management

In most companies, PM is an annual process with a series of meetings between the employee and the manager throughout the year (see Figure 1.1). It starts with a planning meeting at the beginning of the year where goals are set. Informal feedback typically occurs during the year, with formal reviews mid-year and at year end. Performance is evaluated at the end of the year and rewards (merit, bonus) are distributed based on that evaluation. There is very little variation across companies in this basic process.

It is important to note that we cannot talk about PM without talking about rewards. The connection between these two processes has been institutionalized since the 1980s. As we will show in the following chapters, PM has become primarily an administrative process to distribute rewards on the basis of performance ratings. In most companies, these processes are tightly connected.

Over 90% of companies have a "pay for performance" (P4P) philosophy and most tie pay to performance ratings to at least some extent. Seventy-seven

Performance Enablement. Edie Goldberg and Alan Colquitt, Oxford University Press. © Oxford University Press (2026).
DOI: 10.1093/9780197830642.003.0001

Figure 1.1 Traditional performance management process
Source: Authors

percent of companies tie salary increases to performance and 79% tie bonuses to performance.[1]

The Persistent Failure of Modern PM

Douglas McGregor summarized the state of PM nearly 70 years ago, and it's just as true today:

> I have sought to show that the conventional approach to performance appraisal stands condemned as a personnel method. It places the manager in the untenable position of judging the personal worth of his subordinates, and of acting on these judgments. No manager possesses, nor could he acquire, the skill necessary to carry out this responsibility effectively.[2]

Recent statistics tell a similar story. In a recent Gallup study, an overwhelming 95% of companies were dissatisfied with their process.[3] We surveyed 113 practitioners with primary responsibility for PM in their companies (more on our research later in this chapter). Only 7% reported that their PM process had achieved its goals and less than 20% said their process has led to stronger motivation, engagement, and performance. Fewer than one in four companies felt investments in PM were providing a suitable (High or Very High) return on investment in terms of engagement, motivation, and performance. Our findings aren't unique. The widespread dissatisfaction with PM has been well-documented.[4]

Employees' own voices from our own research tell the story candidly:

> Hunger Games is not a PM system.
>
> I just don't think that performance differences are measurable enough to take money from folks that were rated in the "Successful" [middle category]. It is killing innovation and teamwork! It is like sending in the Navy seals to kill Bin Laden, but the only one that gets recognized is the one that shot him.
>
> Our process forces us to choose whether you would like to cut off your right leg or your left arm. What kind of process has you make choices like this?

If PM was working well, organizations and employees should be happy with their reward processes tied to it. Unfortunately, this isn't the case either. Only 20% of companies believe merit pay drives higher performance and less than half believe bonuses drive high levels of performance.[5] A quote from this research report summarizes the state of P4P well:

> Our research shows these P4P tools (merit pay, incentives) are not effective at driving improved individual performance, nor at rewarding it.

A report from the Society for Human Resource Management (SHRM), the premier professional human resources association, expresses a similar sentiment:

> Despite embracing the concept of pay for performance, a surprisingly large number of employers say their programs aren't doing what they were designed to do: drive and reward individual performance.[6]

Despite these perceptions, organizations have no plans to get rid of PM or the reward processes tied to it. Only 6% of companies in one study said that they were likely to eliminate PM in their company.[7] This helps explain why most companies continue to make changes to their process every few years.

Seventy years of disappointing results haven't stopped efforts to improve it. The vast majority of companies have made changes or are planning changes to their PM process.[8] Researchers and practitioners have tried everything, from different rating scales, training managers, and connecting rewards to PM, to focusing on manager behaviors, providing more feedback, using Specific, Measurable, Achievable, Relevant, and Time-bound (SMART) goals and

Objectives, and Key Results (OKRs), and using technology to make the process more efficient. They continue to search for a combination of practices that work, and they continue to be disappointed by the results.

It is no mystery why we keep trying; it's a problem worth solving. This process is tied to many important HR processes including staffing, talent planning, promotion, succession planning, development planning, and career planning. Managers and employees also spend a lot of time on it. Managers spend an estimated 210 hours per year on performance management activities, and employees spend about 40 hours per year.[9] All of this time adds up to a substantial amount of salary costs. According to one survey, a large company with 10,000 employees could spend up to $35 million per year on PM activities.[10] We *need* to figure out how to make better use of this time and cost to the organization. Unfortunately, despite all the efforts, employees, managers, and organizations are as unhappy with this process as they have ever been.

PM Is a Wicked Problem

We argue that efforts to improve PM have failed because they don't match the complexity of the problem. PM is a "wicked problem" for organizations.

> A wicked problem is a "social or cultural problem that's difficult or impossible to solve"—normally because of its complex and interconnected nature. Wicked problems lack clarity in both their aims and solutions and are subject to real-world constraints which hinder risk-free attempts to find a solution.[11]

Examples of wicked problems include obesity, crime, homelessness, poverty, political instability, and climate change. PM seems to fit the definition. Scientists and practitioners have spent 70 years trying to improve it with little progress to show, and most organizations continue to look for solutions, either having recently made changes or planning in the near future. An author of a textbook on PM describes 23 different objectives for the process.[12] Traditional PM practices are deeply institutionalized in organizations; they are taken as a given. There is little motivation to make major changes since most have very similar PM systems. Could everyone be wrong? Moreover, employees themselves say they want the very PM practices they are so unhappy with, and that are so ineffective (performance ratings, P4P, and differentiation). Finally, there are strong forces working against significant change, like benchmarking, technology, and the integration of PM information into many other HR processes. We will discuss these forces in more detail in Chapter 2.

The depth and complexity of the problem, along with the presence of these forces working against change, help explain why we've made so little progress. Our persistent failure can also be traced to our approach to improving PM. Companies focus on changing practices instead of paradigms; they don't confront their fundamental beliefs and assumptions about how to motivate and drive high performance in organizations. Change experts Stewart Black and Hal Gregersen call this a "failure to see."[13] We are stuck in our 50-year-old institutional paradigms. Our problem isn't with rating scales, SMART goals, P4P plans, or with the other standard practices. Our problem is with the paradigms and principles behind these practices and the mental models of the people who design, implement, and control them. Leaders have their own assumptions and beliefs about what works and what doesn't based on their education, training, and experience. Leaders don't see alternatives to traditional PM because they are stuck in traditional paradigms. It is hard to see new possibilities when you are wearing traditional glasses. The alternatives we consider are all based on traditional PM thinking. Organizations need to start with their paradigms when embarking on an effort to change PM, but they rarely start here. Traditional PM paradigms are accepted as truths, so organizations jump right to practices, throwing out the old practices and trying new ones.

Compounding this problem is the penchant organizations have for what Chris Agyris and Donald Schon[14] call "single-loop learning," which involves the detection and correction of error. When something goes wrong, we try something different. If a three-category performance rating doesn't work, we try four or five categories. If a forced-distribution process doesn't work, we relax the requirements and provide "guidance" on the expected distribution and allow some exceptions. When faced with failure, we question our tactics; we don't question our thinking. Argyris and Schon argued we need "double-loop learning." When things don't work like we expect, we need to step back and examine the assumptions, beliefs, and values that underlie our practices. Instead of asking how many rating categories to use or if we should force a distribution across those categories, we need to ask if we should evaluate employee performance at all? Can we really measure performance well enough to tie big rewards to it? Instead of debating the right mix of variable pay elements, we need to ask if we should have variable pay at all.

We need a reset.

Introduction to Our Research

Despite our collective 60+ years of experience designing PM processes for various companies, we wanted to gather our own data to inform our thought process of what this new model for driving performance should look like. We sent a 71-question survey to 335 PM practitioners. Participants were hand-picked professionals who were responsible for PM within their organization (e.g., Performance Management Lead, Director of Talent Management, or Chief HR Officer). The average size of the organization was 7,500–10,000; over half of the participants came from companies with more than 10,000 employees.

Completed surveys were returned by 113 practitioners, for a 34% completion rate. Questions asked practitioners about their perceptions of their process, overall effectiveness, key design elements, the support of senior leadership, the implementation tactics used, and the culture of PM within their organization.

To help us identify the most effective practices, we selected 11 highly desirable outcomes as a measure of effectiveness:

1. Created a more performance-oriented culture (Yes/No)
2. Created a feedback culture (Yes/No)
3. Aligned goals throughout the organization (Yes/No)
4. We hold people accountable for results (Yes/No)
5. We achieved strong employee performance (Yes/No)
6. We motivated and engaged employees (Yes/No)
7. We achieved strong company performance/productivity (Yes/No)
8. Our process has achieved our intended goal (Yes, Somewhat, No)
9. Return on Investment (considering the time/money, resources, dollar value of rewards, vs. what the organization gains in terms of engagement, motivation, and performance) (Very High to Very Low, on a 5-point scale)
10. How good of a job the organization does in recognizing and rewarding high performance (5-point scale, Excellent to Poor)
11. How good of a job the organization does in taking quick action with poor performers (5-point scale, Excellent to Poor)

A composite score was created (scaled from a low of one to a high of five) across these items and we formed three groups based on the composite score in terms of their relative effectiveness (low, medium, or high). We then reviewed practices by group to discover the practices that differentiated these three groups. These findings, which are shared throughout the book, informed our ideas about new assumptions and beliefs about how to drive performance in an organization.[15]

A New Model—Performance Enablement

Our new model has a different starting point from most models (see Figure 1.2). It is grounded in different theories, assumptions, and beliefs. The idea that the performance of employees needs to be "managed" harkens back to antiquated theories from the industrial era and assumptions and beliefs about control, e.g., Taylorism and Theory X, that employees are lazy and unmotivated, and organizations need processes to "motivate" them. We begin with the assertion that PM is a governance or management process—part of an organization's control system. It helps the organization translate strategy and organizational priorities into individual priorities. It provides direction for employees, aligning their efforts to the goals and objectives of the company. It ensures the right things get attention and the wrong things don't. In the research on management control, two approaches dominate: Coercive Control and Enabling Control. We discuss these approaches in detail in Chapter 3. Suffice to say here that coercive control approaches are based on securing *compliance*, while enabling control approaches are based on securing *commitment*. Traditional PM processes are based on coercive control. Our new model is based on enabling control. We will discuss this model in more depth in Chapter 6.

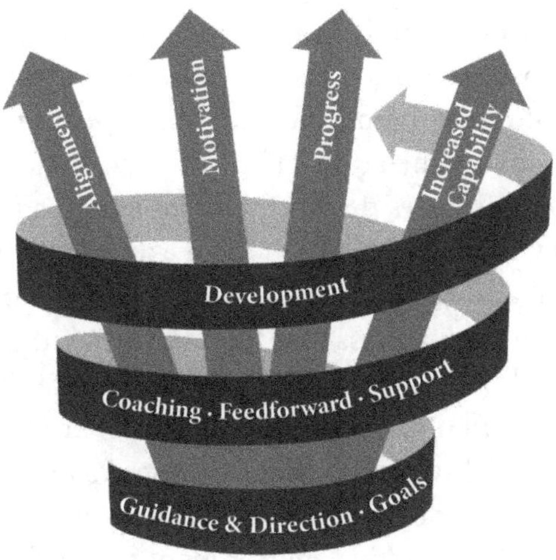

Figure 1.2 Performance Enablement model
Source: Authors

The foundation of Performance Enablement is setting the context—providing guidance and direction on what is most important for the company and *why* it is important. *Why* is especially important as it sets the context for purpose—to what ends are employees working? With this information, individuals and teams can set challenging yet attainable goals.

To achieve these goals, managers enable performance through coaching, feedback, and other types of support including providing information and removing obstacles to success. This coaching activity is a critical and often missing piece. In Chapter 11, we will discuss the idea of feedforward vs. feedback—an important concept for supporting and developing employees.

The final element in the model is development, which is an ongoing effort to develop the skills, careers, and experiences of workers. This is an important part of the model because organizations improve and sustain long-term performance by developing their people. Through an ongoing process of guidance and goal-setting, coaching, and development, teams and individuals perform better, make more progress, and enjoy greater satisfaction. Finally, these actions build on themselves and create an upward spiral of motivation and performance. Context, support, and development build capability, confidence, and self-efficacy, resources that continue to accumulate and enable even stronger performance and satisfaction.

Overview of the Book

The book begins with an examination of current practices and how science has discredited many of the underlying principles driving practice today. We will ask the reader to question the true purpose behind why we conduct performance reviews and urge them to consider that the ultimate goal should be to drive individual and organizational performance. In fact, our own research shows that while practitioners design their PM systems for one purpose (to P4P), they know that it should be designed for a different purpose (to improve and drive individual and organizational performance). Following this introspection, we dive into the business case for change based on how the world of work is changing and the implications this has for paradigms and practices. We wrap the first section of the book by going deeper into our Performance Enablement (PE) Model, which delivers on the goal of improving individual and organizational performance by providing direction and alignment, creating a positive and supportive environment that is focused on goals and individual development.

The next section of the book introduces the eight PE Principles. These principles provide a foundation for how companies should be operating to enable performance in today's business context. These eight principles are broken into three chapters: Aligning How Work Gets Done, focusing on the principles of High Context, Team-Based, and Agile; Being Supportive and Positive for Employees, focusing on the principles of Positive, Enabling, and Progress-Oriented; and Making the Process Simple and Continuous, focusing on the final principles of making PE Simple and Continuous.

The next section will focus on the four key PE practices: Make Goals Central, Create a Feedback Culture, Coach for Future Performance, and Focus on Development. These four practices are designed to help practitioners focus on what is important. What makes this book unique is that we will be sharing evidence-based principles and practices that reinforce our model for PE. We need to use rigorous scientific evidence to inform our decisions about PE. Experts call this evidence-based practice (EBP). EBP is concerned with making decisions about practices by integrating the best available evidence from research. In this case, "research" means more than finding out what other people do; it means the systematic collection of data through observation and experimentation and the formulation of questions and testing of hypotheses. Our goal is to synthesize the research that is available and make it more accessible to the typical manager or HR professional who may not be exposed to scientific research.

We will share research from various disciplines that illustrate why the old principles and practices of traditional PM are not supported and how the new principles and practices of PE are supported by research. We will also bring these principles and practices to life by sharing modern examples of case studies demonstrating how cutting-edge companies are leaning into PE.

In the final section of the book, we discuss the practical steps needed to implement these new principles and practices. We begin with a critical look at why PM has largely been concerned with performance evaluation, and why this does not serve the purpose of PE. In our experience, the first question companies ask about when reducing the focus on ratings (or eliminating ratings altogether) is "How will we reward our employees if we don't rate them?" We share contemporary practices of how companies can think about rewards in this new practice.

As we continue our focus on implementation, we dive deep into new technological advancements (e.g., generative AI, nudge technology, automation, and organizational network analysis) that are propelling PE forward.

Next, we share our experience regarding the critical implementation practices that truly drive change. Without following good change management practices, a practitioner's success will be limited. We close the book with a tool to help companies assess where they are on the continuum from traditional PM to PE. This chapter will provide some guidance for practitioners on how to "flip the script" on the process.

To summarize, we are trapped by our past and our paradigms. Our discussions of improving this process are constrained by a view of PM that has been institutionalized over the past 50 years as a way of managing and distributing rewards. It is about "managing performance" which means we are telling our employees what to do, managing a distribution of performance ratings, and managing a merit and bonus budget. It has become an administrative task. We don't believe "managing performance" is what drives individual and organizational performance. We should be focused on how we can enable, support, sustain, and improve the performance of employees and the organization. Read on and imagine a new positive paradigm that enables individuals and teams to grow and develop, which motivates performance by tapping into one's inner desire to make an impact and deliver results that no one believed was possible.

Key Takeaways

- Performance Management (PM) Needs a Paradigm Shift: The failure of PM is not due to flawed practices but outdated philosophies and paradigms. Instead of "managing" or "evaluating" performance, organizations should focus on enabling performance.
- Modern PM Is Largely Ineffective: Despite widespread use, PM systems are failing, and few believe they improve motivation, engagement, or performance.
- The Connection Between PM and Rewards Is Problematic: PM has become a mechanism for distributing rewards (bonuses or merit pay) rather than driving performance. Research shows that pay-for-performance (P4P) is not effective at driving performance, yet it remains deeply entrenched.
- PM Is a "Wicked Problem": PM is a complex, deeply institutionalized process resistant to change, with strong forces making meaningful reform difficult.

- Organizations Change Practices, Not Paradigms: Companies continually tweak PM processes but fail to challenge the underlying assumptions about how performance management should be designed.
- A Reset Is Needed: The book calls for a fundamental rethinking of PM, starting with questioning long-held assumptions and shifting toward an approach that truly supports employee and organizational success.

2

Current State of Performance Management

As we discussed in Chapter 1, despite decades of efforts to improve performance management (PM), it remains a poor-performing HR process, and yet few have plans to get rid of it.[1] Organizations feel it is important to their business.[2] It touches nearly every employee and manager, and it significantly affects the work lives and careers of most employees through the ratings it produces. It assists in distributing an estimated $345 billion in merit and bonus budgets each year, in the United States alone.[3] Overall, the investment companies make in PM and the rewards processes tied to it can be staggering.

The History of Performance Management

If you want to transform something, you need to understand it. The foundations of PM go back over a hundred years. Several major influences have shaped contemporary PM practices.[4] The first influence from the early twentieth century came from performance appraisal. Performance appraisal aimed to measure job performance so companies could improve promotion decisions. Historically, promotion decisions were based on familial ties, relationships, or seniority. More concrete performance measures were needed to improve the fairness of these decisions. Early performance appraisal systems included ratings of employees on traits such as judgment, integrity, and attitude. These types of ratings are still ubiquitous in contemporary PM systems.[5]

The second influence was Management by Objectives (MBO), which emerged in the late 1950s and early 1960s and attacked the inhumane rating of employees in performance appraisals.[6] With MBO, the focus moved from rating traits to setting and measuring objectives. Employees have objectives with quantitative targets, and progress is measured against these targets. This practice was seen as more objective and fair. Objectives and targets had the added benefit of aligning employee efforts with company objectives and direction. The influence of MBO on PM today is still strong. More than 90 percent of the companies we surveyed had a goal-setting process that

Performance Enablement. Edie Goldberg and Alan Colquitt, Oxford University Press. © Oxford University Press (2026).
DOI: 10.1093/9780197830642.003.0002

translates company and organizational objectives into individual objectives and assesses progress against them.[7]

To this point, performance reviews were predominantly one-way conversations. Norman R. F. Maier describes this conversation as "tell and sell," where the manager does most of the talking and passes their judgment onto the employee.[8] He also discussed a second style, "tell and listen," where managers share their feedback and then listen to the employees' reactions, responding to those reactions. Our experience suggests this style is probably the most prevalent today. Interestingly, his third style, the "problem solving interview," anticipated the move toward performance enablement. In this style, the employee and manager engage in a two-way dialogue about what is working and what is not working. Unfortunately, this approach never became popular, likely due to the rise of pay for performance, which we mention below and discuss in more detail in Chapter 14.

A third influence came in the 1980s when several new elements were introduced to address problems with performance appraisals and MBO.[9] Performance management processes became more forward-looking, planning future performance versus measuring past performance. They also distinguished what outputs and results are expected (the WHATs) from the behaviors expected when delivering results (the HOWs). Newer PM processes also introduced a development planning process separate from the performance review. Finally, as employment law changed in the United States in the 1960s and 1970s, the legal defensibility of decisions tied to PM processes became an important consideration. As a result, documentation became important, which led to longer PM forms, more detailed documentation, and formal signatures on forms.

Finally, perhaps the most important influence on contemporary PM systems came with the connection of PM to reward processes. These links became more explicit as pay-for-performance (P4P) philosophies became popular in the 1980s.[10] We will discuss this development in more detail in Chapter 14. All of these changes have been cumulative; most PM processes today retain many, if not all, of these historical features, making them cumbersome, complex, and unwieldy.

Paradigms and Mental Models

History provides helpful context for understanding contemporary PM processes. They are tasked with accomplishing multiple objectives, and they have many different stakeholders, each with potentially conflicting expectations.

It's no wonder they perform poorly. A deeper understanding of the principles behind the design of contemporary PM processes can also explain this poor performance.

Management scholar Henry Mintzberg explained the problem we face with PM in his book "The Rise and Fall of Strategic Planning":[11]

> Every manager has a mental model of the world in which he or she acts based on experience and knowledge. When a manager must decide, they think of alternatives within their mental model.

He worked with managers at Shell Oil Company to shift their perspectives on important issues, altering their mental models, mindsets, and worldviews by enabling them to become more explicit about their key assumptions. He writes about their breakthroughs, quoting the managers themselves:

> From the moment of this realization, we no longer saw our task as producing a documented view of the future business environment 5–10 years ahead. Our real target was the mental models of our decision makers.

As we discussed in Chapter 1, we face a similar problem with PM. Our problem isn't with PM practices but with the paradigms behind these practices and the mental models of the people who design, implement, and control them. In our search for why PM hasn't fundamentally changed despite 50 years of research critical of its practices and despite persistent calls for change, we landed squarely at the feet of these paradigms as a chief cause.

As Mintzberg learned, the problem with paradigms is that they rarely get examined. When people get together to fix PM, they talk about practices, not paradigms. The foundational paradigms behind traditional PM processes have their roots in a handful of theories from economics and psychology. These theories and their principles have dominated the education and training of leaders and HR professionals and strongly influenced how they design and implement PM processes. Anyone wishing to transform PM needs to understand these foundations and will ultimately need to replace them with more contemporary paradigms.

Economic Foundations of PM

The primary influences on contemporary PM processes are from classical economics and labor economics. Classical economic assumptions and beliefs are familiar to us: People are rational, self-interested, motivated by money, and strive to maximize their gains and minimize their losses.[12] These assumptions lead organizations to emphasize reward systems to motivate employees. However, the impact of standard economic principles on PM goes beyond a focus on financial rewards. People are *self*-interested; they look at their *own* costs and benefits. Organizations design reward systems that prioritize rewarding *individuals* for their efforts (versus the efforts of teams or the organization as a whole). These theories caution us against making rewards contingent on group or organizational performance, believing that self-interested, utility-maximizing individuals will reduce their efforts and "free-ride" on the group's efforts. Finally, standard economic principles also assume that people are rational and behave in ways that maximize their individual outcomes.

Labor Economics has also had a major influence on traditional PM practices. Agency Theory (as it applies to PM) involves a principal (a company) delegating work to an agent (an employee), who performs the work.[13] Principals and agents need to cooperate so that each of them gets what they want. Agency Theory describes the relationship between these two parties using the metaphor of a contract, and there are assumed to be inherent problems with this relationship:

- Agents are assumed to be self-interested; their goals will not be aligned with the goals of the principal. As a result, other mechanisms are needed to achieve this alignment (e.g., rewards, incentives, monitoring, threats, and fear of being fired).
- Principals are assumed to have difficulty verifying whether the agent is upholding their part of the bargain. This means employees could slack off and do poor work, and the principal wouldn't know. This creates costs and risks for principals, reinforcing the need for regular monitoring and surveillance of agents.

The solution to these problems is presumed to be good contracting between the principal and agent and effective performance monitoring. Agency Theory's influence on PM shows up in several ways. First, there is a heavy emphasis on individual rewards and incentives to align employee goals and efforts with company goals. Second, feedback in an agency relationship is primarily about monitoring employees to ensure they aren't doing things that maximize their own utility at the expense of organizational goals. Third, Agency Theory sees goal setting as a process to spell out the terms of a contract and specify the reward contingencies for the successful (or unsuccessful) fulfillment of the contract.

Agency Theory also epitomizes the "tenor" of contemporary PM practices. It uses terms like "moral hazard," "conflict of interest," and "agency costs" to describe the relationship between employee and company. The relationship is assumed to be adversarial with an embedded structural tension, especially from the company's perspective: "Employees don't share my goals" (conflict of interest); "I bear all the risks and incur all the costs of employee misbehavior" (moral hazard); and "I incur the costs of preventing employee misbehavior" (need for monitoring and surveillance).

Tournament Theory is another Labor Economics theory with a strong influence on PM.[14] Tournament Theory was developed to explain flaws in classical economic thinking, such as when differences in wages don't reflect productivity differences or where pay is not proportional to one's skills, abilities, experience, or qualifications. For example, imagine a golf tournament with one hundred participants where the winner receives $1,000,000 and the last-place finisher receives $1,000. Is the winner 1,000 times better than the last-place finisher? Probably not. Tournament Theory suggests that in some cases, performance is judged relatively, not based on some objective evaluation.

An important premise of Tournament Theory is that a certain amount of wages from employees at a given level is withheld and given to employees at higher levels. In a golf tournament, for example, the lower finishers give up prize money to the higher finishers to motivate players. In organizations, for example, the salaries of vice presidents are high in part to motivate those in the lower ranks to work hard to become vice presidents in the future and to motivate current vice presidents to work hard to keep their high salaries. The theory holds that employees compete in "tournaments," with the prizes being promotions, top rewards, or top prizes (e.g., in a sales contest). Tournament Theory has several important implications for PM. First, ratings and relative comparisons are essential, so employees know where they stand. Second, competition among employees and transparent feedback on their standing and performance are important elements of motivation. Finally, differentiation of rewards among employees is important—more differentiation translates into higher motivation and performance levels.

Psychological Foundations of PM

Three theories have heavily influenced PM practices: Behaviorism and Reinforcement Theory, Expectancy Theory, and Control Theory. Thorndike's law of effect in Reinforcement Theory holds that responses that are followed by satisfying outcomes become more likely to occur, and responses that are followed by unsatisfying outcomes will be weakened.[15] Similarly, Operant Conditioning, popularized by B. F. Skinner, holds that individual behavior may change in form, frequency, or strength as a function of the consequences of the behavior.[16] These theories have two important implications for PM. First, behavior is externally mediated. Behavior and actions are driven by external consequences (not by internal desires, motives, or goals). Second, if you want to change behavior, modify the consequences of that behavior (rewards, punishments). These theories have been applied in organizations for decades to motivate and control employee behavior, primarily through feedback and rewards, incentives, recognition, threats, and punishments.

Expectancy Theory views motivation as a function of two factors: (1) expectancy—a person must see their efforts lead to successful performance; and (2) instrumentality—successful performance must lead to outcomes employees value.[17] Expectancy Theory has influenced PM in three important ways. First, motivation is seen primarily as an individual phenomenon—individual outcomes should be based on individual performance. Second, it further reinforces that external contingencies matter; effort and behavior are a function of what happens after that behavior, which puts a premium on extrinsic rewards. Finally, while Expectancy Theory allows for various outcomes to be rewarding for employees, much of the attention is focused on financial outcomes.

Finally, Control Theory has influenced PM practices primarily in the area of feedback.[18] According to Control Theory, feedback is essential to resolving discrepancies between a goal or target (e.g., the speed set on a car's cruise control) and the system's actual performance (e.g., the car's actual speed). When a discrepancy is noted (the car is going faster or slower than the target speed), the appropriate action is taken (engage or disengage the engine). An important implication of control theory for PM is that feedback is primarily focused on gaps—discrepancies between demonstrated performance and expected or target performance. Feedback happens when employees get "off course," so negative feedback is emphasized. Many of the associations we have with feedback are negative, for example, the feedback in a sound system (when an open microphone is too close to a speaker).

From these foundational theories, we can summarize the assumptions, beliefs, and principles that form the foundation for contemporary PM practices:

General

- The relationship between a company and an employee is adversarial, with inherent structural problems, conflicts, and risks that need to be mitigated.

- The relationship between a company and an employee is contractual.
- Motivation is externally mediated.

Planning

- Alignment of employees with company priorities is externally mediated by contracts, contingencies, consequences, and threats.
- Goals are contracts that specify what needs to be done by when.
- Goals have instrumental value. They are important only insofar as rewards and outcomes are tied to them. They specify what accomplishments will be rewarded.

Feedback

- Monitoring and surveillance are necessary to hold employees accountable and ensure they are fulfilling the terms of the contract.
- Feedback is primarily negative, correcting employees when they get off track.

Evaluation

- Ratings and rankings motivate.
- Competition and relativity are essential for motivation.
- Performance can be evaluated reliably and validly by managers.

Rewards

- Money motivates.
- Behavior and performance are best controlled by external reward contingencies.
- Rewards need to be contingent upon individual performance to motivate.
- More differentiation in performance and rewards is better for motivation.

We argue that these assumptions and beliefs represent the biggest barrier to change for PM. The mental model they create blinds leaders and HR professionals from envisioning different alternatives.

It's also clear from research that these assumptions and beliefs are outdated. As we will show in Chapters 4 and 5, organizations, jobs, and employees have changed in response to seismic shifts in the environments many organizations face. We will argue that many traditional HR processes and practices need to change accordingly, and changes in PM have not kept pace with these changes. And scientific research has been critical of these theories for decades. Two revolutions dramatically changed how behavioral scientists viewed the topics of motivation and performance.

The cognitive revolution of the 1950s would significantly weaken behaviorism and reinforcement theory as the dominant explanatory theory of behavior. Pioneering scientists began to dispute the principle that behavior was solely a function of its consequences.[19] Leading researchers began using new terms like tasks, intentions, motives, and needs to explain behaviors that never extinguished long after the reinforcements were gone, and activities that people engaged in apparently because of their own intrinsic interest. Tasks were seen as the causal explanations of most behavior, not reinforcements. By the 1960s, psychologists like Edwin Locke were studying conscious factors like intentions, goals, or purposes in task performance, and motivational theories like goal setting were born.[20]

Twenty years after the cognitive revolution, the behavioral economics revolution was beginning. Richard Thaler observed that people ascribe more value to things they own, merely because they own them. People who own a coffee mug require twice the price to sell it than they would pay to acquire it. This is not rational. The mug has a fixed value, and the minimal acceptable buying and selling price should be the same. Owning it should not change its value. Thaler called this effect the "endowment effect."[21] At this same time, Herbert Simon was questioning the idea of the "rational man." He suggested that our minds must be understood relative to the environment in which they evolved.[22] Decisions are not always optimal. There are limits to a human's knowledge and their ability to process information, and as a result, they make bad decisions. He called this "bounded rationality." Finally, research by Amos Tversky and Daniel Kahneman at Stanford in the late 1970s and 1980s was also chipping away at the credibility of classical economics.[23] They developed prospect theory, which shows decisions are not always optimal and our choices are influenced by the way they are framed—by their context. The work of these early pioneers would converge in a new discipline—behavioral economics—which would explain the failures of classical economics.

Despite these two revolutions, traditional economic and psychological principles remain the foundation of how leaders today are trained to motivate their employees and manage their behavior and performance. These principles are still at the core of many of our human resources practices, including PM. A deeper understanding of these principles and how they shape our thinking is an essential starting point for any PM change effort.

Barriers to Change

The durability of traditional paradigms and a "failure to see" goes a long way toward explaining why little progress has been made in improving PM. However, another compelling reason why companies don't change is what is known as "A failure to move."[24] Many organizations realize their PM processes are deficient, but they don't take the action necessary to improve. Several factors explain why.

Benchmarking

The use of benchmarking surveys by consulting firms and HR think tanks has exploded over the past two decades.[25] These surveys purport to identify "best practices." However, this work confuses *best* practices with *common* practices. An excessive focus on benchmarking to guide organizations pushes organizations toward modal practices ... "if a practice is popular, it must be right." But it's not always clear why firms adopt certain practices; did they adopt them because they are effective or because other companies adopted them? Benchmarking has had another, more subtle effect on the discussion around HR practices. Benchmarking reports are seen and marketed as "research." Many companies base their actions on this information and believe their actions are "research based."

> We need to differentiate benchmarking research (what companies do) from research based on theory, hypotheses, and rigorous experimentation and control (what companies do that works).

The evidence-based management movement argues that we should adopt practices based on evidence (research) that they are effective.[26] The standard for "evidence" is getting weaker.

Institutional Envy

When notable, successful companies adopt certain practices, especially when those companies and practices are widely publicized, other companies flock to them (e.g., GE and forced distributions in the 1990s). They adopt these practices regardless of whether they make sense for their company or whether those practices contributed to that company's success.

Institutionalization

The traditional approach to PM is deeply embedded in organizations. It is hard to change something so common and so institutionalized as "best practice" in organizations. When something is institutionalized, other companies adopt it to attain legitimacy.[27] One of the authors experienced the power of this firsthand at a PM conference several years ago. An attendee at the conference was from a well-respected regional hospital system. They had no formal PM process, nor did they have individual merit pay or bonuses or a P4P philosophy. At the same time, they were very successful, had no difficulty attracting top regional talent, employees were generally happy, and turnover was low. It wasn't clear to the author why the company would risk its success by introducing modern PM practices, given their poor track record of success. The answer was institutionalization ... legitimate companies implemented these practices, so they needed to as well.

Fatalism and Rationalization

Another reason for the lack of meaningful change in PM is the fatalism and rationalization that comes from decades of trying and failing to improve it. We have heard these rationalizations firsthand in our own PM work:

> All PM processes have problems; you simply pick your problems. No process will please everyone; there will always be noise. Every few years companies trade one set of problems for another.
>
> Good medicine tastes bad. An effective PM system tells employees what they don't want to hear, and they won't always like it. Unhappy employees is unavoidable.
>
> Not everyone can get a trophy. Some people come out on top, and some don't. That's life.

Sentiments like these are discussion-killers when discussing PM reform.

Technology

The proliferation of big Human Capital technology applications in organizations makes these processes difficult to change. We will have more to say about these applications in Chapter 15. These applications are designed around standard (common) practices. It can be costly and difficult to make significant changes to PM because this means reconfiguring the software. Sometimes, change can't be made, and if workarounds can be created, they may not survive future releases of the software.

These forces, when combined, are formidable, and overcoming them to make significant changes to PM won't be easy.

Key Takeaways

- PM has been studied and written about for more than fifty years, and yet most stakeholders see it as ineffective.
- Despite its ineffectiveness, companies have no plans to abandon it.
- The root cause of problems with PM is flawed paradigms and mental models, which rarely get examined.
- The paradigms and mental models behind PM are outdated. Their roots are in classic theories from psychology and economics that have long since been discredited as sufficient explanations of complex behavior in organizations. The cognitive revolution in psychology and behavioral economics has provided more contemporary explanations for work behavior.
- Companies rely on external benchmarking to guide them, and this causes them to focus on common practices instead of effective practices.
- Common practices become institutionalized, and companies imitate them to achieve legitimacy. This leads to a homogenization of practices and makes practices difficult to change.

3

The Purpose of Performance Management

Any effort to transform performance management (PM) needs to start with a discussion of purpose. Researchers discuss several purposes, ranging from strategic, organizational, and administrative purposes to communication and development.[1] However, those living and working in organizations experience a much more singular purpose. In our survey of PM professionals, when asked the purpose of their current PM process, "evaluating employees to pay for performance" was the most frequent answer by a large margin.[2] Others have reached similar conclusions.[3] PM has evolved to serve a more administrative process to allocate rewards, a key part of a company's pay-for-performance (P4P) philosophy. This purpose is deeply institutionalized in organizations. Quotes below from two widely read articles illustrate this bias:

> Performance is the value of employees' contributions to the organization over time. And that value needs to be assessed in some way. Decisions about pay and promotions have to be made.[4]

> ... you really do need some form of a documented administrative evaluation of the year to make any employment decisions, or you treat everyone exactly the same. This is just a basic legalese version of 'you need something.'[5]

Others have argued similarly.[6] In fact, editors of a journal recently sent out an email asking researchers to submit papers to a special issue devoted to the subject of PM. An entire issue of a journal was to be dedicated to this topic, reflecting the best thinking available on the topic. In their communication to prospective contributors, the editors lamented the noise in the popular business press about stories of companies getting rid of their PM process or of getting rid of performance ratings and evaluations. The editors then weighed in with their views (and bias), reflecting this same institutionalized purpose:

> The fact remains that as long as there are individuals performing some kind of work in organizations, there will be a need for some manner of performance management in order to evaluate, compensate, and reward those individuals.

Performance Enablement. Edie Goldberg and Alan Colquitt, Oxford University Press. © Oxford University Press (2026).
DOI: 10.1093/9780197830642.003.0003

We find the durability of this purpose surprising, given the overwhelming evidence that PM has failed to deliver on it. We will discuss evidence of this failure in Chapters 13 and 14. The problem with this institutionalized purpose is it limits our consideration of alternatives. As we will discuss, the origins of this purpose cast doubts on its logic, legitimacy, and value.

PM and Rewards: The Rise of Pay for Performance

As is the case with PM in general, the principles behind P4P are grounded in the same familiar theories. Stimulus–response psychology (the law of effect and operant conditioning) and classical economics formed the foundation of early evaluation and reward practices. They were the basis for Fredrick Taylor's scientific management approach, for example, the precursor to modern management and reward practices. However, two developments in the late 1980s and early 1990s would significantly tighten the connection between PM and reward processes.

The first was the emergence of agency theory, which we discussed in Chapter 2. This theory dramatically increased the focus on incentives in organizations. A second set of developments significantly increased the popularity of incentives. In 1993, US tax laws eliminated the deductibility of executive compensation in excess of one million dollars, unless it qualified as "performance-based."[7] The use of performance-based incentives (primarily in the form of stock options) exploded after this legislation was enacted. The percentage of executive compensation contingent on stock price increased from 10% in the 1990s to 70% by 2003.[8] Today, variable pay makes up nearly 90% of executive pay in many organizations, and the practice has cascaded through organizations.[9] Since the 1980s, variable pay has become more popular at all levels of organizations, increasing from just 3% of pay in the 1980s to 13% or more today (and the increase has been much higher at higher levels), and the percentage of employees eligible for variable pay has increased steadily.[10] Most organizations today link P4P for the majority of their employees.[11]

The increasing popularity of P4P put pressure on the "performance" part of the equation. For most jobs, especially managerial and knowledge work jobs, there are few good objective measures of performance on which to base rewards. PM provided a solution in the form of manager ratings of job performance. PM began to evolve in now familiar ways to align with this purpose. When reward and reward differentiation are the goals, PM must not only *measure* performance, it must also *differentiate* it. Forced ranking and forced distribution practices emerged at this time, popularized by Jack Welch at

General Electric. Many organizations still use this practice today.[12] Reward budgets also became a central concern. Budgets are set at the beginning of the year and can't be overspent. Oversight is necessary to ensure that rating targets based on these budgets are hit and appropriate standards are being followed. This led to the emergence of calibration processes, which are still very popular in organizations.[13] Performance differentiation requires performance *evaluation*, which means ratings remain a central and indispensable element of PM.[14] And finally, when rewards, evaluation, and differentiation are the goals, PM plans and objectives function as contracts, requiring specificity and detail, with metrics, targets, and documentation to support and defend decisions based on them.[15] PM became a zero-sum game, driving employee inequality and competition for top ratings and rewards.[16]

With the benefit of hindsight and 40 years of research, we can judge the legitimacy and value of this strong connection. We will review this research in detail in Chapters 14 and 15. Suffice it to say here that these practices are not well-supported and don't align well with the way organizations are changing to adapt to environmental disruptions (discussed in Chapters 4 and 5). We are also now aware of the well-documented problems with agency theory as a model for many organizational practices.[17] It is also widely acknowledged now that tying executive pay to company performance isn't recommended.[18] Many factors outside of their control affect the outcomes for which they are being held accountable. In fact, the relationship between CEO pay and company performance remains low today despite upward of 90% of their pay being composed of variable pay tied to company performance and stock price.[19]

Finally, the logic behind the expansion of these practices throughout the organization was questionable. Expansion at the executive level was driven by changes in tax laws and regulations, not because it effectively drove performance. The expansion of P4P deeper into the organization was similarly not based on evidence of its effectiveness. The logic was simple, "if it's good for executives, it's good for everyone else." More variable pay and less merit pay (base pay increases) have the added benefit of limiting increases in compensation costs, which is a top concern for HR leaders.[20]

Stepping Back—PM as Organizational Control

If PM shouldn't be focused on reward distribution, what should it be focused on? We use an organizational design lens to help answer this question. Organization design configures the organization (process, technology, people, structure, and culture) to operationalize the strategic decisions made by an organization. Many organizational models have an element that reflects an organization's management, control, and governance processes. These processes "steer" the organization. We will argue that this is where PM best fits, and others argue similarly.[21] In fact, the goal of an organization's design is expressly to *control* and influence what employees do.

We use the word "control" here not in a derogatory way but to convey the predictability an organization needs to ensure efforts are directed at activities that will further the organization's long-term performance.

These processes have less to do with the horizontal workflow and more to do with vertical governance, planning, and decision-making that sit on top of the workflow. They define and prioritize strategic objectives, allocating scarce resources (e.g., money and talent) to those objectives. Strategic planning, portfolio planning, business planning, and budgeting are examples. PM is an extension of these processes, translating organizational decisions and priorities into unit, team, and individual priorities.

There is a rich history of research in this area, dating back to Max Weber's study of bureaucracy and Henri Fayol's study of the four functions of management.[22] There is also research in sociology in the areas of state formation, civilization, and governance that explore the balance between more central external steering of organizations and more autonomy and self-control.[23]

Control processes are defined as "mechanisms that managers use to direct attention, motivate and encourage individuals to act in ways that support the organization's objectives."[24] Research in this area describes two broad types of control mechanisms: coercive and enabling.[25] The tools of coercive control are familiar: hierarchy, chain of command, written policies and procedures, management directives, centralization of decisions, and formalization of processes and roles. These mechanisms are formal, codified, and bureaucratic; they limit employee action in more rigid ways with little transparency. Traditional PM and reward practices are tools of coercive control. Managers set or approve objectives that specify what an employee will do and the consequences of doing it (or not). Employees are evaluated based on the achievement of these objectives, and financial rewards and other administrative consequences are tied to those evaluations. Traditional PM processes also involve regular monitoring, surveillance, and feedback to ensure that employees stay on track and are not surprised by their final performance evaluations and rewards.

Given our discussion about the principles underlying traditional PM and reward processes above, it is unsurprising that coercive control mechanisms are popular in organizations. The vast majority of studies of control processes in organizations focus on coercive control mechanisms.[26] Research also highlights several problems with coercive control, pushing organizations to shift away from it for many of the same reasons we discussed in Chapter 2:

> Research in the control domain in many ways has failed to evolve effectively. Instead, research appears to over-rely on theories and approaches based on an understanding of organizations that dates back to the 1950s, 1960s, and 1970s, thereby limiting our ability to better understand organizations and advise managers today and in the future. Dominant theoretical foundations have underlying assumptions that have slowed empirical progress. These foundations do not fit current organizational challenges and environments because their prevailing emphases lend themselves to applications that encompass a singular view of control (vs. a more holistic view), a focus on coercive control (vs. enabling control), and a focus on formal control mechanisms (vs. informal mechanisms). All three foci are becoming increasingly outdated for modern organizations as both organizations and the world have changed.[27]

Management researcher William Ouchi foreshadowed the problems we would encounter with more bureaucratic and coercive controls more than 40 years ago:

> It has recently become fashionable among organization theorists to argue that relatively few real organizations possess the underlying "rationality" which is assumed in bureaucratic forms of control. If there is any truth in this very considerable attack on our notions of the orderliness and rationality with which organizations function, then we must guess that the forms of control which are dominant today may be inappropriate in future organizations.[28]

PM and Enabling Control Systems

An advantage of using this lens to examine PM is that it allows us to see alternatives. Enabling control approaches have been discussed since the 1970s but they have not been widely adopted by organizations. They use a lighter touch. They provide support, guidance, clarification, and assistance to employees instead of constraining them. They are more informal, and they rely more on intrinsic motivation. They allow employees flexibility to adjust when conditions change. They provide transparency so employees understand the larger context for their work, the logic of the systems they work in, and the "why" behind rules and policies. Enabling control mechanisms rely more on social, psychological, and cultural mechanisms to influence employee behavior, and they have important implications for PM and reward practices.[29] Organizational sociology discusses a similar approach, referring to managerial and organizational "civilization." Central steering and coercive mechanisms become internalized and more discipline and a stronger sense of responsibility develops and is internalized. This, in turn, allows for more autonomy. Gradually, the need for more direct coercive control and direct supervision and attention is reduced. As organizations mature and evolve, direct external control can be replaced by more indirect, subtle "binding" approaches.[30]

Social and Psychological Mechanisms

Decades of research has shown that other factors influence employee behavior beyond the need to obtain rewards or avoid punishment. Employees work hard to satisfy other important social and psychological needs like purpose, autonomy, mastery, competence, and belonging[31] A recent review of all research to date in this area shows supporting these needs has positive effects on motivation, well-being, and performance.[32]

Purpose and Meaning: People want to be a part of something bigger than themselves. There is substantial historical research showing the effectiveness of this need in motivating employees.[33] Management researcher William Ouchi discussed purpose and commitment to the organization's objectives explicitly as an alternative to traditional bureaucratic controls in the late 1970s.[34] And research demonstrating the importance of feeling a sense of purpose has recently enjoyed a resurgence.[35]

We will discuss the motivational power of purpose and meaning more in Chapter 10, but this research suggests that goals should be at the center of PM rather than evaluation and rewards. Managers should use goals to direct, inspire, and create a line of sight for employees and their work. Making goals central also emphasizes the need to assess progress. Feedback is important, but it needs to be in the service of making progress toward meaningful goals instead of judging performance to decide future rewards. And managers need to do more than just provide feedback to help employees make progress; they need to provide information, resources, support, and encouragement. In short, managers need to *enable* performance and progress.

Belonging: People are social animals and have a deep-seated need to belong.[36] People do things because others they admire, respect, and identify with do them. When a group of people have something meaningful to accomplish *together* and know clear ways of accomplishing it, they behave and interact differently. They bring more enthusiasm to the work, and they communicate better, cooperate more, work harder, and accomplish more.[37] And work is increasingly being done in teams, and competencies like teamwork and collaboration are becoming critical organizational capabilities.[38] This research suggests that PM should be designed around teams as well as individuals.

Autonomy: Instead of forcing compliance with rules and procedures and extrinsic rewards, employees are more likely to engage when they have the freedom and latitude to manage and control their own work.[39] It's important to note, however, that autonomy is more than just freedom. Thought leader Otti Vogt makes this point forcefully in discussing Sociologist Norbert Elias' work. True autonomy or self-control as a governance process doesn't happen without the right organizational context and socialization process that emphasizes self-discipline, shared responsibilities, and contextual controls. That context is created by the right selection, recruiting, hiring, onboarding, training, socialization, and other processes.[40] Vogt suggests this context creates a more mature form of governance and control, which we see as more consistent with enabling control.

This doesn't mean all bureaucracy is bad. Even formal rules and policies can be enabling when information, transparency, direction, and guidance are the goals rather than coercion and compliance.[41] PM should be a high-involvement process with employees providing input to goals and having the latitude to shift their focus and approaches as the needs of their work change.

Culture and leadership

Another important enabling control mechanism is the culture of the organization. Organizations use socialization processes to inculcate employees on the values and beliefs of the organization and to shape their experiences. Ouchi explicitly discusses the power of culture as an enabling control mechanism (referring to these broader groups as "clans").

> A Clan requires not only a norm of reciprocity and the idea of legitimate authority but also social agreement on a broad range of values and beliefs. Because the clan lacks the explicit rules of the bureaucracy, it relies for its control upon a deep level of common agreement between members on what constitutes preferred behavior, and it requires a high level of commitment on the part of each individual to those socially prescribed behaviors.[42]

Many HR processes in addition to PM create this kind of environment. It happens through recruiting, onboarding, and employee integration processes and programs as well as through formal and informal coaching. Coaching by coworkers, peers, managers, and mentors reinforces important values, beliefs, and norms. Performance management should enable these processes by designing it to be a continuous, ongoing process with regular conversations among managers, teams, and employees about the work to be done, the goals being pursued, and why they are important. We will go deeper into the topic of culture in Chapter 11.

Context

Formal processes are effective control mechanisms, but individual behavior and performance are also influenced by the context in which they occur.[43] Employees want to understand the larger context for their work. We will have more to say about context and why it's important in Chapter 7. Employees want to know why they are pursuing certain goals and not others, why decisions are made, and why certain policies and rules are in place. Sharing this context enables them to make the right decisions "in the heat of battle," when managers aren't around. This context doesn't get created for employees in one PM-planning meeting. It happens over time, reinforcing the importance of a continuous PM process where managers and employees have regular, ongoing discussions about their work and how it aligns with the needs of important stakeholders in the company. These discussions create a "high-context" environment where the purpose, meaning, and direction for their work become internalized and part of the background environment for the workgroup and organization,[44] which increases motivation and performance.[45]

In Chapters 6–13, we will explore in more detail how these enabling control mechanisms translate into Performance Enablement practices and share research supporting their effectiveness. We deliberately chose the term "*Enablement*" in this book. This term isn't just a trendy, more palatable alternative to "Management." The use of this term intentionally signals the need for organizations to move to a more enabling control philosophy, including a more enabling approach to sustaining and improving individual and organizational performance.

Key Takeaways

- The purpose of PM today is primarily to facilitate reward distribution as a part of an organization's pay-for-performance philosophy.
- This purpose remains deeply institutionalized in organizations despite little research support and a shaky philosophical and historical foundation.

- An organization design lens suggests that PM should be a part of an organization's management control processes.
- PM should adopt a more enabling approach to control instead of a more coercive approach, relying more on social, psychological, and cultural mechanisms to influence employee behavior versus evaluations, differentiation, and pay for performance.
- Performance Enablement shows how taking a more enabling control approach to PM can improve employee motivation and individual and organizational performance.

SECTION I
THE BUSINESS CASE FOR CHANGE

4

The Changing Nature of Work

The landscape of professional environments has undergone significant transformations and disruptions since the time performance appraisals were first introduced in the early twentieth century. Yet the methodologies used for assessing performance have struggled to evolve accordingly. In this chapter, we provide some context for the massive changes occurring, and how they are affecting how we work, and their logical implications for performance management practices are covered in Chapter 5.

The world has navigated through four pivotal phases of the Industrial Revolution, each powered by breakthroughs in technology that have radically altered economic and social frameworks. These shifts have sparked major transformations in society. During the First Industrial Revolution, society transitioned from an agriculture-centric to an industry-centric existence. The advent of electricity and the rise of mass production during the Second Industrial Revolution fundamentally altered the dynamics of how people lived and worked. Subsequently, the Third Industrial Revolution introduced the digital age, reshaping people's ways of living, working, and communicating while accelerating the pace of change.

The Fourth and Fifth Industrial Revolutions

The concept of the Fourth Industrial Revolution (4IR) was first introduced and popularized by Klaus Schwab, Founder and Executive Chairman of the World Economic Forum, in 2016. Schwab detailed his vision in his book titled "The Fourth Industrial Revolution."[1] This era was characterized by a fusion of technologies that blurred the lines between the physical, digital, and biological spheres, encompassing advancements such as artificial intelligence, robotics, the Internet of Things (IoT), genetic engineering, quantum computing, and other technologies.

The 4IR has been exciting and the pace of change has been exponentially faster than any prior period. This stage has presented an enormous challenge

Performance Enablement. Edie Goldberg and Alan Colquitt, Oxford University Press. © Oxford University Press (2026).
DOI: 10.1093/9780197830642.003.0004

for business and the practice of human resource management in particular. The skills required to succeed and compete were changing almost overnight, with fewer people in the broader labor market possessing the skills needed by companies. This has implications for Performance Enablement (PE). At the heart of driving a business forward, growing these new skills and capabilities and leveraging them for high performance have become a new urgent priority.

The Fifth Industrial Revolution (5IR), also known as the Cognitive Revolution, began in discussions in various forums and publications in the late 2010s and early 2020s. It represents a gradual shift in thinking and priorities within the technology and industrial sectors. It is often associated with the integration and collaboration between humans and machines, and it will be driven in large part by the continued evolution of artificial intelligence (AI). The Society for Human Resources Management (SHRM) summarizes this idea with the equation AI + Human Intelligence (HI) = Return on Investment (ROI). These new technologies offer a future of human and machine interaction that enables people to improve decision-making, creativity, and productivity.

While characterized by noteworthy technological advancements, the 5IR will also be characterized by its focus on personalized and sustainable technologies. It emphasizes the importance of returning to a more human-centric approach, leveraging the advancements from the 4IR to enhance human creativity, environmental sustainability, and social cohesion. The most visible example of this shift occurred in 2019 when the Business Roundtable Group redefined the purpose of a corporation as not only maximizing shareholder returns but also delivering value to their customers, investing in their employees, and supporting the communities in which they operate.[2] What emerges from this discussion is the concept of business as a powerful force for doing good. This ethos suggests that companies should be required to lift their people up and develop them so that all people, companies, and communities can thrive.

The technologies and workplace advancements that characterize the 4IR and 5IR are impacting the pace of change faced by organizations and are forcing companies to rethink the way they operate and manage their workforce. Traditional PM practices like annual goal-setting, cascading goals, and annual reviews are too slow and cumbersome for the current business environment. Considering the rapid rate of change, it's crucial for employees to consistently focus on the appropriate objectives, adjust their goals as circumstances evolve, and develop new skills needed to thrive in today's workplace. As business priorities shift, it's essential for employees to swiftly reorganize their tasks and maintain attention on the most significant matters. The methods we use to manage performance need to be as flexible and responsive as the business itself.

Digital Transformation

The 4IR and 5IR are driving extensive digital transformation in organizations. These changes go beyond just making your current processes faster or more efficient. Companies are now reimagining the whole way they approach work, thanks to breakthroughs in technology like AI. These technologies aren't just fancy tools; they're changing the game by allowing managers and employees to monitor how work gets done in real-time and offer instant feedback. With improved data and new data analytics tools, organizations can now make data-driven decisions to improve performance. Imagine being able to guide your team in real-time, helping them adjust their approach to improve and sustain their performance.

This isn't about big brother watching; it's about using technology to sustain and boost what we're already doing. Tools like nudge technology, which gently pushes employees and managers toward more productive habits, or micro-coaching, offering bite-sized, personalized advice, are becoming part of your toolkit. These aren't just ideas for the future; they're tools you can use right now to help everyone on your team do their best work. And yes, there's solid evidence that when you monitor and guide performance with the help of technology, people actually do perform better.[3] These technologies are discussed in more depth in Chapter 15 of this book, including examples designed to measure and monitor performance.

Rapid technological advancements are requiring companies to continually innovate to stay ahead. Technology has leveled the playing field in many industries, allowing smaller companies or those in emerging markets to compete directly with established players. Given the acceleration in the pace of innovation, market conditions and customer preferences can change rapidly. Continuously developing talent and fostering new skills required to innovate have become a critical issue for many organizations.

Globalization and Increased Competition[4]

The expansion of global business has significantly fueled growth in emerging markets, which now contribute to nearly two-thirds of global GDP growth. This growth, coupled with technological advancements, has enabled companies to more easily tap into labor markets in these regions, often at lower costs.[5] Competition for top talent, regardless of where they are, has become fierce over the last few decades. This has significantly impacted the cost of talent to an organization and has been a major driver of off-shoring for the past several decades. This shift has increased the pressure on organizations to manage costs more efficiently, affecting compensation budgets, the primary motivational and coercive control mechanism used by most organizations (base pay, merit pay, and bonuses).

As businesses become more global and teams more dispersed, it's not uncommon for team members and managers to be spread across many countries. This trend, enabled by technology, challenges the traditional model where feedback and performance evaluations come primarily from a direct manager. Instead, there's a growing need to adopt a more holistic approach to performance management, one that incorporates insights from a broader array of sources, particularly those who work closely with the employee on a day-to-day basis. This method acknowledges the complexity of global teamwork and leverages diverse perspectives to provide a more accurate and comprehensive view of an employee's performance.

In summary, the globalization of work has created a dynamic and complex environment where competition is fierce due to expanded markets, higher consumer expectations, the need for constant innovation, and the pressure to operate efficiently and cost-effectively. How companies manage talent in this environment is quite different from the more stable, predictable business environment of the early 1900s when performance appraisal first emerged.

The Growing Complexity of Work and Increase in Collaboration

According to Deloitte's *Global Human Capital Trends 2016*, to adapt to the changing nature of work, companies are shifting from siloed, functional, and hierarchical corporate structures that do not serve the needs of companies to structures that are more responsive to changing business conditions. These structures are more adaptable and team-based, which are grounded in agility, customer orientation, and cross-functional integration.[6]

The complexity of modern business challenges often exceeds the problem-solving capabilities of a single individual or team. In response, organizations are adopting cross-functional teams and networks to harness diverse perspectives and expertise, a strategy evident within the biotech sector for product development. It takes the expertise of people from multiple functional specialties to turn a molecule into a marketable drug.

According to research by Rob Cross and colleagues, collaborative activities consume 85% or more of people's work week. The amount of time managers and employees dedicate to collaborative tasks has surged by at least 50% over the last two decades.[7] In today's professional environment, the ability to collaborate effectively is an essential capability. Yet, despite the clear premium placed on teamwork today, nearly 90% of the companies we surveyed focused their PM process solely on individuals.[8]

Moreover, many companies have transitioned to matrixed organizational structures, underscoring the importance of cross-boundary collaboration. Within such structures, employees often report to multiple managers, complicating the traditional oversight functions of direct managers. As organizations flatten and spans of control expand, direct managers see less of what their employees are doing on an ongoing basis. Traditional PM processes have not been designed to deal with this complexity. Your work ecosystem demands feedback from all the people you work with, regardless of where they sit in the organization.

Furthermore, traditional performance management processes assume that employees should set goals for themselves individually—although often they are part of a team or department with broader goals. Regardless, individuals are held accountable for their own goals, and usually, only the employee and their manager have insight into progress against these individual goals. Despite the fact that coworkers may benefit from understanding what these goals are and how they are progressing due to interrelated goals, they typically do not have access to this information.

While people have worked in teams for centuries, the complexity of work has driven an exponential increase in the amount of collaboration in the contemporary workplace. Setting just individual goals does not accurately fit how we operate today. More often than not one individual's performance is not the determinant of whether or not a goal can be accomplished. It requires the input and support of others. Thus, setting team-based goals seems to be a better fit for a contemporary organization.

The nature of jobs is also changing. A job was traditionally thought to be fairly static. It could be well-defined by a clear job description, with a set of key responsibilities, and a core set of skills. However, in today's dynamic work environment, the work required from an employee can change and evolve over time. While a job description may have accurately represented the work to be done when the employee was hired, within a short period of time, responsibilities can shift and change to meet the current business environment and changing business priorities. This trend was accelerated by the global pandemic as businesses pivoted to address pressing priorities. Today, jobs are melting into fluid tasks and projects that leverage specific individual skills to get work done.[9]

Hybrid and Remote Work

While the remote work trend began well before the COVID pandemic, only about 7% of employees were working remotely in 2019, and the term "hybrid work" did not yet exist. Today, approximately 13% of full-time employees in the US work fully remotely, while 27% follow a hybrid schedule. Among employees who can perform their jobs remotely, 46% of employees work a hybrid schedule, with 21% fully remote, while only 32% work full-time in the office.[10] Although there has been a lot of press about "return to office" in 2025, the research shows that remote and hybrid working shows no sign of declining significantly.[11]

Teams with dispersed members pose unique challenges for managers in leading, managing, coaching, and evaluating their employees. Before the pandemic, "management by walking around" was a common approach. Managers can no longer rely solely on observation to determine if and how employees work. Obviously, dropping by someone's office to check on their progress is impossible if the employee is not in the office, or if they simply work in a different location. Thus, managers need new ways of managing and measuring performance in distributed work environments. This puts greater importance on clear goal-setting and aligning on expectations, and getting feedback from peers on collaborative work efforts.

These new work arrangements also require robust communication practices to ensure that employees can collaborate effectively at a distance. This has resulted in a proliferation of new digital tools for communication and collaboration (e.g., video conferencing, instant messaging, document-sharing tools, and collaborative project management platforms). All of these new technologies and ways of communicating can negatively impact productivity if not properly streamlined and coordinated so they do not overwhelm employees. Thus, it is important to ensure that PE activities occur in the flow of work, and technology supports this activity.

Understanding the Changing Nature of Our Workforce

The changes affecting organizations go beyond the nature of jobs, work, and work practices. The makeup, needs, and expectations of our workforce have also changed. In this section, we will discuss the changing nature of the workforce itself. This discussion includes both worker needs and expectations, as well as a discussion of exactly who comprises our workforce today (hint: it is not just your organization's employees).

Knowledge Workers

As we stated in Chapter 2, PM was first developed in the early twentieth century. During this period, employees often performed tasks in an industrial setting that were repetitive in nature. There were strict hierarchical structures, work rules, and limited autonomy. The workforce of today has shifted toward knowledge work. Today's *knowledge workers* value autonomy and flexibility in how they get their work done. They are more likely to be motivated by an internal sense of fulfillment—by doing interesting work and having autonomy in how they do their work, by finding meaning in their work, and by developing their expertise.[12] They do not want to be "managed." They want to be inspired and supported to help them achieve their full potential. Unfortunately, many organizations still lean heavily on more coercive control mechanisms to ensure employees meet their objectives. This approach relies on threats and punishments for underperformance and rewards for success. This practice, however, tends to focus more on compliance and short-term results rather than fostering an environment where employees are motivated to surpass their own expectations and capabilities and are driven by commitment instead of compliance. The coercive-control method focuses more on adhering to specific objectives and less on creating a supportive atmosphere that encourages creativity and growth. For knowledge workers, a greater focus on enabling workers' success by instilling a sense of purpose and possibility allows them to achieve more than what was thought to be possible.

Another challenge in managing performance for knowledge workers is that performance is more complex and challenging to quantify. Unlike traditional factory work, where productivity can be measured in units produced, defects found, or hours worked, knowledge work involves abstract concepts, problem-solving, and creative thinking, which are harder to measure and evaluate.

Progress in knowledge work can be uneven and influenced by various factors beyond an individual employee's control. Performance may depend on the collaboration and productivity of others, the overall work environment, and the quality of resources and information available. Consequently, an employee's output might be impacted by team dynamics, cross-functional cooperation, and even external market conditions. This interdependence requires a different management approach that appreciates the collaborative nature of knowledge work and recognizes that success often relies on a network of interconnected contributors.

To summarize, today's knowledge workers are fundamentally different than workers of the past in how they work, what motivates them, and what prevents them from achieving their best.

Expectations of Millennials and Gen Z

Baby Boomers (born 1946–1964) are moving into their retirement years and now only make up a small portion of the workforce population. While Gen X (born 1965–1980) was a small generation, based on the number of people born during this period, this generation is now assuming more leadership roles in the workplace today, and they comprise 31% of our current workforce. According to the US Department of Labor, Millennials (born 1981–1996) make up the largest segment of the workforce in 2025 (36%).[13] The representation of Gen Z (born 1997–2012) in the workforce is also growing, making up approximately 18% of the workforce. So when we think about PM at work, we are primarily focusing on Millennials and Gen Z (aka Zoomers). These generations have grown up in a digital age, shaped by rapid technological advancements and changing social dynamics, leading to specific characteristics and values that influence how they view work and career progression. Here's an outline of their key needs and expectations regarding managing their performance.

Millennials and Gen Z seek purpose and meaning in their work.[14] They will be positively motivated by goals that give their work meaning (e.g., curing cancer, democratizing access to information, creating products that support the environment). Managers will need to move beyond assigning goals without context, helping employees see how their work makes a positive impact (on the team, company, or broader society).

Their upbringing, schoolwork, and sports were all about teamwork, so they are likely to be more team-oriented at work as well. Rigid hierarchical structures do not sit well with these employees. They will follow the individual they trust, who they think has the expertise to lead the group, regardless of their actual position.

Millennials and Gen Z, with their experience with digital tools, are accustomed to instant feedback. In the workplace, they will *expect* ongoing feedback. They value regular communication with their manager to understand how they're performing, what they can improve, and how they can grow. This constant dialogue helps them feel supported and engaged.

Given their relative comfort and familiarity with technology (they are digital natives), they will expect the use of technology to help facilitate communication, feedback, and collaboration. Transparency is important to these generations (especially Millennials) and the use of some technology-enabled performance tracking will be welcomed, as long as it does not infringe on their private behavior and is in line with data privacy laws.

While this desire for feedback is about knowing what they need to do to improve their performance, they also want insight and direction on how to grow and advance their career. Millennials and Gen Z workers do not lack ambition, and helping them to continuously learn and grow is crucial to both keep them motivated and to retain them.

These generations also thrive on recognition and appreciation for their contributions. They grew up in the era of participation trophies. They really want to know that you value them and their contributions. They expect regular acknowledgment of their achievements, both in formal and informal settings. This recognition can boost morale and foster a positive work culture. This, in turn, positively influences performance.

Overall, to meet the needs and expectations of Millennials and Gen Z, PE must be flexible, collaborative, and focused on continuous growth. It should create a supportive environment that values career development and gives a sense of purpose and provides recognition while embracing technology and diversity. These elements are essential for engaging and retaining these younger generations in the workforce.

Alternative Employment Arrangements

Today's workforce reflects a mix of full-time and part-time employees working alongside external collaborators, including freelancers, contractors, consultants, vendors, and other partners. According to McKinsey's American Opportunity Survey, 36% of workers today are independent workers—which equates to 58 million Americans.[15] In all likelihood, this is a significant undercount of this population because consultants and other partners are not counted in these figures.

Some of the best and brightest workers today want to work on their own terms, picking and choosing both what work they do and with whom they do it.[16] While companies spend months (sometimes years) looking for employees with a rare set of capabilities, often these "unicorns" are not interested in working full-time or on a permanent basis for one company, but they will work on a project basis on their own terms. Hiring freelancers on a temporary basis enables managers to access the talent they need when they need it.

Leveraging external talent has enabled companies like Procter & Gamble, IBM, and Microsoft to accelerate project execution by hiring staff with specific skills temporarily to meet a critical deadline.[17] The tremendous growth in digital capabilities has facilitated the *open talent marketplace.* Talent platforms like Topcoder, Guru, Toptal, and Upwork provide plenty of opportunities for freelancers to market their capabilities to companies that may hire them for specific projects. Technology-driven talent platforms enable companies to find individuals with critical, cutting-edge skills that are in short supply in the labor market.

Traditional performance management often overlooks these external contributors because they aren't officially part of the company's internal talent management systems. However, if PM aims to boost the success of individuals, teams, and the organization as a whole, it should also encompass these external partners. The traditional PM model, focusing on individual employees under direct managerial oversight, doesn't work in this broader context.

Joint Ventures Require Managing Performance across Organizational Boundaries

Similar to the issues cited for contractors who are contributing to the company's goals, today, teamwork can extend beyond an organization's boundaries. We have already made the business case that the complexity of work today requires the collaboration of different sets of capabilities to execute on business priorities. While traditionally all of this collaboration has happened internally, with our very complex business world, it is also true that companies collaborate across their organizational boundaries in the case of joint ventures.

For example, in 2022, Honda and LG announced a joint venture that would lend LG's expertise in producing lithium-ion batteries to Honda's efforts to ramp up the production of electric vehicles. Employees from across these companies must work together on projects that are important to both companies. This requires collaborative goal-setting and managing the performance of these teams across organizational boundaries. Our traditional ways of managing talent, which have most, if not all, of the feedback coming from one's direct manager, do not translate to an environment where individuals are working together across two different organizations.

Key Takeaways

- As technologies quickly advance, the speed of change in organizations is accelerating, requiring greater organizational agility.
- Technology has not only enabled us to leverage talent and access markets globally, it has also enabled small businesses to compete with larger more established companies, rapidly shifting the landscape for competition. Organizations must quickly build new capabilities to stay in the game (which means employees need new skills).
- The growing complexity of work requires greater levels of collaboration both across disciplines and sometimes across organizational boundaries.
- Knowledge workers are motivated by doing interesting work, finding meaning in their work, and by developing their expertise. They don't want their performance to be "managed," they want to be inspired to achieve great accomplishments.
- Younger workers want purpose and meaning in their work. They expect more feedback and development than organizations have previously given. Our processes need to change to meet these new expectations.
- Companies no longer rely solely on employees to achieve their objectives. We need to consider the best ways to enable the performance of workers of all types (full- and part-time employees, contractors, consultants, business partners, etc.).
- These changes will have significant implications for how companies think about managing performance.

5
Implications of the Business Context for Performance Management Practice

Most people in business today can remember where they were on September 11, 2001, when the World Trade Center Twin Towers were destroyed in a terrorist attack. Two other planes flew to Washington, D.C. One struck the Pentagon while the other crashed in rural Pennsylvania, taking the lives of brave people on board who had received word that their plane was repurposed as a weapon in a terrorist attack. Many readers will also remember the prior year when the dot.com bubble burst, many start-ups failed, and larger companies lost a significant portion of their market capitalization. Then, there was the start of the Iraq War in 2003 that ushered in a massive and sudden shift in the geopolitical landscape.

The early 2000s were a wild ride in the business world. Around this time, business leaders and consultants began to adopt a term that the military had coined in the late 1980s, which was designed to describe the challenging and unpredictable conditions that arose in the wake of the Cold War. That term was VUCA, which stands for Volatility, Uncertainty, Complexity, and Ambiguity. Today, this acronym also characterizes the increasingly fast-paced, unpredictable, and complex global environment in which businesses operate. These conditions have profound implications for performance management (PM) practices. For example, in the past, organizations operated with a relatively stable workforce. Jobs were well-defined, with clear responsibilities and boundaries. Roles were stable over time. Job responsibilities and competencies rarely changed. Employees could expect to follow linear career paths, often progressing within a specific function or role over many years. Managers measured performance against static job descriptions and goals, which aligned with the stable environment. PM systems were built around the assumptions of predictable, fixed roles and skills, where goals set at the outset of the year were still a priority at the end of the year.

In today's VUCA environment, however, the global workforce is increasingly dynamic, and the concept of a fixed job is evolving. Job descriptions

Performance Enablement. Edie Goldberg and Alan Colquitt, Oxford University Press. © Oxford University Press (2026).
DOI: 10.1093/9780197830642.003.0005

have become more fluid as roles adapt to evolving business needs. Employees are often given the opportunity to take on tasks outside of their traditional responsibilities while crossing functional boundaries and working on short-term projects that address critical business needs. These "internal gigs" let employees leverage all their skills and experiences to get critical work accomplished.[1] Between shifting skills, changing customer expectations, organizational restructuring, and a dynamic business environment, a job description may change from 10% to 40% in just one or two years.

The evolving work landscape demands a significant overhaul of traditional PM practices. Common practices are no longer working. These outmoded practices include setting fixed, annual goals, offering feedback only yearly or twice a year, making managers the sole arbiter of employee performance, and managing and rewarding individuals instead of teams. Yet, organizations stubbornly cling to these traditional PM practices. We need new practices that enable employees to work successfully in a changing world.

This chapter explores the implications of the changing business context for PM practices. It will address the mismatch between our current practices and what our business world requires and lay the groundwork for a new approach to PM for the twenty-first century.

Table 5.1 summarizes the shift in business practices discussed in the prior chapter, which defines the current business state for which we need to design our talent practices.

These macro trends in the business environment have numerous implications for PM. The following practices are a good beginning toward managing performance in a VUCA world.

Table 5.1 The world is changing and our management practices are not aligned

From	To
Stable jobs with specific, well-defined responsibilities	Constant change (VUCA, Agile), Skill sets rapidly changing
Traditional hierarchical organizations, low spans of control, colocation to monitor performance	Flatter organization, larger spans of control, globally distributed workforce
Production-based work	Knowledge-based work
Jobs where individual effort translates to individual performance	Complexity of work, team-based structures
Office-based work	Distributed work arrangements
Employees	Employees (full- and part-time), consultants, gig workers, contractors

Agile and Continuous Performance Management Processes

While Agile work methodologies were originally created for software development, they are now widely applied in a variety of industries and disciplines, including HR.[2] In Agile environments, rigid, top-down management approaches are no longer tenable. Leaders must now act as facilitators and enablers, supporting teams by clearing obstacles and ensuring alignment with broader organizational goals, rather than by directing every move.

Agile work processes focus on adaptability and customer satisfaction. Elements of Agile have obvious implications for managing performance. For example, the Agile Manifesto[3] emphasizes:

- **Individuals and Interactions over Process and Tools**: The value placed on communication and collaboration over a rigid adherence to tools and processes shows the importance of collaborating with all those involved in a process and making adjustments that work for all, versus sticking with a process (or goals) that may not yield the desired outcome.
- **Working Software over Comprehensive Documentation**: This emphasizes a shift to learning along the way and a focus on continuous improvement. All of the energy should not go into documentation (e.g., such as documenting performance or setting goals for the year), but instead should focus on learning while doing and making continuous improvements. This places an emphasis on understanding the big picture goals and continuous feedback and modifying interim goals along the way to pave a path toward success.
- **Responding to Change over Following a Plan**: Being open and responsive to change is a core tenant of the Agile Manifesto. Goals are not set in stone. They provide direction based on the current business circumstances. They adapt based on changing business needs and learning while doing to provide the customer with the best possible experience.
- **Simplicity**: Focusing on what's essential and eliminating unnecessary work to maximize the amount of work not being done. How do we make our methods for managing performance simple, so they don't get in the way of the work that needs to get done, but rather they support the company's highest priorities? We think the answer is managing performance in the flow of work, not as a separate process.

Agile methods emphasize the importance of adaptability, efficiency, and customer focus. How we manage performance in an organization needs to also be more adaptable (business goals change), efficient (we need to eliminate non-value-added activities, like excessive documentation), and customer-focused (growing the skills we need to deliver on customer demands and adapting to the changing business priorities of our customers). Agile work methods require a high level of coordination and flexibility within and across teams.

Traditional work models that emphasize individual roles and responsibilities are being replaced by team-based approaches. Setting team-based goals aligns and supports an agile work environment. In the Agile methodology, for example, teams work collaboratively on projects in sprints, relying on each other's strengths and skills to innovate and solve problems. This shift encourages a more dynamic and flexible work environment where the team's success is prioritized over individual achievements and the focus is on leveraging strengths vs. developing weaknesses. While many companies rely on traditional hierarchies for broad governance purposes, they also leverage purpose-built networks of teams to get their day-to-day work accomplished. Given our experiences during the COVID pandemic, the practice of staffing project-based teams to shift talent to address new pressing business challenges has taken off like a rocket. Every company is talking about the need to become more agile. (Here, we differentiate between big "A" Agile as in Agile work methodologies and little "a" agile, simply meaning adaptable and flexible.) When business priorities change, employees must be able to change their priorities to focus on the projects that matter the most to business success. Companies are pulling concepts from Agile methodologies to simply understand how to be more agile as a company.

The role of managers and leaders has evolved from supervising and directing the work of individuals to facilitating, coaching, and enabling team collaboration. Leaders must now create environments that support agile practices and cross-functional teamwork, focusing on empowering their teams rather than micromanaging tasks. The implication for managing performance within the company is that managers now need to assess how the *team* is performing and how individuals are collaborating to get important work accomplished. This requires new metrics and evaluation methods that recognize the value of teamwork and collaborative problem-solving.

The changing nature of work also requires a more networked design because of the increasing importance of knowledge and expertise. In the past, roles were defined by function, with workers confined to their particular areas of expertise. Today, however, complex problems demand input from multiple disciplines and departments. Many modern companies rely on collaborative networks where teams come together around common goals. These networks provide the flexibility needed to tap into specialized knowledge, regardless of its location within or outside the company. The result is an organization better equipped to innovate and to deliver solutions at the speed demanded by today's markets.

The final implication is that the traditional goal-setting processes, typically characterized by static objectives and annual reviews, are increasingly misaligned with the dynamic business environment. VUCA necessitates a more frequent and flexible approach to setting and evaluating the objectives and performance of employees. Companies must adjust priorities to meet changing business needs.

Organizations must transition from individual-based, static goals to agile, team-based objectives that can adapt to changing business priorities. Having more frequent touch points for PM supports quicker responses to market changes and fosters a more collaborative work environment.

Continuous and Crowdsourced Feedback

One of the most significant shifts we have seen in PM accelerated by the pandemic is a shift to more frequent check-ins and continuous feedback (although this shift started in 2012). Managers must maintain regular communication with their employees, regardless of where they are working, to ensure that employees have the tools they need for success and that managers are removing obstacles that are getting in the way of progress. This more frequent communication also provides the benefit of keeping employees connected to the company, its mission, strategy, and culture. These frequent meetings may take place as part of the regular manager 1:1s or during weekly team meetings. These meetings need to shift from simple updates to opportunities to solve problems and an opportunity to provide coaching to ensure success as work moves forward.

Furthermore, as more companies have adopted project-based work teams, feedback needs to shift from an annual perspective (once or twice a calendar year) to conducting reviews at the end of each project. This is a natural point to get feedback on what worked well, what did not, and what lessons can be learned and carried forward to other projects. Often referred to as project retrospectives or After Action Reviews, this type of look back helps team members reflect and learn in the moment. While those individuals may move on to work in new teams with different people, they can carry forward the lessons learned and infuse them in their new teams to improve team performance.

Saving feedback for the end of the year is a flawed process to begin with because a great deal of information is lost over the long months between reviews. Employees need support in the moment, not looking in the rearview mirror. If feedback is delayed, employees' ability to learn from their successes and their missteps is greatly diminished. We need to move beyond occasional feedback to ongoing coaching for performance.

In addition, the dispersed nature of modern workforces challenges the traditional model of manager-led feedback. In a geographically dispersed workforce, the manager may not always be the best source of input on performance. Individuals who observe employees in action should be able to provide feedback anytime. Continuous feedback mechanisms, incorporating peer input, are essential to addressing this challenge. Frequent, crowdsourced feedback provides more complete and varied performance insights and supports ongoing development and coaching. Regular check-ins and real-time feedback help employees stay aligned with organizational goals and foster a culture of continuous improvement.

Managing Team vs. Individual Performance

While the shift from production-based to knowledge-based work and the need for agile structures require new ways of thinking about performance metrics, it is also true that work accomplishments are rarely the result of one person's individual effort. Today's complex business environment requires individuals and departments to work together to achieve common objectives.

Team-based work further complicates traditional performance measurement because the impact of one person's contributions may be difficult to isolate from the team's overall performance. Traditional performance reviews, which focus on task completion and individual achievements, are giving way to approaches that consider team success while reinforcing behaviors that support collective goals.

In an increasingly collaborative environment, behaviors, as opposed to static goals, are often a significant driver of what gets accomplished. We have seen many companies shift from a simple system considering "What" was accomplished (e.g., completion of goals or achievements) to also include "How" goals were accomplished (e.g., rewarding behaviors that facilitate collaboration across boundaries to achieve common goals). In fact, many processes today balance the importance of the "What" with the "How" of performance. In our study, 69% of the participating companies included behaviors as part of their process, and 42% weighted goals and behaviors equally.

Measuring the "What" + "How" of performance is not new. What is new is the need to focus on team vs. individual accomplishments. Thus, the "What" refers to collective goal achievement and the "How" is focused on the individual's behaviors that contribute to team success.

Work increasingly centers on project teams, yet companies continue to set individual goals and evaluate and reward employees based on them. PM systems need ways to measure and reward team performance. A shift toward market-based pay, combined with team and organizational incentives, can better recognize and reward collective achievement. This approach aligns with the collaborative nature of today's work and supports a more equitable distribution of rewards.

Including External Partners in Parts of Your Performance Management Process

While the traditional model of full-time employment for professional workers is still the norm, many workers operate outside of the traditional corporate environment as contractors/ freelancers and consultants. Given that so many people are stuck in *the sandwich generation* (i.e., responsible for taking care of both their children and their parents), contract work, which is often not full-time, is becoming an important employment alternative for many seeking to balance their work and personal commitments.

While an external firm may fully employ some freelancers or consultants, they are nonetheless collaborating with your employees in contributing to critical projects. But when we think of managing performance, we often do not include these individuals who are often critical for achieving strategic objectives. While the legal definition of a contractor requires that management has no control over their work, facilitating workers to accomplish organizational goals is always the responsibility of management, regardless of who is doing the work.[4] If a freelancer or consultant needs feedback or coaching on how to navigate the organization better, this does not conflict with their status as an external contractor.

Typically, however, companies handle contractors very differently from how they manage employees. Managers want to honor the fact that contract talent is truly independent. These differences in management practices can create friction between internal employees and contract talent who must collaborate to accomplish important work. Despite their independence, holding contractors accountable for deadlines, achieving agreed-upon goals, including them in team huddles to discuss what is working and not working on a project, and providing feedback to help them be more successful make good business sense. While managers may not conduct a performance review with a contractor, providing feedback and meeting regularly to discuss progress and roadblocks are in both parties' interests.

Clear communication about goals and expectations, along with regular feedback on progress, is essential for everyone involved in the work. When challenges arise, ongoing and open communication helps find solutions faster. To manage performance effectively in today's complex workplaces, which rely on an extended network of contributors, it's crucial to rethink our approach to include all contributors in the PM process.

Development as a Central Feature

Employee development has become crucial in a fast-paced and skill-intensive work environment. In traditional PM processes, managers often overlook or gloss over development because the emphasis is placed on setting and evaluating performance goals. However, prioritizing development is essential for equipping employees with the skills to navigate the rapidly changing business landscape. Organizations should integrate development planning into the PM process, ensuring that it receives the attention and follow-up necessary for effective skill growth and career progression.

In interviews with managers about how their PM process actually works (vs. how HR designed the process), we have heard that by the time managers get to the part of the form that involves development planning, they are exhausted. It does not get much attention and very little, if any, follow-up. But given the changing nature of work, development is more important than ever before. Development needs to be a central part of the process, not an afterthought.

Rethinking the Role and Value of Evaluations

As we will discuss in Chapter 13, traditional performance evaluations rely heavily on numeric ratings. These ratings have increasingly come under fire for being biased and inaccurate indicators of employee contributions. Our ability to differentiate and reward individual performance is compromised by unreliable ratings and the fact that achievement is often a team and not an individual effort. Instead, companies need a holistic approach to discussing performance that's more than a number. This involves discussions focused on achievements, progress toward goals, what got in the way of performance and how to overcome those obstacles in the future, areas for improvement, strengths to leverage, and career development. By moving away from purely quantitative assessments, organizations can better recognize the complex, collaborative efforts that drive success in modern work environments.

Rating and labeling employees isn't necessary for managers. They know who their star performers are and which employees are underperforming. They know this based on people's accomplishments and how they work with others. In Chapter 13, we will detail the research that informs us that rating employees often has a negative impact on employee motivation and performance—even for employees who are rated highly!

Further, measuring performance quantitatively in knowledge work is challenging. There's no pile of widgets next to the production line, which allows managers to see who is working efficiently and where there is a bottleneck. Ambiguity in assigning quantitative measures for qualitative work can cause disappointment and resentment among knowledge workers. Some companies are starting to move away from individual, quantitative assessments toward a more holistic way of measuring performance that credits the value that knowledge-based, collaborative teams truly offer.

For these reasons, we have seen companies either move away from ratings altogether (which will be discussed in greater detail in Chapter 13), or move toward fewer and more descriptive assessments of performance that do not include numbers or labels. The focus is on a dialogue about performance that both recognizes and celebrates accomplishments but also looks for continuous improvement opportunities. Of course, a majority of companies today still have traditional rating systems in place. Our hope in writing this book is to educate you, the HR professional, manager, and research community, on the impact of these ratings on individual performance and provide alternative strategies that will be more effective.

Cost Pressures Change Reward Structures

When PM systems were first designed, they aligned closely with the economic realities of the time. Managers often had access to relatively generous budgets that enabled them to recognize and reward employees who worked hard, achieved goals, and contributed to the company's success. In this environment, pay-for-performance (P4P) models flourished. It was not uncommon for organizations to allocate a 10% merit pool, allowing managers to reward their top performers with increases that significantly differentiated the latter's compensation from their peers. This financial flexibility made it possible for organizations to send strong signals through compensation, motivating employees to strive for higher levels of achievement.

Cost constraints and shrinking budgets mark today's business environment. Merit pools, once a robust tool for recognizing performance, have dwindled. A 3% merit pool or less is now far more common, leaving managers with limited resources to differentiate pay based on individual performance. This shift has diluted the effectiveness of P4P models, creating a situation where even top performers may not see meaningful financial rewards for their contributions. With smaller budgets, the ability to incentivize performance through traditional compensation structures has weakened and managers are often forced to spread limited rewards across entire teams.

Relying solely on financial rewards as a primary tool for motivating and recognizing employees is no longer feasible (nor advisable). Furthermore, we will argue in Chapter 14 that these financial incentives rarely worked and sometimes backfired on employers. As we discussed in Chapter 3, organizations must look beyond coercive control mechanisms like merit pay and variable pay programs and find more sustainable, meaningful ways to motivate and engage their workforce. The focus must shift toward creating environments where employees feel supported, enabled, and valued through development opportunities, feedback, recognition, and alignment with a purpose. To remain effective, PM needs to evolve from a transactional process centered on reward distribution to a dynamic system that fosters team success and personal growth.

By adopting the strategies above, organizations can better align their PM practices with the evolving nature of work, fostering a more adaptable, collaborative, and supportive environment for their employees. The remaining chapters of this book will provide a deep dive on our recommendations for moving forward.

Key Takeaways

- **Agility**: Shift from static, individual goals to dynamic, team-based objectives.
- **Continuous Feedback:** Implement continuous feedback mechanisms that incorporate peer input and real-time coaching in the flow of work.

- **Development Focus**: Prioritize development planning to equip employees with the necessary skills to sustain and improve their performance.
- **Holistic Discussions about Performance**: Move beyond ratings to discussions on achievements, obstacles, progress, and behaviors.
- **Reward Systems**: Transition to market-based pay and team/organizational incentives.

6

Performance Enablement

The Right Model for Today's Business Needs

In the evolving landscape of organizations, traditional performance management (PM) models often fall short in fostering sustained individual and organizational performance and growth. Traditional PM models designed based on more coercive control philosophies typically emphasize evaluation and differentiation over development and focus on past performance rather than enabling future success. Recognizing this gap, we introduce an alternative model: Performance Enablement (PE). This approach reflects a continuous process of actions designed to facilitate an upward spiral of performance and progress toward achieving both individual and organizational goals.

Up to this point, we have set the stage for a new model for managing performance that better suits today's business needs. In this chapter, we lay the foundation for our new PE model. PE should be a core part of the organization's management and control processes. Its purpose should be to translate strategy and organizational priorities into team and individual priorities. It should guide employee efforts, aligning them with important team and organizational goals. It should act as a *guidance system*—helping employees focus on the right activities. It should also be a *support system*—helping employees progress against their daily goals. The new PE process should be about direction, alignment, support, and progress in the service of individual and organizational performance.

As we discussed in Chapter 3, this move toward PE reflects a change toward *enabling* performance instead of *coercing* it. As a result, we are more focused on actions that support and enable individual and organizational performance and not on judging, evaluating, and differentiating that performance so we can distribute rewards. In our research, we asked practitioners, "What is the primary purpose of your PM process as implemented?" Much as you might expect, "evaluate performance to pay for performance" was the top vote-getter. However, a majority of practitioners stated that they believed the primary purpose *should be* to "drive/improve performance." We think

Performance Enablement. Edie Goldberg and Alan Colquitt, Oxford University Press. © Oxford University Press (2026).
DOI: 10.1093/9780197830642.003.0006

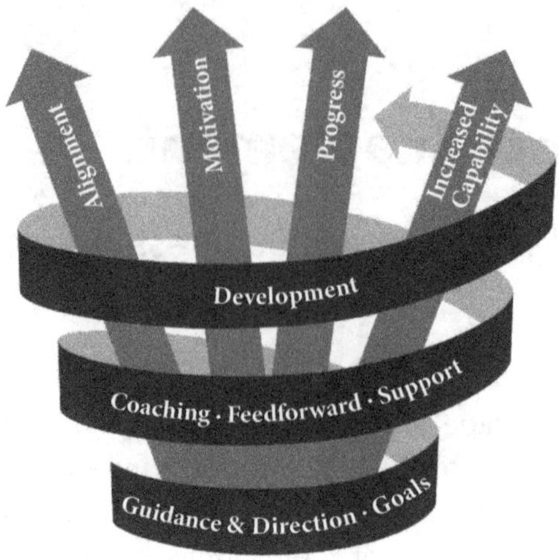

Figure 6.1 The new paradigm of Performance Enablement
Source: Authors

practitioners understand that the current paradigm and their current processes are not effective, but they don't have a different, evidence-based model to use instead—until now!

The foundation for PE is setting the context—providing guidance and direction on what is most important for the company and why it is important. With this information, individuals and teams can set goals.

A critical and often missing piece of PE is the ongoing support of managers to facilitate performance through coaching, feedback (and feedforward), and other types of support, including providing resources and removing obstacles to success. Development is the last critical part of this framework because this is how individuals and organizations improve. With these processes in place, the organization will benefit from increased alignment, motivation, progress against goals, and increased capability. Figure 6.1 shows our new model of PE, a first step in transforming talent management and HR processes using an enabling control philosophy. With this new model, we are focused on driving and improving individual and organizational performance instead of evaluating and differentiating performance so we can distribute rewards.

Setting the Context: The Foundation of Performance Enablement

At the foundation of PE is the necessity to provide a clear context for employees. As we discussed in Chapter 3, this involves providing a comprehensive understanding, guidance, and direction on what is most important for the company and why it holds such significance. When employees understand the overarching goals and the reasons behind them, it is easier for them to commit to those goals, and they are better equipped to align their individual objectives with the company's vision.

Providing context is critical for several reasons. First, providing context for goals provides clarity for employees on why their goals are important and how they fit into the bigger picture of what the team or organization is trying to accomplish. This provides motivational value by giving the employee purpose and meaning in their work.[1] Second, by providing this context, employees can be more agile in changing their approach or goal focus to achieve the desired outcome because they understand the bigger picture of what they are trying to accomplish. Context also helps with the prioritization of activities because it will direct more attention to those activities that are likely to have the biggest impact on desired outcomes. We will talk in more detail about the importance of creating a "high-context" environment in Chapter 7.

Creating Alignment: Translating Strategy to Goals

Creating alignment throughout the organization by translating company strategy to team and individual goals is critical for achieving cohesion and driving performance.[2] It ensures that everyone is rowing in the same direction. According to Kaplan and Norton, the Balanced Scorecard approach demonstrates that linking strategy to performance measures helps organizations translate strategic objectives into operational terms.[3] This alignment ensures that every employee understands how their work directly contributes to the company's success, enhancing their commitment and effort. Alignment provides contextual clarity and helps employees understand the *why* behind their goals.[4]

The seminal research on goal-setting theory found that specific and challenging goals, when understood and accepted, lead to higher performance.[5] This clarity empowers individuals and teams to set meaningful, relevant goals that contribute to the organization's success. Goal-setting should become a collaborative process where the alignment of personal and organizational objectives fosters a sense of purpose and direction.

Clarifying Behavioral Expectations

An important element of providing guidance to employees is not just about goals. It is also being clear regarding *how* employees go about doing their work, or the behavioral expectations of an organization. For some companies, values may be the driver of behavioral expectations. It is important that these values be clearly defined behaviorally so that managers have a guideline against which to coach employees to align with the values of the organization. For example, if a core value of a company is teamwork, then the company should define what this looks like from a behavioral perspective and why it is valued by the company.

Behavioral expectations can also come in the form of either core competencies the company expects from all of its employees (e.g., customer-centric) or role-based competencies that are critical for success in each position (e.g., analytical skills). Whether it is values, core competencies, or role-based competencies, the important point is that a company clearly defines what expected behavior looks like.

Continuous Support: The Role of Managers in Performance Enablement

In today's rapidly evolving business environment, PE is no longer confined to annual reviews or periodic feedback sessions. It's an ongoing, dynamic process that involves providing continuous support to employees in the normal flow of work. This modern approach emphasizes coaching, feedforward, and proactive problem-solving to create an environment where employees can make progress, thrive, and drive organizational success. These activities are described in the middle of the model shown in Figure 6.1. This doesn't necessarily require additional meetings; it can happen in the normal 1:1 meetings and team meetings managers already have with their employees. By embracing these principles, managers can foster a culture of resilience and high performance.

Coaching Employees: Leading to Solutions, Not Providing Them

One of the most critical aspects of continuous support is coaching. Effective coaching goes beyond simply pointing out what needs improvement; it involves guiding employees through challenges and helping them discover the right solutions themselves. This approach empowers employees to think critically, develop problem-solving skills, and build confidence in their abilities.

Rather than giving direct answers, managers can adopt open-ended questions that stimulate thought and reflection. For example, instead of saying "Here's how you should handle this client issue," a manager might ask, "What do you think would resonate the most with this client given their priorities?" Such questions encourage employees to analyze the situation deeply, consider multiple perspectives, and arrive at a solution they can own. This enhances their immediate performance and prepares them to tackle future challenges independently.

David Rock describes a useful framework for managers to help employees make progress. He uses two dimensions to describe how managers approach feedback with their employees: "ask versus tell" and "problem versus solution."[6] The traditional PM feedback approach is for managers to tell employees what they are doing wrong. Rock suggests that 75% of the time, employees know what they did wrong, and they know what the problem is. Managers focus too much on the problem. Effective feedback and coaching involve asking employees questions, helping them think through what the issue is, and focusing on solutions.

Effective coaching requires managers to engage in regular, open dialogues with their team members, asking critical questions and offering constructive feedback that helps them navigate challenges and seize opportunities. This ongoing interaction ensures that employees continuously develop their skills and competencies and stay aligned with organizational goals.

Coaching also involves creating a safe space where employees feel comfortable sharing their struggles without fear of judgment. This trust-building aspect of coaching is essential for addressing challenges head-on and fostering meaningful growth.

Feedforward: A Future-Focused Alternative to Feedback

Traditional feedback often dwells on past actions, which, while informative, can sometimes feel limiting or even punitive. Research also shows that it frequently becomes personal and disconnected from the work and the progress employees are making toward the goals they are pursuing.[7] In contrast, feedforward shifts the focus to the future, providing actionable insights and advice on how employees can handle upcoming situations effectively so they can make progress toward their goals. This proactive approach aligns with the principles of continuous support, as it equips employees with the tools and strategies needed to succeed in real-time.

Feedforward involves asking questions that prompt employees to think about how they might approach similar situations differently. For instance, a manager could ask, "What's one thing you might try next time to streamline this process?" or "How do you plan to prepare for the presentation to ensure it aligns with the client's approach?" This approach not only fosters a forward-thinking mindset but also motivates employees to take ownership of their own professional development.

Additionally, feedforward could be tailored to individual strengths and growth areas. By recognizing employees' potential and offering personalized advice, managers can inspire confidence and encourage innovation.

Removing Obstacles to Enable Success

Even the most motivated and skilled employees can struggle to make progress when facing obstacles beyond their control. Continuous support requires managers to proactively identify and address these barriers, creating an environment where employees can perform at their best. These obstacles might include unclear expectations and skill gaps, insufficient resources and information, bureaucratic inefficiencies and red tape, or even interpersonal conflicts within or across teams.

Managers play a crucial role as facilitators and advocates, ensuring employees and teams have the tools, information, and support they need to succeed. For instance, if an employee struggles to meet a deadline due to conflicting priorities, a manager might help reprioritize tasks or secure additional resources. Similarly, if a team member faces roadblocks due to outdated technology, the manager could escalate the issue and advocate for necessary upgrades.

Removing obstacles also involves being attuned to employees' well-being. Burnout, stress, and work-life imbalance can significantly hinder performance. Managers who recognize these challenges and offer support—whether through flexible scheduling, workload adjustments, or wellness resources—demonstrate a commitment to their team's holistic success.

The Impact of Continuous Support

When managers consistently provide coaching, feedforward, and obstacle removal, the benefits ripple throughout the organization. Employees are motivated by the progress they are making toward important individual and organizational goals. Employees feel valued, supported, and empowered, leading to higher engagement and job satisfaction. Over time, this approach builds a culture of continuous improvement, where individuals and teams are equipped to adapt, innovate, and excel.

Moreover, continuous support strengthens the manager–employee relationship, fostering trust and collaboration. Employees are more likely to seek guidance, share ideas, and take calculated risks when they know their manager is invested in their growth and success. This dynamic ultimately drives better performance outcomes and contributes to the organization's long-term goals. These dynamic effects are symbolized by the upward spiral in our model.

Continuous support is not just a management strategy—it is an enabling control philosophy that prioritizes the development and success of employees as individuals and as contributors to the organization. By embracing coaching, feedforward, and obstacle removal instead of surveillance, evaluation, and reward differentiation, HR professionals and managers can transform the traditional PM paradigm into a dynamic process that inspires growth, resilience, and sustained excellence—and enables performance. This approach not only benefits employees and teams but also ensures that organizations remain agile and competitive in an ever-changing world.

Development: The Engine for Improvement

Development is the final critical component of the PE framework, seen at the top of Figure 6.1. Continuous learning and skill development are essential for sustained individual and organizational performance and growth. This involves creating opportunities for employees to expand and deepen their capabilities through training, mentoring, and experiential learning, empowering them to meet their current or future challenges. Of course, coaching and feedforward also contribute to individual development.

Development, often treated as a secondary or closing segment of performance discussions, must instead take center stage. This shift in philosophy is critical because facilitating growth directly fuels collective success. When employees and teams have the skills, mindset, and opportunities to continuously improve, the organization as a whole becomes more agile, innovative, and competitive.

Too often, development planning is relegated to the end of performance discussions, where it risks being rushed or overlooked entirely. Managers, having spent significant time reviewing past performance and setting future goals, may feel fatigued or pressured by time constraints, leaving development as an afterthought. It is also possible that managers lack the skills and knowledge of how to have these conversations, linking development to future performance. This undervaluing of development undermines its potential to transform both individual and organizational performance. By elevating development as a core element of PE, leaders signal its strategic importance and ensure that it receives the focus it deserves.

Development should not be treated as a "nice-to-have" but as an integral, ongoing process woven into the fabric of PE. Organizations today face dynamic challenges—from technological advancements to shifting market demands—that require employees to continuously adapt and evolve. By prioritizing development, organizations equip their workforce with the skills and capabilities needed to navigate these changes successfully.

Managers need the tools and training to engage in meaningful development discussions for this shift to occur. These conversations should go beyond identifying areas for improvement to explore employees' aspirations, strengths, and potential. Development plans must be actionable and aligned with both individual career goals and organizational priorities. When employees see that their growth is a cornerstone of the organization's strategy, they are more likely to embrace accountability for their development and contribute at higher levels.

Organizations committed to PE invest in their employees' growth, recognizing that enhanced skills and knowledge translate to sustained and improved performance. This commitment to development fosters a culture of continuous improvement, where employees are motivated to learn and innovate.

Benefits of Performance Enablement

Implementing the PE model yields numerous benefits for employees, managers, and the organization as a whole. These benefits are displayed as the energetic arrows that come out of engaging in the PE process in Figure 6.1. These include the following:

1. **Increased Alignment**: Clear context and continuous support ensure that individual and team goals are aligned with organizational objectives, creating a cohesive effort toward common goals. When everyone is moving in sync toward the same vision, the company is more likely to reach its objectives.

2. **Enhanced Motivation**: When employees see how their work contributes to the larger picture and receive ongoing support, their motivation and engagement levels rise. Through continuous conversations, goals stay in front and center and employees have a clear understanding of their most important priorities and how they are contributing to the organization's success.
3. **Progress against Goals**: Continuous feedback and development enable employees to make steady progress toward their goals, resulting in tangible improvements in motivation and performance. Getting feedback on progress toward goals enhances motivation to continue, even in the face of obstacles. Research from positive psychology highlights the importance of recognizing progress toward goals in motivating employees. When managers acknowledge small wins and incremental progress, they can significantly boost an individual's intrinsic motivation and overall performance.[8] By regularly celebrating achievements, managers can sustain employee engagement and drive continuous improvement.
4. **Increased Capability**: A focus on development leads to a more skilled and capable workforce, enhancing the organization's ability to adapt and thrive in a dynamic environment.

In conclusion, PE offers a transformative approach to managing and enhancing performance within organizations. By shifting the focus from mere evaluation to facilitation and development, organizations can foster an environment where employees are empowered to achieve their full potential, driving sustained success and growth.

Key Takeaways

- At its core, PE shifts the focus from evaluating past performance to actively facilitating present and future performance. It replaces coercive control mechanisms with an enabling control philosophy—one that helps people succeed. This reframing allows PE to become a vehicle for progress, not just appraisal.
- Without a deep understanding of what matters and why, employees are directionless. Providing meaningful context—the "why" behind goals—is foundational. It helps individuals prioritize, adapt, and remain motivated. High-context environments don't just communicate tasks; they build shared understanding and purpose.

- PE is not simply about individual effort—it is about synchronized movement across the organization. Translating strategy into aligned team and individual goals ensures that everyone is rowing in the same direction. But goals alone are not enough; clear behavioral expectations define *how* the work should be done, reinforcing values and competencies in action.
- Through coaching, feedforward, and removing barriers, managers help employees progress in real-time. These manager–employee interactions are not extra tasks—they are the way effective management happens.
- Rather than treating development as a postscript, PE embeds it at the heart of performance. Growth is not "nice-to-have," it's essential for organizational agility and individual advancement. When development is prioritized, organizations cultivate future-ready talent and empower employees to stretch, adapt, and thrive.

SECTION II

PERFORMANCE ENABLEMENT PRINCIPLES

7
Aligning to How Work Gets Done

The foundation of our Performance Enablement (PE) model focuses on providing employees with *Guidance, Direction, and Clear Goals.* This chapter focuses on this underpinning, which is critical to aligning how work gets done across the organization. While we will briefly discuss goal-setting in the modern world of work, we are putting a larger frame on this topic—providing employees with context. While goal-setting is critical to setting the foundation, we will discuss this as a practice in Chapter 10.

Context is critical because, without understanding the "why" of work, motivating employees and aligning work and desired behaviors across the organization is challenging. If employees understand the context for their work, then every team member is on the same page. Success becomes a shared journey, and you are able to reach the destination faster. With alignment across the organization, teams can work together to achieve common goals. When employees deeply understand the company strategy, strategic goals, and the why behind them, they know better how their work contributes to the overall strategy, they are more motivated by their work and have greater satisfaction, persist longer, and know what activities to engage in to get results.[1]

This chapter is divided into three core themes that support organizational alignment: Providing Context, Team-based Alignment, and Agility and Alignment. Each section will further illustrate the value of aligning interests across the organization to improve organizational productivity and performance. Effective alignment connects employees to purpose and facilitates collaboration and adaptability, enabling organizations to thrive in a complex and fast-changing environment. These themes dive deep into three of our eight core principles referenced in the first chapter: providing High Context for work, making PE Team-Based, and creating an Agile process.

Providing Context

Employees need guidance and direction to understand both where they should focus their efforts and what is expected of them in behavioral terms.

Performance Enablement. Edie Goldberg and Alan Colquitt, Oxford University Press. © Oxford University Press (2026).
DOI: 10.1093/9780197830642.003.0007

Organizations achieve the former by sharing a compelling vision of the future and helping employees understand their role in achieving that vision. They achieve the latter by sharing with employees how the company's values are defined or other detailed behavioral models the company has that share how employees should go about doing their work (e.g., customer orientation, moving fast and breaking things, respecting others, being bold, etc.).

Gallup research shows that just a 10% improvement in employees' connection with the mission or purpose of their organization leads to an 8.1% decrease in turnover and a 4.4% increase in profitability.[2] When employees understand the broader context for how their work contributes to a broader organizational goal (e.g., to create innovative products for their customers, cure cancer, improve the work experience of others, help everyone in the world access the world's knowledge), they are more committed to these goals and more motivated to expend effort to achieve their goal. However, when employees do not have a clear understanding of the company's strategy and their business circumstances, it is difficult to align personal goals to organizational goals. In a study with over 8,000 managers across 250 companies, researchers found that *only* 55% of middle managers could properly name one of their company's top five business priorities.[3] These are the leaders in charge of explaining the strategy to their employees. So, if they don't get it, how do we expect people deeper in the company to understand the context in which they are setting their goals? Despite management's role in communicating about business priorities, helping employees understand those priorities and how they fit together is often the missing link.

The book *Firms of Endearment* shares research that tracked the financial performance of organizations over a 10-year period. They found that companies that were purpose-driven significantly outperformed companies that scored lower on their index of a purpose-driven company (13.1% average return on equity vs. 4.12%).[4] A purpose-driven company is a company that operates with a clear purpose, beyond simply making a profit for shareholders. This purpose often falls in the category of social or environmental benefits (e.g., curing cancer, saving the planet, putting a man on the moon). Purpose-driven companies leverage this mission when making decisions at all levels and functions within the organization, impacting not only their culture but also their interactions with customers. A purpose-driven company that engages employees in that purpose is a powerful combination.

Other research also shows that people need meaning and purpose in their lives. When they have purpose and meaning, they experience a variety of positive outcomes (motivation, engagement, performance, well-being, and health) and fewer negative outcomes (dissatisfaction, disillusionment, stress, strain).[5] A meta-analysis found a strong positive relationship between meaningful work and positive work outcomes (e.g., work engagement, commitment, and job satisfaction).[6] (A meta-analysis looks at the results across many studies on the same subject to determine the true overall impact or relationship between variables.)

Dan Pink wrote about the power of purpose as a motivator in his bestselling book *Drive*.[7] Research on transformational leadership also shows that leaders who can foster and inspire a sense of purpose can improve the performance and well-being of their employees.[8] Nine of ten people said they would be willing to earn less money to do more meaningful work, and people are willing to forego 23% of future earnings to have a job that is always meaningful.[9] Despite all of this research evidence, a survey by Deloitte found that 68% of employees and 66% of executives believe businesses are not doing enough to create a sense of purpose and to deliver a meaningful impact.[10]

While much of the literature on context is about connecting employees with purpose and meaning at work, sometimes employees just need to understand the *why* behind management decisions. What is happening in the business environment that is impacting our company's performance? Why is the company implementing this new strategy, which will reduce the firm's investment in the work my team does, and how do I prepare for the future? Why are we implementing this new technology, and how will it change how I do my work? Why are my performance goals 10% higher than last year, and how does that compare to my peers? Context helps employees understand what is happening in the business and why. Decisions can seem random to an employee. Long gone are the days when employees would blindly follow management's direction. As we discussed in Chapter 4, Millennial and Gen Z employees seek purpose and meaning in their work, and they want to know that their efforts will have a positive impact. Employees need to understand how decisions are made so they can commit to the path forward. This is why context matters.

Creating a Line of Sight to Purpose

The next step in providing context is providing employees with "line of sight" (LOS). Providing LOS is about creating a mental map for an employee of what the company is trying to achieve and connecting that to the goals/tasks/activities the employee is engaged in so that the employee understands how their actions are supporting the larger company goals. While this is part of providing employees with context for their work, this literature is more focused on the psychological impact of providing employees with LOS. When employees understand how their work connects to higher-level goals, they become more committed to achieving their goals.

The research in this area makes a very important clarification that this is a switch from a coercive control-based approach, where employees are supposed to follow orders, to managing employees toward a new focus on shaping employee mindsets. This quote encapsulates the idea perfectly:

> "For an organization to work well, it is not enough for employees to accept commands literally... What is required is that employees take initiative and apply their skills and knowledge to advance the achievement of their organization's success."[11]

Context for goals and creating LOS is critical for creating purpose and meaning, which is a key mechanism of enabling control. This shift in mindset is important in today's business environment, where goals may shift quickly as business conditions change. Achieving organizational success comes from the discretionary and unspecified behaviors that lead to accomplishing organizational goals. When employees understand the direction of the organization, when business conditions change, they can make adjustments to their previously assigned goals to deliver on the broader company strategic objectives. LOS helps employees go beyond what is detailed in their job description or established goals to make adjustments that will lead to improved outcomes. They remain aligned to the strategic objectives but adjust their actions to meet the moment.

One outstanding example of how LOS impacts the bottom line comes from JetBlue. JetBlue employees attend JetBlue University where they learn about the company's business model and the company's values. All employees are sent a monthly newsletter that reports on the company's progress, competitors' standings, and information about the company's financials. In 2004, the company's CEO said that the key to the company's growth to over $1 billion in revenue, coupled with the improvements the company has made in overall performance, stems from their employees' understanding of and commitment to the larger goals of the company.[12]

Goals serve the purpose of directing attention to the activities and behaviors needed to achieve organizational outcomes. For goals to work, employees need to be committed to them—and this is where context comes in. Difficult goals are, by their very nature, hard to achieve. This requires extra work by employees to accomplish these goals. When managers provide the context for employees about *why* they should work hard to achieve these goals, they provide the meaning that influences commitment to achieve a goal.

As we have said, when employees understand the big picture and how the work they are doing fits into the company's strategy, we don't need to handcuff them to the work or micromanage them. This is the essence of enabling control—employees are enabled to take the initiative to make adjustments along the way to achieve better outcomes.

Team-Based Alignment

In Chapters 4 and 5, we made the business case for why companies need to shift from a strict focus on individual performance to include team performance. An excellent illustration of the importance of this change comes from Microsoft. In early 2000, Microsoft experienced company-wide performance issues because of the competitive nature of its individual-based performance management (PM) system.[13] Employees set individual goals and were evaluated on their performance against goals using a forced distribution curve. Employees were stack-ranked based on their performance against their goals. This determined the size of the reward an employee would receive. We will talk in more detail about this practice and the dangers it can pose in Chapter 13. This competitive situation led to several issues:

Decreased Collaboration: Employees were incentivized to compete against their colleagues rather than work together. This led to information hoarding and discouraged teamwork.

Talent Drain: Many skilled employees left the company because of the stressful, cut-throat culture. Performance reviews were viewed as unfair because even if the team was all high-performing, managers were forced to rate their team on a bell curve, leading to artificial and unfair evaluations.

Innovation Stagnated: Their system, which focused on short-term individual goals that could be easily achieved, discouraged risk-taking and long-term innovation projects. This caused Microsoft to fall behind its competitors.

Toxic Culture: The PM process fostered distrust and undermined morale among team members. This led to a drop in employee engagement, which in turn led to a decrease in productivity.

When Satya Nadella became CEO in 2014, he played a crucial role in shifting the culture within Microsoft. The company ended its stack-ranking practice and implemented a new PM approach that encouraged greater collaboration with a focus on continuous feedback, coaching, and individual growth. Their new system promoted teamwork and collective success over individual rankings.

These changes led to significant growth for Microsoft, with its stock tripling within four years of Nadella shifting the company's culture and focus, and its market cap growing from around $300 billion in 2014 to over $3 trillion in 2024. While much of this success had to do with a shift in company strategy, even the CEO would attribute much of the success to improved collaboration.[14]

Team-Based Goals Create Alignment

As we think about what PE looks like through a work group lens, we need to think about how we set goals, how performance is evaluated, and how we recognize and reward performance. Although subsequent chapters will discuss these issues in depth, from a principles perspective we will briefly touch on these factors.

Although many organizations today set company and department or team-based goals, most do not focus individuals on those higher-level goals. They still have employees set individual goals, which are theoretically aligned with company goals. But as the Microsoft example demonstrated, individual goal-setting can create a competitive environment. Furthermore, as discussed in previous chapters, it is rarely the case that an individual has sole control over the outcomes of their individual goals. Outcomes require the collaboration of many individuals, often across organizational boundaries. This sets up the conditions that are ripe for team goals.

When teams focus on their collective responsibilities, employees can jump in and help out (discretionary effort) when they see that their accomplishments may be for naught unless another aspect of the project is executed as well. Unfortunately, research informs us that 71% of colleagues are not committed to helping each other by offering feedback, and 74% don't believe they are being held accountable to shared goals.[15]

But when a group of people has something meaningful to accomplish together and they know clear ways of accomplishing it, they behave and interact differently. They bring more enthusiasm to the work, and they communicate better, cooperate more, work harder, and accomplish more.[16] This creates a team spirit and taps into the power of belonging. The need to form and maintain social bonds is among the most powerful human motives.[17] Our thoughts, feelings, and behaviors are profoundly influenced by our need to maintain quality relationships and avoid rejection by others. In fact, the relationships and commonalities we have with others are a big part of the way we define ourselves.

Our case study will provide a great example of how team goals can work in practice and tie to individual goals while still retaining a focus on team outcomes. This creates a strong alignment between team and individual goals.

How Can Companies Align Teams and Create Team-Based Goals?

From the Front Lines—Edward Jones

Edward Jones, founded in 1922, has a rich history evolving from a small, family-run brokerage firm based in Missouri to a major player in the financial services industry. Today, they have 2.2 trillion dollars of assets under care. From the 1950s to the late 1980s, the company experienced rapid growth as it brought Wall Street to Main Street and opened over 1,000 offices across the country and eventually internationally. In recent years, the company has undergone a significant transformation to adapt to changing market conditions. They shifted from their traditional single-advisor office model selling investment products to creating financial advisor teams that can provide more comprehensive financial planning and advice, becoming a diversified financial services organization, now with more than 20,000 financial advisors. This is not unlike IBM's big shift from a product to a services company.

This shift from individual brokers to financial services teams required the company to rethink how it manages performance. It required a shift from focusing on individual performance to talking about team-based (shared) objectives. How does each individual contribute to the team objective? That is, how does what each person does contribute to the team's performance? This has the effect of keeping individual focus fully aligned with team focus.

Unlike traditional goal-cascading processes, this company establishes the team's goal and then cascades each individual's contribution to that goal. This keeps them more closely aligned and committed to what is being accomplished as a team and makes it clear how individual performance matters.

"As we have become more and more of a team-based firm, setting and managing performance for teams rather than individuals fosters greater collaboration, accountability, and shared business outcomes. It transforms isolated efforts into

continued

continued

a unified, aligned force, driving collective achievement and innovation, while ensuring that every member's strengths are leveraged for the greater good."

— Suzan McDaniel, Principal, Chief Human Resources Officer

Edward Jones knew that they wanted to focus on improving team performance and holding individuals accountable for their part in that shared commitment. But they began with the premise that if you don't set clear goals and expectations, you can't provide quality feedback and people won't be clear about what they need to do to make progress and move the goal post toward a win. Beyond their team-based approach to goal-setting, Edward Jones also established clear performance expectations with their framework of Purpose, Mindsets, and Behaviors.

Purpose: This represents *why* the firm exists. *The purpose of Edward Jones is to partner for positive impact to improve the lives of their clients and colleagues, and together, better their communities and society.*

Mindsets: These are the set of beliefs and attitudes that influence how they view situations and how they may act. Examples of the five mindsets include:

- Leadership: How they hold themselves accountable to help others thrive.
- Continuous Learning: Embracing and learning from new experiences and perspectives.

Behaviors: The firm has nine core behaviors clustered under three key themes:

- Be purpose-driven
- Be human-centered
- Lead with courage

Thus far, the company is getting positive feedback from employees that by setting the foundation for performance, with clear team goals, and an understanding of how each individual contributes to that success, managers are better able to give clear feedback that helps individuals perform. The company has been asking employees two questions: "Are you having a conversation with your leader about your performance?" and "How is it going?" The results indicate that employees feel the frequency and the quality and candor of those conversations about that performance had increased significantly.

This case study is an excellent example of how a company sets context for employees and focuses individuals on team-based goals, while also focusing them on their individual accountabilities for achieving the team goal.

Aligning Behavior with Evaluation and Rewards

Evaluation is not the purpose of PE, but when it is done, the performance of the team is a critical focus, not just the individual. Measuring performance at the team level, as is done in our example from Edward Jones, is important for reinforcing team alignment. Then, team performance can be linked to rewards based on what the collective team, department, or company has achieved. These are the principles that facilitate alignment and best match the needs of our modern business environment. When you measure performance at the team level and hold employees accountable for the workgroup's performance, performance increases across many metrics, including collaboration, financial performance, and customer service.[18] It is important to put more weight on team goals than individual goals to reinforce the need for collaboration.

Agility and Alignment

In a traditional PM process, companies set their annual goals, goals cascade down the organization until individual goals are set, and then everyone expects those goals to remain in place for the entire year. In reality, what happens is that the business environment changes, new competitors come in, new technologies are introduced, innovations happen both within the company and externally, and this forces business priorities to shift. Then, at the end of the year, managers "revise" the goals to better fit what the employee really did, and they rate employees on those revised goals. In other words, often, the goal-setting process is a process of "revisionist history." Not that it set out to be that way, but a year is a long time in today's business cycle.

In Chapter 5, we shared how the principles of the Agile Manifesto have implications for traditional PM practices. Here, we want to emphasize how the principles of PE facilitate a more agile operating model. PE encourages frequent communication as an essential practice that facilitates continuous improvement and learning while doing. Real-time feedback is put to use. Time spent documenting is much less important than making the time for communication.

Being open to changing what you are doing because business conditions have changed is at the heart of being agile. Strategic goals provide direction, but frequent reviews allow individuals to update their goals based on conditions on the ground rather than how we thought things would play out for the year. In Chapter 10, we will introduce goal-setting methods that are designed to respond to a more agile work environment; the key is reviewing goals frequently and making adjustments based on progress and new information. While goals may still focus on key outcomes the team is driving toward, individual tasks may change to achieve the desired outcomes.

Key Takeaways

- Employees need to understand the "why" behind their work, not just what tasks to complete. Providing context is the foundation for high performance; it aligns work with organizational goals, increases engagement, and improves job satisfaction.
- Employees who see how their individual contributions fit into the larger organizational strategy are more proactive and adaptable. Organizations like JetBlue provide a great example of how creating LOS drives business success and employee engagement.
- We know from the research that setting specific, difficult goals is important to performance. But clarifying expectations is important as well. Unfortunately, a major issue in business today is unclear expectations.
- Relying solely on individual goals can lead to competition, knowledge hoarding, and disengagement. Shifting to team-based goals fosters alignment, collaboration, discretionary effort, and overall company success. Our case study from Edward Jones shared how one company approached team-goal-setting and individual accountability to facilitate alignment for the collective good.
- Traditional annual goal-setting is problematic in today's dynamic business environment. Agile methodologies provide flexibility by focusing on outcomes over rigid tasks, ensuring continuous alignment with shifting priorities.

These insights highlight why investing in a PE approach—grounded in context, collaboration, and agility—is critical for driving organizational success.

8
A Focus on Being Supportive and Positive

Another principle at the center of Performance Enablement (PE) is a shift from evaluating and differentiating performance to supporting and enabling performance. This happens not just by providing feedback, but by providing other support, resources, and information that employees need to make day-to-day progress toward their goals. It also reflects a more positive approach to support employees, emphasizing positive feedback, recognition, and leveraging their strengths. This chapter describes three of our eight core principles referenced in the first chapter: Positive, Enabling, and Progress-Oriented, and it shares the supporting research and key practices based on these principles.

Progress

To enable performance, employees need to know how they are doing—they need feedback on their progress toward their goals. From Control Theory, we know that an effective feedback system involves multiple "tests" to detect a gap between the goal and current status.[1] Assume your goal is to lose 20 pounds. If the initial test shows a gap (you are 20 pounds from your goal), you will take action to reduce the gap (eat less and exercise more). After taking these actions, we need a second feedback system—a monitoring feedback loop—to compare results from the initial test with subsequent tests to see if the gap is shrinking—are we making progress. You get on the scale every day and see if the gap is shrinking. Researchers refer to the rate at which the gap between the goal and current state is shrinking as velocity. Research shows velocity (rate of progress) can be as important or even more important than the size of the discrepancy (feedback) in driving satisfaction, motivation, and performance.[2]

Progress keeps the focus of feedback on the work itself and on the goals employees are working toward. Ryan Hawk, host of The Learning Leader Show podcast, captured the essence of this mindset in a recent interview

Performance Enablement. Edie Goldberg and Alan Colquitt, Oxford University Press. © Oxford University Press (2026).
DOI: 10.1093/9780197830642.003.0008

with the author Dan Pink. Ryan reflected on an exchange he had with Drew Brees, a famous US football quarterback. Brees advice to future quarterbacks was to focus on "moving the chains," getting first downs, 10 yards at a time. If he did this, the touchdowns would come.[3] Organizations should adopt a similar mindset. Big ambitious goals are fine, but it is the moment-to-moment, day-to-day progress toward important goals that keeps employees feeling positive and coming to work every day. Teresa Amabile captured this sentiment in her mantra for organizations and managers: *Progress in meaningful work*.[4]

Feedback is a means to an end, and that end is progress toward goals. People don't weigh themselves every morning just to see how much they weigh; they want to see if they are making progress toward their goal (e.g., lose 20 pounds before their class reunion). Feedback and progress are essential companions to goal achievement and performance.

While research in the areas of progress and monitoring goal achievement is relatively recent, the practice has early roots. Benjamin Franklin, a US politician, diplomat, author, and scientist, was an early practitioner. He wanted to make 13 virtues the centerpiece of his life, but he found it difficult to achieve in practice. To help, he created a calendar and scorecard to assess his progress.[5] Every night before bed, he would review his day and ask himself what good he had done that day (see Figure 8.1). On days when he succeeded, this question would be a chance for him to recognize and acknowledge his successes. On days when he fell short, this question was a nudge to reflect on what's important and how he could get back on the right path.

Research shows that progress toward goals is more important than achieving goals in predicting happiness.[6] This makes sense; people can experience a letdown after they achieve their goals. Even thinking about goal achievement can decrease motivation by mentally transporting people to the point where they have achieved their goal, which can decrease energy levels.[7]

Progress is the premise of research by Harvard professor Teresa Amabile.[8] She studied employees working in 26 project teams in seven organizations over a period of several months. She was interested in the psychological experiences of employees as they went about their daily work, which she called "inner work life." Employees completed diaries describing how they felt on a day-to-day basis and rated their engagement. They described their daily work activities and the emotions, perceptions, and motivations associated with these activities. She then compared employees' descriptions of their best and worst days. When employees described their best days, they talked about the progress they had made and when they described their worst days, they talked about the setbacks they experienced. Simply making progress, even if it was

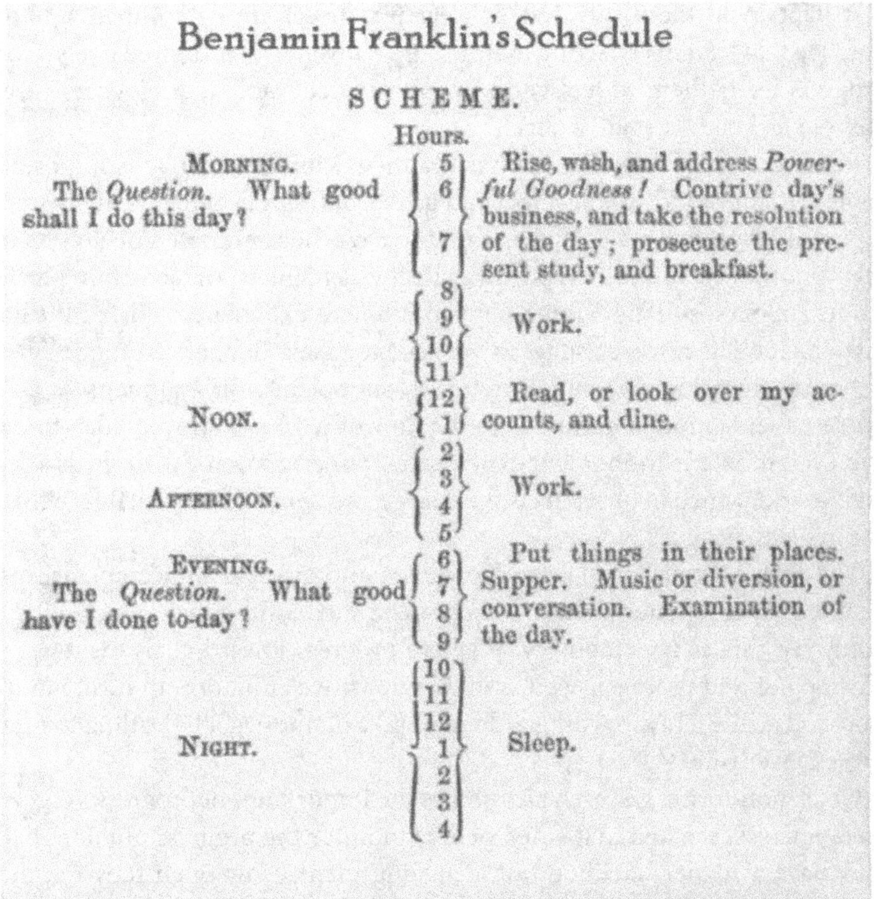

Benjamin Franklin's Schedule

SCHEME.

	Hours.	
MORNING. The *Question.* What good shall I do this day?	5, 6, 7	Rise, wash, and address *Powerful Goodness!* Contrive day's business, and take the resolution of the day; prosecute the present study, and breakfast.
	8, 9, 10, 11	Work.
NOON.	12, 1	Read, or look over my accounts, and dine.
AFTERNOON.	2, 3, 4, 5	Work.
EVENING. The *Question.* What good have I done to-day?	6, 7, 8, 9	Put things in their places. Supper. Music or diversion, or conversation. Examination of the day.
NIGHT.	10, 11, 12, 1, 2, 3, 4	Sleep.

Figure 8.1 Benjamin Franklin's calendar

Source: Public domain

small, affected all aspects of inner work life. When people made progress, they reported more positive emotions, they were motivated by the work itself, and they saw the work and their teams in a more favorable light. These effects were more pronounced when employees were working on something meaningful. Employees were most engaged when they "made progress in meaningful work." Unfortunately, Amabile also found that progress is not something managers think about when motivating their employees. She asked managers to rank order the importance of five different motivation factors. Only 5% of managers ranked progress high, and most ranked it last.

Other researchers also find that making progress is important for happiness, engagement, and performance. People's emotional responses to events that happen to them (positive or negative affect) are determined by how they see these events affecting their progress toward their desired goals. Goal progress leads them to feel good—positive affect, and goal blockages lead them to feel bad—negative affect.[9]

Research by Harvard Researcher Matthew Killingsworth adds important context to the work-linking affect and goal progress. Participants in his study reported emotional states throughout the day when prompted by an app on their phones. He found that positive affect was highly variable within participants.[10] Small, situational, moment-to-moment experiences during the day matter a lot. His research suggests we need to take a "higher resolution" view of how to support and enable employees, supporting our argument for a PE process that is more continuous in the flow of work. Employees' day-to-day and even moment-to-moment experiences working toward their goals affect their mood, which in turn affects the energy and enthusiasm available to them to pursue their goals.

The relationship between goal progress and affect is important because people who feel better are more likely to be successful in work and in life.[11] Many see this as a virtuous cycle where progress toward goals makes people happier and more engaged, and these positive emotions, in turn, build a storehouse of energy to work harder and take on more goals, leading to more success over time.[12]

Goal-monitoring research also shows the importance of progress. A recent meta-analysis showed that when people monitor the progress of their goals, they have a higher likelihood of achieving them. How often they monitor progress also matters, the more frequently they monitor progress, the more likely it is they will achieve their goals.[13]

This principle has clear implications for PM practices. It suggests we focus more on how managers work with employees on a continuous basis to monitor the progress they are making toward their goals and train them to support employees in making progress. It also reinforces the importance of helping employees see the value and meaning of their work by connecting it to broader organizational goals.

Positivity

Feedback is an important topic in this book and plays an important role in enabling performance. Discussions of feedback naturally raise the question about the effectiveness of different types of feedback—positive versus negative and different theories and approaches to motivating employees. Different theories make different predictions about which is more effective.[14]

There are many areas of research across several disciplines on the effectiveness of positive and negative feedback. This research suggests that whether the feedback was positive or negative doesn't matter much when it comes to employee performance. The effectiveness of feedback had more to do with the nature of the feedback and how the individual interpreted it; the more personal the feedback (vs. feedback on the work), the less effective it was in improving performance.[15]

The effectiveness of positive or negative feedback also depends on the type of goals employees are working toward. Negative feedback seems to be more effective where prevention is the goal (e.g., safety, compliance), where accuracy and adherence to rules, policies, and procedures are important. Employees want to avoid punishment, and negative feedback can increase motivation and performance. In contrast, for more traditional goals where individuals hope to achieve something (versus avoid something) and are looking for rewards (versus avoiding punishment), positive feedback is more helpful for motivation and performance.[16]

Managers play an important role in feedback delivery, and unfortunately, they are biased toward negative feedback and against positive feedback.[17] Managers believe they are more effective when they give negative feedback. This negative bias makes sense given our earlier discussion of the underlying assumptions organizations (and leaders) hold about employees: They are lazy, unmotivated, and self-serving; they behave instrumentally and work hard only when extrinsic rewards are at stake.[18] These assumptions reinforce the need for a more coercive approach to motivation, which emphasizes negativity. And, as we discuss later in this chapter, feedback is frequently pointed at weaknesses, which also reinforces a negative bias.[19]

While managers are biased toward negative feedback, research suggests that a positive feedback bias is more effective. Researchers studied 60 strategic business unit leadership teams from a large information-processing company. They tracked the verbal communication among team members along three dimensions: Positivity/Negativity (P/N), Inquiry/Advocacy, and Other/Self. They measured the performance of these teams using financial performance, customer satisfaction, and 360-degree feedback ratings among the team members. They found that the P/N feedback ratio was the strongest differentiator between the high- and low-performing teams. High-performing teams were nearly three times as positive as medium-performing teams and nearly 15 times as positive as low-performing teams.[20]

Findings from positive psychology also support a positivity bias. Positivity is more typical of the human experience, and a higher ratio of positivity to negativity (a "positive offset") is associated with optimal mental health and human functioning.[21] Interventions that focus on positivity increase satisfaction, fulfillment, motivation, well-being, and performance and can provide a reservoir of energy to draw on under more difficult circumstances.[22] Extensive research on marriage reinforces these findings. Unless couples can maintain a high ratio of positivity to negativity (five to one is optimal), it is not likely they will be able to sustain the relationship.[23]

A positive bias also makes sense given the potency of negative feedback. Responses to negative feedback, experiences, and emotions are stronger than their positive counterparts. Leaders who approach employees critically ignite stronger neural responses and activate areas of the brain that impair thinking and perceiving and inhibit learning.[24] Researchers studied the power of many different types of events—life events, relationship outcomes, social network patterns, interpersonal interactions (including feedback), and learning processes. In nearly every case, bad events were more potent than good events.[25] Teresa Amabile's research discussed earlier also found that negative experiences (setbacks) were two to three times more potent than positive experiences in affecting engagement and the quality of inner work life.[26]

Leaders play an important role in maintaining this positive bias. Research shows that different leaders produce different effects in the brains of their employees, which produce different attitudes, moods, and behaviors.[27] They find that "Resonant" leaders (who are more positive and compassionate) activate areas of the brain associated with being open to new ideas and other people. "Dissonant" leaders (who are more negative and critical) deactivate these areas and activate areas associated with narrowed attention, decreased compassion, and negative emotion. This research suggests that leaders "infect" employees with feelings and emotions that can either help or hinder them from performing well.

Strengths

A key aspect of the more supportive and positive approach of PE is a focus on strengths. Many organizations have deficit-focused cultures.[28] Traditional PM processes reflect this culture by identifying and focusing on weaknesses.[29] Managers focus on employee failures and remediating skills, abilities, attitudes, or behaviors that need to be improved through training, feedback, and coaching. This approach tends to emphasize preventing failure versus facilitating success. Many researchers and practitioners agree that the best strategy for individual development is to invest in employees' strengths and not in managing their weaknesses.[30]

Research on strengths has accelerated, and interventions to identify and leverage strengths have been developed. These interventions have been successful in a wide variety of contexts and have had positive effects on a broad range of outcomes, including well-being (positive affect, life satisfaction, depression) and job outcomes like work performance and work engagement.[31]

Researchers have integrated these principles into an alternative to traditional performance appraisals at Soda Stream. They incorporated more positivity and a focus on identifying and leveraging strengths with encouraging results and positive reactions from employees and managers.[32] Others have used a similar approach to help leaders develop effective relationships, implementing it effectively at FifthThird Bank.[33]

How Does a Company Fix a PM Process That Is an Administrative Burden and Uniformly Disliked?

From the Front Lines—Supporting Employees in a Public Sector Organization

Shonna Waters, PhD, CEO and co-founder of Fractional Insights, shared her experience with redesigning a PM process for a high-profile public sector organization. The project began with a top-down directive to improve the PM process. It was uniformly disliked by everyone with a heavy emphasis on administration and paperwork. The project began with a pragmatic objective:

If no one liked the process, the least we could do was make it less of a burden.

In the end, the team had three simple goals:

1. Increase efficiency
2. Improve organizational performance
3. Reduce administrative burden

They simplified performance ratings, clarified key decisions and how ratings would affect them, and reduced documentation. By working backward from those goals, it became clear that simply changing the performance management (PM) process wasn't enough. To "make it better," they wanted more two-way conversations and introduced several tools to enable this. Yet the organization needed to make deeper,

continued

continued

more fundamental changes still. They realized that if they didn't instill a culture of coaching and trust, a new process and new tools wouldn't matter. The culture needed to evolve to support the new process. Like many organizations, their culture was more of a "telling" culture (vs. an asking culture). Managers weren't always aware of issues employees were facing and how they could better support them. To help with this, they introduced a new quarterly check-in process.

They sent out a simple pulse survey of three to five questions every quarter to better understand where employees were getting stuck. The questions were simple: Did employees know what was expected of them, and did they know what success looked like? Did they have the resources and support to deliver on what was expected? Were they getting feedback on the value they were adding to the organization? What other types of direction or feedback would be most helpful to have from their managers?

The organization acknowledged that employees may not have a fair chance to be successful; they may be getting stuck because of things beyond their control. They wanted managers to know what issues they were facing and what could be done to improve their situation. Without quality information in both directions—what success looked like and how they were measuring up against it and where employees were unclear or under-resourced—any process would still fail to unlock performance potential.

The feedback was aggregated and sent directly to the manager. The goal wasn't the numbers—it was the dialogue. Managers needed some structure to facilitate this dialogue. Managers discussed the results with their employees to better understand the issues, causes, and possible solutions for better supporting their employees and to address issues getting in the way of performance. If a manager's score was low and didn't improve, results were shared with their managers. This introduced more accountability for the managers, but it wasn't punitive. The goal wasn't to place blame but to surface issues and identify managers' development needs to help them get better. Some studies suggest that as high as 98% of managers believe they need more training.[34] It didn't seem fair to assume managers were aware of the issues employees faced nor to assume they knew how to help employees address them. The managers may be as stuck as the employees.

They developed several resources to train and support the managers in facilitating these quarterly check-ins: learning journeys, microlearnings, and implementation playbooks. A key piece of the training for managers was on how to receive feedback. Managers are accustomed to training on giving feedback but get little help in how to receive feedback—yet they are a powerful model for their employees.

The process worked well. There was an increase in the amount of bidirectional dialogue and a distinct move in the direction of asking vs. telling. Overall, employee engagement scores went up significantly over the years. The organization has evolved reward guidance in the last couple of years to set a minimum value. This helped move the organization from the "peanut butter spread" reward approach to more focused impact rewards to ensure meaningful performance distinctions.

This research has several implications for PM and PE practices: monitor employee mood and attitudes regularly, focus more on positive feedback, and train managers to use positive feedback and interventions. This case study also provided a great example of how a company can be more supportive and enabling, by asking questions that raised managers' awareness that more help was needed to achieve goals.

Enabling and Supporting

An important piece of context we take from Chapter 7 is the role of self-efficacy and self-esteem in motivation and goal achievement. Self-efficacy is an individual's belief in their ability to successfully complete a task or achieve a goal. Higher levels of self-efficacy leads employees to commit to goals (especially challenging goals) and that commitment is necessary for motivation and goal achievement.[35] Employees need to feel confident to accomplish their goals which motivate them. It is through their interactions with managers and others and their own success that self-efficacy develops. These interactions involve more than simply providing feedback. They involve actively supporting employees by providing them with the resources and information they need, problem-solving with them, removing obstacles, connecting them with role models and others who can help, and expressing confidence in them. If employees know that their manager and others fully support them, they are more likely to feel confident and they can achieve their goals. These insights aren't new. Management icon Rensis Likert talked about the value of managers being more supportive and enabling over 50 years ago. He discussed four management systems that describe different types of employee–manager relationships, which lead to different levels of satisfaction and productivity for employees. "Consultative" and "Participative" systems are more supportive and enabling, with higher levels of trust, participation, cooperation, and autonomy, and therefore more satisfying and productive for employees and managers.[36]

Teresa Amabile's research discussed earlier illustrated the benefits of supporting and enabling employees. They found that, on their best days, employees received the support, help, and encouragement they needed from others (which she calls catalysts and nourishers). In contrast, on their worst days, not only didn't employees get the support they needed, but they also frequently encountered events that actively blocked or undermined their work (she calls these inhibitors and toxins).[37]

A recent meta-analysis study confirmed that supportive behaviors within interpersonal relationships are core determinants of an employee's motivation, well-being, and performance.[38] Recognition from a teacher can build a student's sense of mastery and sustain and reinforce their efforts.[39] Trust from a manager can develop an employee's initiative and proactivity.[40] Expectations established by a coach can engage an athlete and sustain their efforts to improve.[41] The positive effect of supportive behaviors on motivation, behavior, and wellness is well-established in research on self-determination theory.[42] This research has focused primarily on interpersonal behaviors that help satisfy employee needs for autonomy, competence, and relatedness, and we presented evidence earlier showing the benefits of supporting these needs.[43]

Autonomy support involves recognizing the employee's perspective (empathy) and encouraging more self-directed behavior. It requires providing more decision authority and less reliance on external controls (rewards or sanctions) to motivate behavior. Competence support involves promoting self-efficacy and mastery by providing feedback, structure, and guidance about how to perform activities, sharing knowledge and expertise, and establishing clear and realistic expectations. Relatedness support involves expressing interest, care, warmth, and positive regard toward employees and encouraging teamwork and collaboration. Providing these kinds of supportive behaviors helps satisfy these needs and, in turn, increases employee motivation, well-being, and performance.

Finally, research in organizational support theory also reinforces the value of enabling and supporting employees. It holds that employees develop global beliefs concerning the extent to which the organization values their contributions and cares about their well-being. Perceived Organizational Support (POS) reflects a belief that help will be available from the organization when it is needed to carry out one's job effectively. A meta-analysis of 70 studies found that several areas of employee support (e.g., fairness, manager support, organizational rewards, favorable job conditions) were associated with POS. POS, in turn, was related to favorable employee outcomes (job satisfaction, positive mood) and organizational outcomes (affective commitment, performance, and retention).[44]

Employees develop similar views about the degree to which managers value their contributions and care about their well-being (Perceived Supervisor Support—PSS). Research has consistently shown that PSS is a positive contributor to POS and is directly related to favorable organizational outcomes (turnover, engagement, and performance).[45]

To summarize, PE has at its core a focus on treating employees in a more positive, supportive, and humane way and leveraging employee strengths so they can make day-to-day progress toward their goals. Implementing practices based on these principles provides employees with a reservoir of motivation and energy to approach (versus avoid) the day-to-day challenges they face.

Key Takeaways

- PE emphasizes supporting and enabling employees rather than merely evaluating performance. This includes providing feedback and resources and recognizing strengths to foster day-to-day progress.
- Regular feedback on goal progress, rather than just outcomes, enhances motivation, performance, engagement, and satisfaction.
- Studies indicate that making progress in meaningful work leads to greater motivation, engagement, and positive emotions, whereas setbacks negatively impact workplace morale.
- Positive feedback is more effective for motivation and engagement, especially in goal-achievement contexts.
- Traditional PM focuses on fixing weaknesses, but research supports leveraging employees' strengths for better performance, well-being, and job satisfaction.
- Effective managers foster self-efficacy and goal commitment by providing resources and encouragement and removing obstacles, leading to higher motivation and productivity.
- Employee motivation improves when organizations support autonomy (self-directed work), competence (clear expectations and guidance), and relatedness (positive relationships and teamwork).

9
Making It Simple and Continuous

Making It Simple

When we first envisioned our Performance Enablement (PE) model, we knew we wanted to shift the process to something easy to implement and manage. Making it simple became one of our key principles for design. But what does making PE simple mean? This takes on many forms, but they all add up to shifting away from a complex process with heavy documentation that every manager dreads. It should be a process that adds value to the individual and organization, not an administrative burden. A widely reported industry statistic is that performance management (PM) activities (e.g., setting goals, providing feedback, evaluating, and documenting performance) take a single manager about 210 hours per year to complete.[1] That equates to 26 days a year! We think this time could be better spent supporting employees and teams to accelerate performance.

Goal-Setting

Throughout this book, we make it very clear that the process of goal-setting is very important to driving performance. While goal-setting is not easy per se, organizations tend to make it time-consuming and complicated when it comes to goal alignment. Some companies cascade goals from the top. Each leadership level must wait until the leader above them has set their goals. Then, the next level down sets goals that align with the higher-level goal. This cascades down the organization until months later, when everyone has set their goals. Unfortunately, all this effort at alignment is misspent because business conditions change, and there is little appetite to go through the cascading process once again when top-line (or mid-level) goals shift.

We believe that directional alignment is good enough, and we recommend simpler, directional goals that are more flexible. Once the senior leadership team has set the company's direction and goals, everyone can align to those goals, with someone in management responsible for reviewing the collective

Performance Enablement. Edie Goldberg and Alan Colquitt, Oxford University Press. © Oxford University Press (2026).
DOI: 10.1093/9780197830642.003.0009

goals to ensure that all critical areas are being addressed. The senior leadership team usually sets goals both for the company and their own area of responsibility. Thus, enough direction is set in a context appropriate for teams and/or individual contributors to set goals that support these higher-level goals.

Simplify Rating Systems and Calibration Process

A lot of complexity has crept into the performance evaluation process without adding any value. We rate employees on each goal, each behavior, and often an overall score. That overall score is sometimes calculated based on an algorithm that weights each component based on its relative importance. While early research advocated that a seven-point rating scale was optimal for reliability, a frequently cited research article found that reliability really drops off after five points.[2] Today, it is quite common for companies to use a five-point rating scale.[3] However, in practice, we have seen companies end up with a ten-point rating scale, or more, because they allow managers to provide +/− or the use of ½ points in addition to whole-scale numbers (e.g., 3.5). In Chapter 13, we will discuss the issues of accuracy and bias in ratings and why most rating systems are flawed. However, here we simply want to say that managers have a difficult time making some of these fine-tuned ratings in any reliable or accurate manner. Whether using a ten-point rating scale or even a five-point scale, managers stress over what rating to give and how the employee will respond.

Our rating scales, whether they be five-point, seven-point, or ten-point scales all assume that performance is normally distributed. But is it? Some Industrial/Organizational Psychology research suggests that performance may better fit a power-law distribution curve instead of a normal distribution.[4] Unlike a "normal" (bell curve) distribution, a power-law distribution curve drops off quickly and flattens out, showing that very large values (like super-rich people) are rare, but do happen, and most people have much less wealth. In Figure 9.1, you can see that in a normal distribution curve, most scores fall around the average, and the small tail ends have a few high and low performers. In contrast, with the power-law distribution curve, the research shows that in numerous settings (e.g., business, sports, arts, etc.), there are a few high performers who make a disproportionate impact on company performance. This suggests that we may need to focus more on identifying, recognizing, and rewarding these high performers rather than focusing on differentiating the masses. So why not simplify our rating scale to three points (or even two if you are handling low performers through another process)?

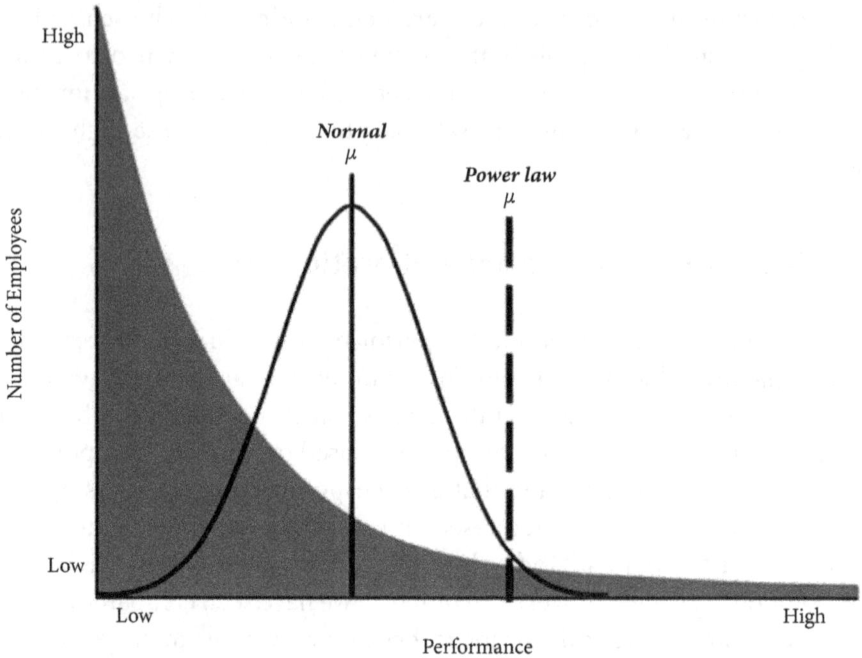

Figure 9.1 Normal distribution curve superimposed on a power-law distribution curve

Reprinted from Organizational Dynamics, Vol 44 /edition number 3, Aguinis, H., & Bradly K. J. "The secret sauce for organizational success: Managing and producing star performers, 161–168."

Another way in which we make the rating process complex is through the calibration process. In a rating calibration process, managers discuss and align performance ratings for their employees in a group setting. The goal of this activity is to reduce bias and subjectivity and to ensure employees are being rated using the same criteria and standards, regardless of their manager or department. While a few companies may calibrate on the level of goal difficulty for the goals that are being set, most companies calibrate on the rating of performance. In our study, 72% of participants said that they conduct calibration sessions on ratings. By doing so, all employees who receive a four on a five-point rating, for example, are deemed to contribute to the organization's success in a similar manner. Calibration meetings consume lots of time from managers and senior leaders. It can also be an emotionally exhausting process with managers fighting for the ratings of their employees. But does it make ratings more accurate and fair? You will see in Chapter 13 that the answer is "no." The strongest manager often gets their way. Criteria other than performance (such as political influence, likeability, and forced distributions) all influence the accuracy of ratings. Many organizations have roll-up meetings as well, where rating distributions are reviewed for face validity (e.g., it looks right) and for fit with distribution guidance. If ratings are not accurate, then why do we spend so much time trying to fine-tune differences and debate with others the accuracy of our comparison of one employee against another, which is what happens in the calibration process. We spend a lot of time trying to make the best decisions, but ultimately, they are flawed. So why not simplify and get the basic information you need to help make the decisions needed.

Documentation

PM documentation is something most managers dread. It is emotionally exhausting because judging an employee's performance and differentiating performance among groups of employees and feeding that information back to employees can feel stressful. It's a similar experience for employees. They feel they need to make their case and document everything they've done. It isn't uncommon for employees to attach other documents to their forms (e.g., sales reports) and have final forms that are 15–20 pages long. Spending time documenting performance takes hours away from making progress against goals, and it feels like an administrative burden. Most PM processes are designed as if they are documenting performance of the 1% of employees who are having performance issues versus serving the needs of 99% of the employees who are performing well.

We need to design the PE process for the majority of employees who are performing adequately and create a separate Performance Improvement Plan (PIP) process for employees whose performance is not acceptable. Underperformance doesn't just suddenly appear; it is identified in regular 1:1 meetings. There is plenty of time to recognize these individuals and then move them to a process more specific to their unique needs.

One reason for this shift to simplified documentation is that the effectiveness of performance documentation in supporting disciplinary actions is often thwarted by poor or inadequate documentation. So, the documentation we have today does not stand up to legal scrutiny and, in many cases, works against the company or manager rather than supporting them. Organizations need to focus more on ongoing performance conversations and providing light documentation that summarizes performance status.

Our advocacy of less documentation does not mean we believe employees should not get feedback on their performance. To the contrary, we believe that on a regular basis, managers and their teams and/or employees should be meeting to discuss their work and progress toward goals and what type of support is needed. Every conversation does not need to be documented (unless performance begins to falter), although notes may be taken to document key points of the performance conversation.

It is in this area of light documentation that technology can facilitate improved performance reviews by connecting data from 1:1s, real-time performance metrics, and ongoing feedback from peers, customers, and the manager. Thus, technology, especially recent advances in Artificial Intelligence (AI), can not only help connect lighter documentation to a more complete end-of-year performance picture, but it can also improve the accuracy of the overall evaluation by tracking performance throughout the year versus a typical human bias of being swayed by recent performance.[5] We will have more to say about what role technology can play in PE in Chapter 15.

Finally, if we embrace PE as a practice we engage in during the context of our day-to-day work, then the need to document becomes reduced, and PE becomes how we drive day-to-day progress and performance in the organization, versus an administrative task meant to justify HR actions and compensation decisions. When done in the flow of work, PE is no longer seen as something a manager does, separate from managing the team. We will provide a more extensive discussion of how the PE framework impacts HR decisions in Chapters 13 and 14.

In conclusion, simplicity means less focus on complex rating scales and procedures and detailed documentation, and more focus on ongoing performance conversations that support and enable performance. It means not getting so lost in the process of cascading goals to perfection that we lose sight of the fact that what we are really trying to accomplish is creating a line of sight as to why the work that employees do matters to achieving critical organizational goals.

Continuous

Our eighth and final key principle for PE is that it is a Continuous process. The traditional PM process is event-driven and calendar-driven, versus taking place in the flow of work. Managers set goals at the beginning of the year. In some companies, they have a formal mid-year check-in to discuss progress. Some companies even conduct a light evaluation process at this point. Then, at the end of the year (or performance period), a formal review is completed. In our survey, 74% of participants indicated that their process was event-driven, with only 26% stating that it was continuous. However, our research showed that those companies that had a continuous process were significantly more likely to achieve their desired outcomes than companies that had an annual/semiannual or event-driven process ($p < .001$, see Figure 9.2).

So what does a continuous process look like? We like to use a diagram like Figure 9.3 to describe the continuous process.

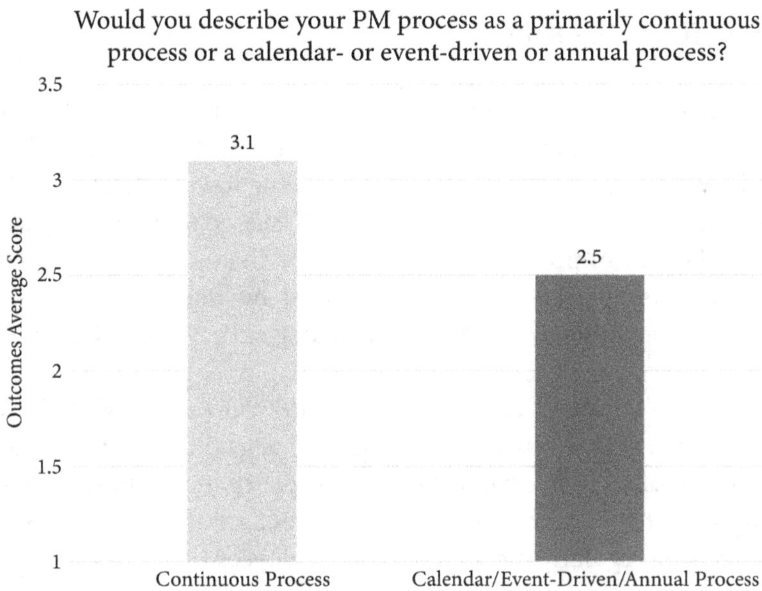

Figure 9.2 Is the PM process continuous or event-driven?

Source: Colquitt, A. L., & Goldberg, E. L. (December 2020). *Designing performance management for impact: Practices that make a difference.* Unpublished Participant Research Report.

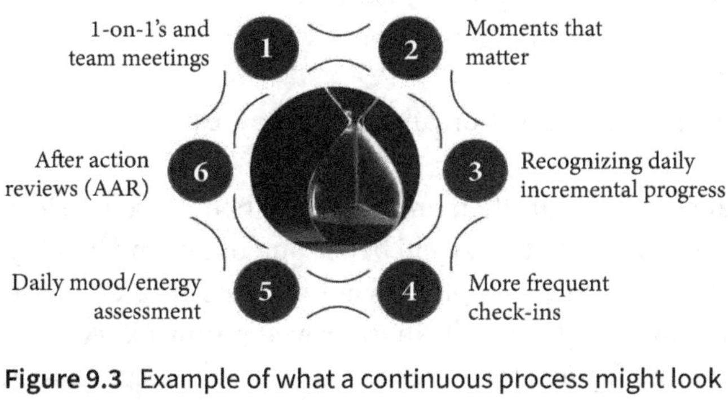

Figure 9.3 Example of what a continuous process might look like

Source: Authors

Research from the field of Positive Psychology supports a more continuous approach to managing engagement and performance.[6] In working with product development teams, research found that day-to-day events made a big difference in employees' moods and productivity. This suggests we need to use a much higher "resolution" when looking at supporting employees and facilitating performance than once or twice a year.

1:1s and Team Meetings

Ground zero for PE is the regular 1:1s and/or team meetings. It is during these weekly or biweekly meetings that managers and employees talk about their daily work and the progress they are making toward their shared goals. What is getting in the way of performance is discussed to unlock any blockers getting in the way of progress. This is the time that a manager can provide coaching and support to employees to understand what obstacles are in the way of progressing forward and how the manager may help overcome these issues.

We often don't think of 1:1s as part of the PE process, but we believe they are a critical part. This is where the magic happens. Formal steps in a traditional PM process are backward-looking drudgery that both managers and employees don't get a lot out of because the feedback is not timely. However, when managers regularly meet with their employees to discuss performance and progress, this is where managers can motivate their employees and provide coaching and support to accelerate performance. In a recent *Harvard Business Review* article, *Managers Can't Do It All*, the authors shared research that found that weekly 1:1s during uncertain times lead to:

- 54% increase in employee engagement
- 31% increase in productivity
- 15% decrease in burnout
- 16% decrease in depression among employees[7]

When managers support their employees by helping to reprioritize, coaching them on behaviors that will yield better outcomes, and helping employees manage work/life balance, employees are more connected to their manager and the company, and this results in improved performance.

When teams are a part of the organization's work design, managers should be meeting with their teams regularly as well. In this context, the team gathers to discuss progress, problems, and work together to overcome any barriers they are facing. We can learn from the practices that make Agile teams high-performance teams and then borrow practices that drive individual and organizational performance. Daily stand-up meetings (DSMs) are a key feature of Agile work design. They are based on the principles of transparency, collaboration, self-organization, regular reflection, continuous improvement, and iteration.[8] Compared to traditional team meetings, DSMs are characterized by (1) their daily cadence with a strict 15-minute time limit, (2) a focus on quick updates without extensive discussion or problem-solving, (3) self-organization of the team, and (4) a focus on goal achievement and identification of potential obstacles.

These stand-ups help provide visibility into what everyone is doing and how they contribute to the team's success. They ensure that the team is aligned on what they need to be focused on, to identify and address roadblocks, and to share lessons learned so the group can continuously improve. They also have the added benefit of holding all members of the team accountable for their responsibilities. Recent research has shown that teams using these meetings have higher satisfaction and better performance.[9] While all work groups may not be as deeply interdependent as an Agile team, having brief meetings to achieve the same general goals is an exceptional practice.

Moments That Matter

Part of continuous PE is about creating the "moments that matter" for employees. Managers need to connect with their employees to establish a trusting relationship where performance problems can be openly discussed so that solutions can be found. Managers need to help connect employees to one another to facilitate collaboration to get big problems solved. These moments that matter provide employees with the context they need to understand their role and responsibilities in light of what the company is collectively trying to achieve.

Recognizing Progress and More Frequent Check-Ins

In Chapter 8, we shared the importance of discussing progress against goals. Thus, recognizing progress is another touchpoint in the continuous PE process. This recognition usually happens either during team meetings or during a check-in. These are light-touch conversations about performance and progress. While notes may still make it into a performance-tracking system, these check-ins are less about documentation and more about keeping an open dialogue going about goals, progress, and performance. Check-ins can take many forms. While in most companies, this refers to manager–employee discussions or 1:1s or team meetings, other companies also employ daily or weekly pulse checks on their employees to monitor mood and intervene when energy or positivity is waning within a team. Some companies do this with a one-question poll to ask how employees are feeling (e.g., "How excited are you to come into work each day?" or "I feel motivated to do my best work in this role."). But let's be clear, check-ins are not a process to review performance four times a year. It is a light-touch conversation meant to both keep the manager informed and to really support the employee in their success.

Companies like Adobe, GE, Synaptics, and Gap Inc. have changed their PM processes to either eliminate or, in most cases, deemphasize the end-of-year review. They have moved toward regular check-ins, where managers and employees can meet to discuss progress against goals and on-going performance in the workplace. This allows course corrections to be made along the way, and recognition can be given for excellent work to keep motivation strong and reinforce positive behaviors.

The important point we would like to make is that the discussion that companies like Adobe or Gap, Inc. have eliminated the PM process is an overstatement of the facts. They are simply shifting from a focus on an annual review, which is focused on evaluation, to an ongoing conversation about performance. They have flipped the script on performance reviews, but they are still trying to drive individual and organizational performance.

After Action Reviews

Event-driven performance reviews and check-ins usually happen at a time based on the calendar, versus how work flows within a company. Mid-year check-ins are in June, regardless of whether or not the project is at a meaningful point to review. In contrast, After Action Reviews (AARs) take place at the end of a project or after major milestones. The purpose of an AAR is to learn from past activities to improve performance in the future. The focus of the conversation is on learning, not blaming or evaluating. The goal of these discussions is to drive actionable insights to help the team improve. This approach to continuous improvement originated in the US Army from the Center for Army Lessons Learned (CALL). The US Army has a well-developed process for conducting these reviews.[10] There is a general structure to most AAR processes that asks four basic questions:

1. What was supposed to happen (e.g., what was the goal of the project)?
2. What actually happened (an objective assessment of the outcome)?

3. Why were there differences (root cause analysis)? This might be positive, as in what led to successful performance, or it might look at root causes of failure.
4. What can we learn from this experience that we can apply in the future?

This introspective process is meant to help the team develop a culture of continuous improvement so that they can drive for improved results. Continuous PE leads to results. Research from the Conference Executive Board demonstrated that the leaders who engaged in these types of behaviors on a regular basis had the highest impact on organizational performance.[11] These behaviors included:

- Providing real-time feedback and coaching
- Helping employees solve problems
- Adjusting goals as situations change

In conclusion, transforming PE into an easy and continuous process is not just about reducing administrative burden; it's about unlocking the potential of employees and organizations. By shifting from complex, ratings-heavy, and documentation-heavy systems to streamlined, value-added practices, we can reimagine PE as a driver of employee growth and engagement.

Simplification is not an excuse to do less—it is a commitment to focus on what really matters: providing employees with the appropriate context and direction, setting clear goals, fostering meaningful conversations, and providing real-time coaching, feedback, and support.

Ultimately, when PE becomes a part of the day-to-day workflow, it stops being an administrative management task and becomes a transformative business practice. The path forward is clear: simplicity and continuity are the cornerstones of a PE process designed for today's dynamic and demanding business environment.

How Does a Continuous PE Process Work in Practice?

From the Front Lines: Adobe Role Models a Continuous Process

Adobe's Check-in Process—Thirteen Years Later

Thirteen years ago, Adobe Inc. innovated the Check-in process. They did away with annual reviews and ratings of employees in favor of quarterly conversations. These

continued

continued

conversations were relatively unstructured and required no formal documentation. There were standard questions for each check-in, but they were pretty generic (e.g., "What's one thing that worked well? What's one thing that could have gone better?"). Keeping it simple was a core design principle that remains true today.

What worked well for 10,000 employees was not holding up as well for a 30,000-person organization that experiences frequent change. Employees and managers wanted a system that moved with them and provided continuity. Some documentation was considered highly valuable for sharing employees' goals, accomplishments, and development plans. This makes it easier for a new manager to pick up where the old manager left off. Goals change over time because the business shifts. But if those goals were never documented, there was no way to have discussions about the alignment of employee priorities with company priorities.

So, Adobe made some changes to their Check-in process in 2022. Employees kick off the process by documenting what they have accomplished and how they are developing. The questions asked each quarter reflect what is going on in the business at that time. For example, at the beginning of the year, the conversation focuses on ensuring employees have set goals and that they understand the few items that are the most strategically important. In the middle of the year, they focus more on discussing progress, development plans, and feedback for the manager. Then, late in the year, they discuss how they performed against their goals and progress against development plans. (e.g., What did you learn? What do you wish you had done differently? What do you want to focus on for the next year?).

> **"While 1:1s for them are very focused on the day-to-day tasks that need to get accomplished, they have found that these quarterly Check-ins make space to step back and reflect on both progress and personal development."**
>
> *—Lauren Doyle, Adobe's Director of Talent Management*

According to Lauren Doyle, "The business is driving what conversations need to happen in terms of performance." In contrast to the typical process where HR develops a set of standard questions that get asked each quarter (and get more and more stale each time), Lauren and her team meet with business partners, leaders, and employees about what is happening in their business. Then, their team crafts the quarterly questions that are relevant for that moment in time. They are constantly iterating and adapting the process to meet the needs of the business. This attention to detail is rare and a big part of their success story.

Lauren shared with us a little about their Check-in journey. She said, "We piloted a lot of things before we launched company-wide. At first, we started with too many questions and too many activities. So, we stripped it back to what was essential to get the best conversation, not the best documentation, not the perfect written record, but to exchange feedback that will help employees perform and grow.... Most people are strong performers with opportunities to improve. We could all get better. The process is not designed to capture underperformers or to fire people, it is to help everyone get better."

To keep their process simple and flexible, they offer the ability to ask for or get feedback from peers at any time. However, there is no structured process, so all employees are not asked to give feedback at the same time. About one-third of their employees ask for feedback through their formal system. They are also aware that many people are asking for feedback informally and not through the system, which is just fine. They just want people to share feedback.

Adobe tracks their success in a variety of ways. First and foremost, are people doing it? But Lauren was very clear that having a Check-in is not the end goal. They were seeking behavior change. So they ask questions on their employee survey, read all the comments from the survey, and hold employee and manager focus groups. All of this data tells them that employees are getting more feedback from their manager, which helps improve their performance. They are also clear on what they need to do to be successful. They have seen sustained improvement in their survey scores and an increase in positive comments on their surveys.

Adobe's advice to other HR professionals is:

1. Ensure the process fits your company's culture and needs. Quarterly Check-ins fit with Adobe's continuous improvement culture. At Adobe, managers have a lot of discretion, flexibility, and trust. They want simple systems that are flexible so that managers can respond in the moment. A company that is rigid with lots of formal processes may not be able to execute this with the simplicity that makes their process work.
2. Be willing to continuously adapt and improve the process based on employee and business feedback.
3. Manager training is essential to building the skills and behavior change for effective performance conversations. They started with in-person training given right before a quarterly conversation and then leveraged the conversations as the practice of what was learned. Over time, they have supplemented this training with short, on-demand videos and job aids to help employees and managers in the process.
4. Focus on enabling meaningful conversations, not just documentation. For Adobe, employee documentation is a preread for managers to help them understand the employee's perspective and prepare for the conversation. After the meeting, the manager provides straightforward documentation

continued

continued

(e.g., What is the one thing you want to make sure the employee takes away from the conversation? Were you misaligned, and what do you want to reinforce?)

5. The process does need some structure. You need to have a timeframe for the Check-ins. Be mindful of the rhythm of your business and do not schedule Check-ins for very busy times (e.g., end of the quarter).

The key is to view PE as a tool for continuous improvement, not a static HR program. By keeping the process simple, minimizing documentation, and adapting the process to meet the organization's evolving needs, Adobe has been able to sustain its effectiveness over the long term.

In practical terms, we see that Adobe's Check-in process is really a quarterly process that allows employees to lift their heads up from their day-to-day work and take stock of how they are progressing on both their personal and professional goals, and if those goals are still relevant. But we also want to point out that this is married with regular 1:1s that are more focused on supporting employees with their weekly tasks.

Key Takeaways

- Focus on simplicity: PE should be easy to implement and manage. This involves eliminating complex processes, like over-detailed goal alignment or extensive documentation, to reduce the administrative burden on managers. Performance should be tracked through ongoing conversations, not just formal reviews.
- Goal-setting should be flexible; instead of rigid, cascading goals, organizations should focus on directional alignment. Employees should set their goals based on company direction.
- Simplify rating and calibration: Traditional rating systems, with multiple scales and calibration meetings, often add complexity without increasing accuracy. The focus should shift to identifying top performers and providing feedback, rather than stressing over rating nuances or calibrating employees against one another.
- Less documentation, more dialogue: Focus on light-touch documentation that summarizes key points from ongoing discussions. Performance should be managed through continuous check-ins and coaching, not

only formal reviews. Create a separate PIP when you need to document performance.

- Traditional, event-driven PM should shift to a continuous process with regular check-ins and 1:1 meetings. This supports ongoing performance development, fosters real-time feedback, and ensures issues are addressed quickly, driving better employee engagement and productivity.

SECTION III

PERFORMANCE ENABLEMENT PRACTICES

10
Make Goals Central

Ensuring employees have a sense of direction, purpose, and meaning is the foundational element of our model of Performance Enablement (PE) and is an essential part of shifting to a more enabling control philosophy in general. Companies need to think differently about the role goals play to make this shift. As we discussed in Chapter 7, PE is "high context," it requires that employees understand deeply the context for their work. If employees are committed to the organization's goals and see their work making an important contribution to those goals, managers won't need to coerce and micromanage employees.

Effectiveness of Goal-Setting

Nearly all companies we surveyed (93%) set goals as a part of their PM process. Goals are important for motivation and performance, they direct and energize, they cause people to persist, and they require people to think, plan, and strategize.[1]

The effectiveness of goals in driving motivation and performance is among the most well-established findings in the social sciences and is corroborated in the education literature as well.[2] There have been hundreds of studies to guide leaders and HR professionals on how to use goals to support and enable performance.[3] Below are the key insights from this research:

Specific and challenging: People and teams with specific, challenging goals perform better than people with "do your best" goals or no goals.
Feedback: As we shared in Chapter 8, employees need feedback to know if they are making progress toward their goals.
Commitment: For goals to work, employees need to be committed to them. Several factors increase commitment:

- Importance: As we discussed earlier, if employees see their work in the service of something important and meaningful, they are more likely to commit to that work.[4]

Performance Enablement. Edie Goldberg and Alan Colquitt, Oxford University Press. © Oxford University Press (2026).
DOI: 10.1093/9780197830642.003.0010

- "Self-Efficacy": As discussed in Chapter 8, employees need to believe they can achieve a goal to commit to it. Managers can increase self-efficacy by:
  - Involving employees in the goal-setting process and getting their input.
  - Providing employees with the resources, support, training, skills, and experience necessary to accomplish the goal.
  - Breaking goals into pieces and structuring the work so employees experience early successes, which builds confidence.
  - Connecting employees with others who have accomplished similar goals who can coach them.

  It is important to note that one of the factors discussed in early goal-setting research to increase commitment to goals (and therefore achievement of goals) was making rewards contingent on goal attainment. We will come back to this point in Chapter 15. Suffice it to say that now top goal-setting researchers like Garry Latham and others point to voluminous studies showing that money does not have to be tied to goal pursuit/attainment for a significant increase in employee performance to occur.[5]
- Other Factors: It's worth noting that the ability of specific and challenging goals to drive achievement and success is also dependent on three additional factors: (1) the ability of the employee (e.g., do they know enough to do the work; (2) complexity of the work to be done (e.g., the work is too complex for their skill level); and (3) situational constraints (e.g., they don't have the resources to do the work effectively).[6]

Goal-Setting in Teams

As we discussed in Chapter 4, work is increasingly being done in teams, and skills like collaboration and teamwork are becoming more important.[7] Research shows that goals may even be more effective in improving motivation and performance in teams.[8]

Where Goals Go Wrong in PM?

While goal-setting is common practice in PM, companies' efforts seem to be missing the mark. Benchmarking statistics show that only 44% of employees can connect their own goals to the goals of their organization.[9] And companies are not doing a good job of setting clear and specific goals, nor are they clarifying the behavioral expectations for employees. Research from Gallup shows only 45% of employees said they knew what was expected of them at work.[10]

There are several issues with the way companies approach goals that reinforces a more coercive approach in PM.

Goals aren't central

Despite the overwhelming evidence that goals drive high performance, only 16% of companies we surveyed see goals and objectives as the most important contributor to employee motivation and performance. Nearly half the companies we surveyed only discussed goals once or twice a year. Talking about goals once or twice a year isn't enough to create and sustain commitment and motivation.

Goals play an instrumental role

PM plans in many organizations are more like contracts or service-level agreements. A quote from a leading provider of PM software expresses this sentiment:

> Goals are a contract between employee and manager. They provide the framework for accountability and promote conversations between the manager and employee to monitor progress throughout the year. Goals are also a contract between the individual and the organization.[11]

This encourages employees to look ahead to the implications of goal achievement instead of at the meaning and value of the goals themselves.

> Traditional PM processes view the *consequences* of goal achievement as the source of motivation, not the goals themselves or the meaning attached to them.

In many traditional PM processes, there is also a heavy focus on metrics and targets to support goals, which become ends in themselves. Goodhart's law identifies the danger associated with this practice: "Once a measure becomes a target, it ceases to be a good measure."[12] This practice is frequently accompanied by a strong emphasis on accountability—putting "teeth" in goals by tying goal achievement to rewards. This is a hallmark of coercive control. We would extend Goodhart's law to say, "Once a measure is tied to rewards, it will be corrupted accordingly." When goal achievement "counts," it creates a "results at all costs" mentality (we will discuss this more in Chapter 14). This practice also teaches employees only to pursue work that will be rewarded, encouraging them, like students in school, to ask, "Will this be on the test?"

Some have unfairly laid this problem at the feet of goals themselves.[13] We disagree; corruption of goals and measures is a problem with targets and rewards tied to the targets, not with the goals or measures themselves.

Focus on individual goals

In our survey, 87% of companies focused their PM process more on individuals versus teams. When individuals working in teams set goals focused on their individual work ("egocentric" goals), employees on the team end up competing with one another and the performance of the team suffers.[14] The Microsoft example we shared in Chapter 7 is a perfect example of this. We will come back to this point in Chapters 13 and 14. The design of many PM rating and reward processes reinforces competition among employees, especially those with forced distribution requirements, which can set up conflict between individual and team goals. Individual goals also tend to be private, which makes collaboration within and across teams difficult.

Lack of flexibility

As we mentioned in Chapter 7, goals set at the beginning of the year can quickly become outdated as priorities change. Employees and teams need flexibility to change course and revisit goals as circumstances change. Companies that cascade goals top-down are particularly vulnerable to this problem. By the time goals reach employees, circumstances may have changed. As we discussed in Chapter 5, many managers and employees simply rewrite the goals to match the work done during the year.

It's clear from the discussion above that our current goal-setting practices are not working effectively. If this is the case, where do we go from here?

Enabling Goal-Setting Practices

PE views goals as a central element of enabling control, and several practices support this shift. We believe these practices leverage what we have learned from the science about this powerful process to drive performance.

Create Transparency and Context

There are several actions organizations can take to create more transparency and a deeper understanding of the context for the work teams and employees are doing:

1. Have senior leaders share the broader company goals and the business landscape with all employees—just like JetBlue. Use storytelling to create a vision for the company's future and enlist the employees to contribute to achieving it.
2. Have managers discuss company and organizational goals with employees and connect broad company goals to department or team goals and then to individual goals. Create the line of sight for employees. You don't need to cascade goals from one level to the next, but rather simply show the logical connection between goals at various levels. Be clear about current goals but be flexible enough to adjust these goals as needed. Goals provide direction and focus action in the right place.
3. In these discussions, ensure managers and leaders emphasize the positive impact achieving these goals will have on the important customers and stakeholders of the organization. Employees need to feel good about what their work is contributing to; this will make their work more meaningful and increase their commitment to it.
4. Be explicit about behavioral expectations. By clearly defining the behaviors expected, you can help your employees understand how to be successful. Many companies set behavioral goals, for individuals or teams and research suggests a focus on behaviors drives improved performance.[15]

This deeper understanding will allow employees to adapt in the moment when doing their work without cumbersome and time-consuming monitoring and review processes.

Have Continuous Conversations about Goals

Context (and the motivation and commitment it creates) isn't created in a single meeting at the beginning of the year. Managers should have regular 1:1 meetings and team meetings, and these meetings should include regular reminders and discussions of context:

- Importance of goals and objectives they are pursuing.
- How their work is connected to the important goals of the workgroup, organization, and the company (line of sight). Why do those goals matter? What are the benefits to customers and other key stakeholders?
- Progress they are making toward these goals and the benefits they are seeing.

- What, if anything, has changed about the goals based on progress or change in context?

These discussions will continually prime employees, keeping their attention focused on their goals and the meaning attached to them, sustaining their commitment to their own goals.

Create Flexibility and Agility

As we discussed in Chapter 7, an important principle behind PE is agility. Organizations should encourage managers and employees to write goals that are more flexible and directional, so they don't become out of date so quickly, allowing them to adjust more easily during the year as circumstances change. Organizations should also design the goal-setting process, so it is flexible, allowing goals to be created, changed, accomplished, and deleted or archived in a fluid, continuous way as business conditions change. Research shows that viewing goals in this way leads to higher levels of performance.[16] Research by Bersin and Associates found that companies that reviewed and revised goals more frequently (e.g., quarterly) improved financial performance and reduced costs.[17] This practice may require changes to evaluation and reward processes if ratings and rewards are tightly tied to goals set at the beginning of the year. Finally, the goal-setting process must be flexible enough to fit the wide variety of people, roles, organizations, and circumstances reflected in organizations.

OKRs

In response to the inherent conflicts between operating in a fast-paced business world and setting annual goals, Objectives and Key Results (OKRs) were introduced as a goal-setting framework that was both more dynamic and focused on achieving critical outcomes aligned with the business strategy.[18] This methodology has been around since the mid 90s, beginning at Intel and popularized by Google in their early history. It supported Google's growth from 40 employees to more than 180,000 today. Companies across many industries have now moved to this approach because it is simpler than traditional methodologies (e.g., SMART goals).

OKRs incorporate agility by encouraging short-term (often quarterly) goal-setting cycles, regular check-ins, and flexibility to adapt to changing circumstances.

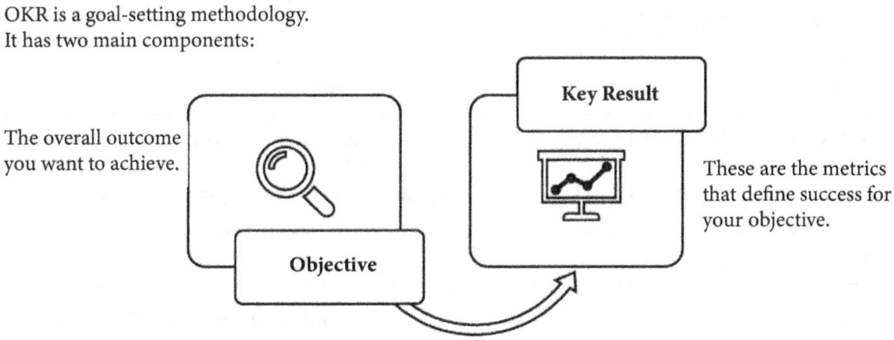

Figure 10.1 What is an OKR?
Source: Authors

There are two parts to an OKR (see Figure 10.1).

1) The objective, or the overall outcome you are trying to achieve. By design, this is supposed to be a ambitious goal that stretches the team or individual. Because of changing business dynamics, sometimes the task needs to change. But often, the objective "delight our customers" does not. So, it is important to remain clear about the objective employees are trying to achieve.
2) What are the key results an employee will use to measure their success in achieving their objective? Sometimes, a goal (e.g., increase sales by 10%) is too broad to understand where to focus your energy. In this case, you can include specific measurable activities that are known to produce the desired outcome. For example, calling on 1,000 accounts, should yield 250 new contracts, or conducting interviews with 20 former customers will yield actionable information to improve customer churn. Being clear about how you will measure your success is very important. With OKRs, accomplishing tasks is not good enough. The question at the forefront is, "To what end?" What does your work impact?

One key difference between OKRs and other goal methodologies is they should not be used for evaluation purposes. Employees need to feel safe setting challenging OKRs, so they won't be negatively affected if they don't achieve all of them. Our experience and our survey results show that this principle is frequently not followed. Many companies find it hard to resist connecting OKRs to their PM process and use them as a basis for evaluations. This practice can significantly limit or even eliminate their benefits.

Table 10.1 Examples of OKRs

Objectives	Key Results
• Qualitative and inspirational • Aspirational • Actionable by the owner	• Measurable and timebound milestones • How you achieve the objectives (Measurable activity → results)
Example:	
• Break growth records • Delight our customers • Transform the team to be the highest-performing Customer Service team in the company	• Schedule and perform 100 demos in Q1 • Achieve Net Promoter Score (NPS) of 60 or reduce detractors by 5% • Review four calls/rep each month and provide feedback • Reduce customer complaints by 10%

Table 10.1 provides some examples of OKRs.

How Can Goal-Setting Facilitate Agility and Alignment?

From the Front Lines—OKRs and the Transformation of Arcesium

Arcesium, a financial technology company founded in 2015, delivers advanced data, operations, and analytics capabilities for some of the world's most sophisticated asset managers, hedge funds, and banks. Bhavya Gopalakrishnan, former Head of Human Capital for the United States and United Kingdom, spoke with the authors about their journey in aligning priorities as the company scaled.

"When you're starting a new business, it's easy for everyone to be on the same page about what matters most," says Bhavya. "The priority is crystal clear—build the solution, sell the solution!"

As Arcesium grew, employees naturally began setting their priorities based on their individual and team's focus. Maintaining alignment to the top company priorities across the organization became increasingly challenging.

To address this, Arcesium implemented OKRs. While they had previously used goal-setting methodologies such as SMART goals, they needed a framework that provided both corporate-level alignment and adaptability to shifting priorities. OKRs ended up playing a big role in shifting the culture by improving transparency, prioritization, and alignment.

OKRs helped facilitate tough conversations: If an initiative was truly important, it became an OKR with proper resourcing—which often meant hitting pause on something else. Making them transparent helped enhance cross-functional collaboration.

Like any transformation, adopting OKRs came with challenges. Initially, employees associated them primarily with transformation initiatives, which made it harder for those focused on critical operational priorities to see their relevance. To help bridge this gap, Arcesium took steps to make sure that performance evaluations considered both OKRs and ongoing operational responsibilities as key inputs. For example, while a client success team might have an OKR focused on improving client satisfaction, their broader day-to-day contributions—such as gathering feedback to improve products, proactively addressing potential issues, and building scalable systems to share best practices—were also recognized.

Arcesium has continued refining its approach. OKRs drive alignment at the organizational level, while operational goals provide structure and focus within teams. To support all this, managers have access to training on goal-setting and OKR alignment and employees have quarterly check-ins with their managers where they are able to talk about questions such as:

1. What were you supposed to do? Did you do it? How did it go?
2. What challenges did you face, and what adjustments should be made to your OKRs?

Arcesium also allows business units to customize certain aspects of PM by incorporating stakeholder feedback and team-based goals.

Is it working? Bhavya believes the approach is working but acknowledges that continuous iteration is key. She is sure about three things:

- "We are clearer on what our biggest priorities are now."
- "We are doing a better job of prioritizing the big things."
- "Everyone is aligned on our top priorities."

Arcesium showed how goals and OKRs can be at the center of the transformation of a company by providing direction, focus, and alignment as the company grew.

Agile goal-setting

Agile goal-setting is a dynamic and flexible approach to setting and achieving goals, drawing on the principles of Agile methodology. It emphasizes adaptability, collaboration, and continuous principles, all consistent with a PE approach.[19] There are six core principles.

1) **Alignment with Strategy**: Goals should align with the organization's strategic objectives. This helps individuals understand how their work fits into the organization's broader priorities.
2) **Flexibility and Adaptability**: Agile goals tend to be set and reviewed more frequently (e.g., quarterly) or follow project milestones. This allows more flexibility as circumstances change.
3) **Focused on Progress**: Agile goals are broken down into smaller, manageable milestones, allowing for frequent tracking of progress and regular reassessment of priorities.
4) **Collaboration and Transparency**: Goals are set collaboratively with all key players. Transparent tracking and communication about goals ensure everyone understands how their efforts contribute to the broader objectives.
5) **Frequent Feedback and Review**: Regular check-ins, whether weekly or biweekly, provide opportunities to assess progress, jointly address obstacles, and adjust goals if priorities have shifted. Weekly 1:1s or daily team huddles are opportunities to get coaching on how to overcome barriers or when a change in direction needs to be made. By collaboratively reviewing what's working and what's not working, the team can adjust to ensure they continue to make progress.
6) **Focus on Outcomes, not Outputs**: Agile goals, like OKRs, focus on outcomes that are desired (e.g., improving productivity by 10%, a minimally viable product (MVP) by the end of the second quarter) rather than executing against a task or producing some type of deliverable (e.g., completion of a report, interviewing 20 candidates). This helps employees find meaning in their work and understand the impact they are having.

The use of technology to track progress (e.g., a dashboard) that can be seen by all is helpful in keeping goals top of mind and identifying when priorities need to shift. Regardless of the methodology you are using, the "secret sauce" to making goals agile is embedding a goal-review process into the regular work rhythm. This may happen during weekly check-ins or quarterly reviews. However, the frequency should be at least quarterly to ensure employees remain focused on the most important objective and remain up to date with any relevant changes in the business environment or company goals.

FAST goals

This alternative approach to goal-setting is designed to be more flexible and agile and incorporates many of the principles important to PE.[20] Four core principles underpin this methodology:

- **Frequent Discussion**: Goals should be embedded in ongoing discussions to review progress, allocate resources, prioritize initiatives, and provide feedback.
- **Ambitious**: Objectives should be challenging but not impossible to achieve.
- **Specific**: Goals are translated into concrete metrics and milestones that force clarity on how to achieve each goal and measure progress.
- **Transparent**: Goals and current performance should be made public for all employees to see.

Team goals

PE gives more attention to team goals. This practice can take different forms depending on the work system of the unit or organization:

1) Companies can forgo individual goals altogether and only set team-based goals. Performance becomes dependent on what the team does together. In some cases, individuals may still be rated or receive feedback on their behaviors that drive team success. In other cases, feedback may only formally be provided to the team, and the focus is what behaviors and actions will improve the team overall.
2) Some companies may set team and organizational goals as well as individual goals. If this is the case, managers should work with employees to set individual goals *in the context of team goals* whenever possible to ensure individuals are not working across purposes. Individual goals should be shared transparently to encourage employees to collaborate and coordinate within and across teams. Managers should work to keep these goals to a small few so that what one person is accountable for does not become overwhelming and it is easy for an individual to stay focused on their priorities. Finally, it will be critical for the reward process to be aligned with this practice. Rewards should be distributed based on what the team accomplished, not what any one individual did. This promotes collaboration and ensures that all individuals are working together to achieve their common goal—not to forsake the team goal to improve one individual's personal gain.

With team goals in place, the practice of team huddles and team feedback becomes all the more important to ensure that everyone is aligned in their actions and working together to achieve outcomes. If one person is stuck, the team can work together to overcome any challenges or setbacks. For example, companies that have adopted an agile work model, daily standup team meetings, and regular milestone meetings where progress is assessed and problem-solving occurs.

Individual and Team Goals in the Biotech Industry

We illustrate how these team and individual goals might look using an example from the biotech industry. Often in these companies, cross-functional teams are pulled together to take a molecule through the drug development process. The new product development team needs expertise from many different disciplines (e.g., Chemistry, Molecular Biology, Clinical Development, Quality Control, Product Management, Regulatory, etc.). The members of these new product development teams would have collective goals tied to specific milestones in the drug development process. Individual members of the team might also have specific goals related to their functional role both within the product development team as well as more broadly to support the entire company.

Here is an example of what this might look like:

Team Goals

1) Develop and validate a novel diagnostic kit for early cancer detection with 95% sensitivity and 98% specificity within 12 months.
2) Implement monthly interdisciplinary team meetings to increase cross-functional collaboration, resulting in a 50% improvement in knowledge sharing and ideation by the end of the year.
3) Obtain regulatory approval for the new diagnostic kit within 24 months of project initiation.
4) Conduct 10 customer interviews and two focus groups within the next quarter to identify unmet needs in the diagnostic market, resulting in three new viable products.

Individual Goals

For Product Manager

1) Increase the Net Promoter Score of the new diagnostic kit by 15% within six months of launch by implementing customer feedback and enhancing product features.
2) Create and execute a cross-functional product development plan that reduces time-to-market for the diagnostic kit by 15%, to be implemented over the next 12 months.

3) Produce a comprehensive analysis report by the end of Q2 to identify marketing opportunities and inform product positioning.

For Molecular Biologist

1) Design and execute three experiments to improve the stability of the key enzyme in the diagnostic kit, extending its shelf life from six to twelve months, within the next quarter.
2) Develop and document a new protocol for isolating circulating tumor DNA from blood samples, increasing the yield by 25% compared to current methods, within three months.

For a Regulatory Affairs Specialist

1) Prepare and submit a complete regulatory dossier for the new diagnostic kit to the relevant authority within nine months, aiming for approval within 18 months of submission.
2) Develop and implement a training program on regulatory compliance for the product development team, to be completed by all team members within three months.

Key Takeaways

- Setting goals for employees and teams is a fundamental part of PE.
- Goals provide direction, context, purpose, and meaning for employees and help connect their work to the goals of the organization, reducing the need for micromanagement and other coercive control mechanisms.
- Goals should be specific and challenging, but success depends on commitment, feedback, employee belief in their ability to achieve goals (self-efficacy), and other factors (employee ability, complexity of the work, and situational constraints).
- Many companies fail to align individual goals with organizational objectives, focus too much on metrics and accountability, and set rigid goals that quickly become outdated, undermining motivation and effectiveness.
- Organizations should adopt more agile approaches to goal-setting, allowing for frequent updates, directional goals, and adjustments as business conditions change to keep employees engaged and aligned.

- Objectives and Key Results (OKRs), Agile goal-setting, and FAST are all methodologies that promote adaptability, transparency, and frequent feedback, ensuring goals remain relevant and drive meaningful outcomes.
- Emphasizing team goals as well as individual goals enhances collaboration, minimizes competition within teams, and fosters a collective sense of responsibility for achieving business objectives.

11

Create a Feedback Culture and Coaching for Future Performance

While research on goal-setting theory plays a significant role in the ubiquitous inclusion of goal-setting in most of today's performance management (PM) processes,[1] many PM systems fail because they don't follow through on the additional research finding that feedback on progress toward goals is a *required* component to ensure the motivating power of goal-setting.[2] Companies are great at setting goals at the outset of the year, but far too frequently, they fail to discuss those goals again until the end of the performance period. As a result, those goals are no longer motivating because employees are not getting feedback on progress toward the goal. Often, they have forgotten what those goals are as new priorities are added to their plate.

Today, we are seeing strong signals that companies are recognizing the crucial role that feedback plays in sustaining motivation toward goals and enhancing employee performance. When asked which element of the PM process, if any, is most important for driving employee motivation and performance, participants in our study pointed to feedback (see Figure 11.1).

While 33% of our survey respondents indicated they still adhere to an annual or semiannual process, 67% said they provide feedback quarterly or more frequently (e.g., monthly, weekly, ongoing). Clearly, companies are beginning to understand the importance of providing more frequent feedback.

While many believe in the importance of feedback, the research shows that feedback isn't always effective. A meta-analysis of the impact of feedback on performance suggested a generally positive trend; however, one-third of the studies showed a decrease in performance following a feedback intervention, one-third showed no performance improvement, and one-third showed an improvement.[3] The researchers believed part of the reason for the difference in impact was the focus of the feedback. When feedback was focused more on personal identity and how people see themselves, it was less impactful and potentially damaging. However, when the feedback focused on the task, it was well-received and had a more positive impact.

Performance Enablement. Edie Goldberg and Alan Colquitt, Oxford University Press. © Oxford University Press (2026).
DOI: 10.1093/9780197830642.003.0011

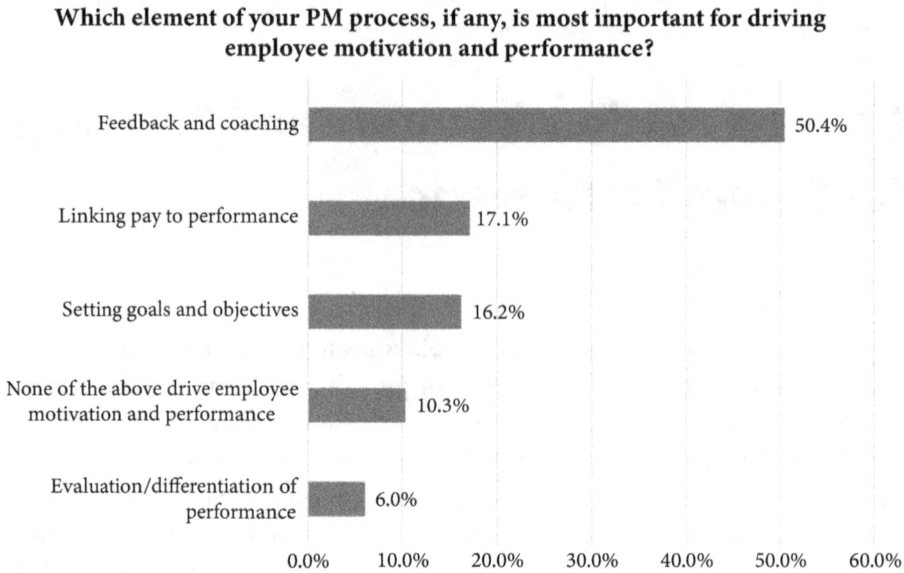

Figure 11.1 Which element of your PM process drives motivation and performance?
Source: Colquitt, A. L., & Goldberg, E. L. (December 2020). *Designing performance management for impact: Practices that make a difference.* Unpublished Participant Research Report.

Recent research suggests that results may be even more nuanced; people at different stages of their careers have different preferences for the type of feedback they receive. Younger employees are open to task-based feedback because it is useful to help them achieve their goals. In contrast, older workers are more confident in their approaches to work, and are more interested and open to feedback that helps them to understand how others perceive them and, thus, how they can influence outcomes.[4]

In practice, it is today's modern theories from disciplines outside of Industrial/Organizational Psychology that are playing a disproportionate role in how PM systems are being designed. These research theories are grounded in how individuals perceive feedback.

Contemporary Research Driving Today's Practices

Growth Mindset

One body of research making a significant impact on practice today is Carol Dweck's work on Growth Mindset.[5] Dweck suggests there are two different mindsets that impact the way people approach their lives and work: the

"Fixed Mindset" and the "Growth Mindset." Dweck's research interest in this area began with her fascination with children's different reactions when faced with a difficult problem to solve. Some children became very anxious, while others got excited about the opportunities difficult problems posed for them. Her research concluded that some people are raised with the idea that they are born with a *fixed* level of intelligence. Others are raised to believe that through persistence and hard work, intelligence can be *grown*.

Her work argues that many managers and companies emphasize the fixed mindset. Employees are selected and compensated for their inherent brilliance or talent. You hire the "A" player because they are smart. This mindset views talent as static. She found that employees with a fixed mindset avoid challenges and obstacles because less-than-stellar performance might cause others to question their initial assumptions about their brilliance. These employees exert minimal effort because things should come easily to them, and exerting more effort will not change the result; you either have it or you don't. Fixed-mindset employees ignore negative feedback because they have been told they are better than others, so why should others' opinions matter? Interestingly, fixed-mindset employees are threatened by others' success because it endangers their relative standing in the world. They should be the only ones with outstanding performance because they are the best.

In contrast, people with a growth mindset embrace challenges and work hard when faced with obstacles because they see these situations as a path to personal growth. Growth-mindset individuals seek out and embrace all types of feedback as a point of learning. They are inspired by others' success and seek out other people to learn from them. For people with a growth mindset, it's exciting to take on a new challenge or learn something new.

Dweck argues that individuals with a growth mindset have a mastery orientation to learning, where the learner's attention is focused on gaining new skills that lead to the mastery of a skill, subject, or task. This is in contrast to individuals with a performance orientation, who are focused on competing against others and thus view feedback as a potential threat. Her work argues that individuals with a learning orientation (or growth mindset) are more likely to be receptive to feedback and make good use of the feedback they receive. Importantly, mindsets can be shaped by the messages of those around us.[6]

This research has resulted in several companies (e.g., Gap Inc., Microsoft) crafting their language to promote a growth mindset. It was Satya Nadella, the CEO of Microsoft, who said he wanted to shift the company's culture from "know-it-alls" to "learn-it-alls."[7] Companies are teaching their managers and employees about a growth mindset in the hopes of facilitating a learning organization that believes that with frequent feedback and an openness to learning, we can improve the performance of individuals and their organizations.

While there is still little research on the effectiveness of mindset in work settings, and some authors have questioned the validity of this construct or its impact on performance, we believe that there are several psychological constructs that support the importance of a growth mindset.[8] Some researchers have made the link between Implicit Person Theory (beliefs about the malleability of personal attributes, e.g., ability and personality that affect behavior) and both managers' coaching employees and feedback-seeking behaviors that lead to personal growth and development.[9] Furthermore, other researchers linked feedback orientation to Dweck's mastery orientation.[10] They define feedback orientation as the extent to which individuals welcome guidance and coaching, which includes a positive reaction toward feedback, the propensity to seek out feedback, to process the feedback mindfully, to value it, to care what others think, and to act on the feedback. Self-Determination Theory also supports the idea that humans have a fundamental need to feel capable and effective in their actions, essentially striving to gain mastery over challenges and develop their skills.[11] Companies like Gap, Inc. and Microsoft have taken the stance that a growth-mindset culture, reinforced by PE, will lead to more innovation and greater learning—both of which will lead to improved business performance. We agree!

NeuroLeadership

The second area of research that has had a disproportionate impact on the practice of feedback in companies comes from David Rock and his NeuroLeadership Institute.[12] He suggests that the brain is oriented toward threats and rewards. He argues that the PM process is filled with elements that create a threat response (e.g., lack of control, explicit monitoring and evaluation, uncertainty of the outcome, threat to one's self-image, etc.). The impact of this is that our brain turns off its creativity center and shuts down to new information in a protection state. While some experts have questioned this research and these conclusions,[13] it's clear this research has struck a chord with practitioners and managers who find it compelling, practical, and helpful.

Rock recommends several changes to the way we approach performance feedback conversations. Placing the employee in the driver's seat of the conversation and having employees ask for feedback was recommended as a critical step to ameliorate the threat response. This changes feedback from unsolicited criticism to invited information. They also recommend having more frequent performance conversations to reduce the employees' uncertainty in the conversation.

Thus, this research suggests that to reduce stress and anxiety in the performance feedback and evaluation process, managers should provide frequent, constructive feedback, with an emphasis on learning and growth, and less emphasis on evaluation, from which much of the threat response emanates.

Creating a Feedback Culture

At this point, you are beginning to get the value and importance of regular, ongoing feedback to drive individual and organizational performance. But how do you create a strong culture for feedback in your organization where individuals continuously solicit, receive, and use both formal and informal feedback to improve performance? Research suggests three categories of organizational practice that will help create a feedback culture.[14]

1. Focus on enhancing the ***quality of feedback*** that individuals receive.
2. Emphasize the ***importance of feedback*** in the company.
3. Provide ***support for using feedback.***

Based on the research and our collective experience, we will share interventions that can positively impact each category.

Enhancing the Quality of Feedback

At the foundation of our PE model, we discuss providing employees with guidance. That guidance usually comes in the form of clearly defined direction and goals as well as behavioral standards and expectations. These performance standards help managers provide quality feedback because they serve as a reference point. The same logic applies to clear, measurable goals. When we know what we are striving to achieve, individuals are able to provide more effective feedback on progress toward that goal.

While most companies are pretty good at communicating and emphasizing the importance of providing regular feedback to employees, the problem is that most managers are not skilled at providing effective feedback. According to Gallup, only 23% of employees say they receive meaningful feedback that helps them to improve their performance. Unfortunately, this statistic is only getting worse over time. The most recent Gallup survey results indicate that only 21% of employees feel they got meaningful feedback from their manager in the past week.[15] But it's clear that those who do receive this type of feedback are better off; they are nearly three times more likely to be engaged at work.[16]

Thus, training managers to deliver meaningful feedback is a critical step in improving the quality of feedback. Drawing on research, we can gain some good insight into how to improve the manager's ability to provide meaningful feedback. They need to ensure that feedback focuses on the work and the tasks, and is not personal in any way.[17] In our study, we found that the companies that rated their managers as being highly skilled at providing feedback were significantly more likely to achieve desirable outcomes as presented in Chapter 1 ($r = .36$, $p < .001$, $N = 115$).

One final way the quality of feedback can be improved is by having the data to support any type of assessment of performance or progress toward goals. In today's highly automated world, organizations have access to much more data regarding performance than they have ever had before (e.g., customer complaints, cases won, number of defects, etc.). When managers review the data with their direct reports, greater insights can be gained into what is working well and what needs further attention.

Emphasizing the Importance of Feedback

Leaders and organizations communicate the perceived value of feedback based on how they act and what they recognize and reward. When senior leaders serve as role models for providing regular, meaningful feedback, their direct reports will see this behavior as valuable. Leadership needs to set the expectation that everyone gives and receives feedback. This includes both formal feedback and informal "in-the-moment" feedback. And of course, that which gets recognized and rewarded gets done. Managers need to be recognized and rewarded for providing feedback and developing their employees, and employees need to be rewarded for taking action on feedback and improving their performance.

Providing Support for Using Feedback

Providing support can take many forms, from having skilled facilitators help interpret feedback results, to providing employees with access to development resources that help them to learn from their feedback and improve. While we discussed the importance of training managers on how to provide meaningful feedback as part of enhancing the *quality* of feedback, under *support*, we want to emphasize the need for managers to develop skills in coaching their employees. Giving employees the answer does not improve their skills. To embed learning, employees need to discover the answers for themselves with skillful coaching to lead them to the right solution.

The Impact of Creating a Performance Feedback Culture

In 2018, the Center for Effective Organizations (CEO) and the Institute for Corporate Productivity (i4cp) conducted a study of 234 organizations, demonstrating that the key to implementing an effective PM process is to create a performance feedback culture (PFC).[18] The researchers define a PFC as one where:

- Managers are focused on providing effective feedback.
- There is regular and varied communication and training on how to provide effective feedback.
- Senior executives model the desired behaviors.
- Managers are recognized and rewarded for doing it well.

This study demonstrated the real impact of a PFC on bottom-line business results (see Table 11.1). The authors found that those companies rated higher on the PFC scale achieved improved business performance. The measures of business performance included: Net Profit Margin, Return on Investment (ROI), Return on Assets (ROA), and Return on Equity (ROE).

Table 11.1 Impact of performance feedback culture on business performance

Use of PFC Practices	Net Profit Margin	ROI	ROA	ROE
Top 1/3	12.08%	14.63%	7.68%	26.26%
Middle 1/3	7.48%	7.96%	4.89%	19.71%
Bottom 1/3	5.09%	6.51%	3.65%	10.63%

Ledford, G.E., & Schneider, B. (2018). *Performance Feedback Culture Drives Business Impact*

We share this research because our Performance Enablement (PE) model is firmly rooted in a PFC. If our goal is to improve business performance through PE, this clearly shows that this critical element makes an impact.

Special Types of Feedback

360-Feedback and Crowdsourced Performance Feedback

Historically, it has been argued that 360-degree feedback should not be used in PM because ratings tend to get elevated when people know that the information will be used for decision-making purposes.[19] We have witnessed this effect within our own work as well. When 360-feedback is used for making performance evaluation, compensation, and promotion decisions, both managers and peers are likely to inflate ratings because they don't want to be responsible for an individual getting hurt by giving them low ratings, which will negatively affect their rewards. However, when 360-feedback is used for development purposes, everyone is much more likely to provide an honest assessment. With that said, another argument against using 360-feedback is that ratings across raters simply aren't measuring the same thing. Ratings of the same person by different people, even if they share the same perspective (e.g., two bosses, two direct reports), simply don't agree very much (correlations from 0.30 to 0.50).[20]

Organizations such as Pepsi Co. have successfully implemented 360-feedback for development and achieved a level of trust within the organization to then proceed to use that feedback for decision-making purposes as well. But this only happens over time when trust has been built within the system.

Some of today's PM technologies have incorporated 360-feedback capabilities using a common set of competencies. Our biggest concern with these applications is that companies are likely to implement this feature without the benefit of experts who would strictly adhere to anonymity rules, and ensure this is used for development purposes only (unless it is a well-accepted and trusted process), provide in-person review of results, and ensure there is follow-through on the feedback provided.

Recent research suggests the use of 360-feedback for PM and decision-making processes is on the rise.[21] With this in mind, we need to ensure that this information is used properly, and when using it for decision-making purposes, appropriate procedures are put into place to ensure the information is valid. Averaging across the perceptions of peers, customers, direct reports, and the manager is inappropriate, as these individuals work together in a different context, and differences in behavior may be real. Reporting this information by subgroup is an important part of feedback. For example, an individual might be very decisive when working with peers or direct reports, but when working with people in authority, confidence may waver, resulting in greater indecision. Perceptions of decisiveness represent true differences in context, and it is important to raise awareness about these differences.

Another practical consideration for using 360-feedback is that while the feedback can be invaluable for development purposes, when using it for development, it is often obtained for leaders at a particular level, and only periodically vs. on an annual cadence. The collection of 360-feedback for the entire organization takes a tremendous amount of time and effort. Doing this on an annual basis as an input to PE is simply not sustainable.

If 360-feedback is not the right answer for PE, but employees today are much more likely to work more closely with peers on teams than they do with their direct manager, what is the solution? Crowdsourced feedback. Feedback from peers, other managers with whom an employee may work, and feedback from customers can still be part of the PE process, just in a lighter-touch format. This feedback can come in the flow of work, during team meetings and via existing collaboration technologies employees are already using. When feedback is given in this manner, it is more disarming and remains deeply tied to the work.

Today's technology systems that support PE also allow a company to include feedback from others. Often, this type of feedback takes the form of structured input from people who work closely with the employees, and it does not represent a traditional 360-degree process that is focused on a set of competencies. This provides the manager with a more informed view of the individual's performance.[22] However, it is important that the request for feedback not be made in a vacuum, but in relation to achieving goals or completing a task or project.

Crowdsourced feedback is often an "always-on" feature, allowing employees to provide or request feedback from anyone at any time. Many organizations seek this type of crowdsourced feedback at the end of a performance cycle to provide additional input to the manager before they complete their performance evaluation.

It is interesting that most vendors and companies using these technology applications report a low uptake of this type of feedback feature. This may be because it requires "extra work," and depending on a company's feedback culture, it may be more oriented to evaluating an employee's performance or providing constructive criticism versus being in the spirit of continuous improvement. Regardless of how widely used this feedback feature may be, we caution against making performance evaluation, compensation, or promotion decisions strictly based on this data, as it is likely to be positively skewed for the reasons we described previously. However, we do believe that the addition of input from people who work closely with the employee does provide more factual points of information that the manager can use in making performance assessments.

Examples of Crowdsourced Performance Feedback Questions

Example A	Example B
What did this person do well? Consider both the employee's OKRs and how they demonstrated the company's core values?	What should the employee **Start** doing to improve their ability to achieve team goals?
Was there anything that got in the way of performance or achievement of objectives? (Company core values may be important here)	What should the employees **Stop** doing, because it is getting in the way of performance?
Is there anything this person should work on or leverage to be more successful in the coming year?	What should the employee **Continue** doing because it is very effective and helps the individual and/or the team achieve their goals?

As we discussed in Chapter 8, feedback systems have two important parts: (1) is there a gap between an employee's goals and their current state? and (2) is the gap closing and how quickly?[23] This second part is related to tracking and monitoring progress.[24] Progress is important because it keeps the focus of feedback on goals and the work. There are several ways organizations and managers can emphasize progress.

- Set clear goals. Focusing on progress requires clear goals to begin with. This starts with clear strategic direction and priorities at the organizational level, translating these into meaningful work unit or team goals and individual goals.
- Have frequent check-ins. Making progress requires frequent, ongoing discussions between managers and employees. Satisfaction, well-being, and performance are the result of continued engagement in important, meaningful goals.
- Improve 1:1 and team meetings. If progress, positivity, and performance is a continuous, day-to-day challenge, improving the quality of 1:1 and team meetings represents ground zero in this effort. These conversations should have a positive, upbeat, and supportive tone to them. Respectful inquiry is a useful approach for conducting these meetings, which uses three components that acknowledge employees' motivational needs for autonomy, relatedness, and competence: asking versus telling, open-ended questions, and listening attentively. These meetings should be focused on working with employees to facilitate (and memorialize) progress by addressing barriers and obstacles they are encountering.[25]

- Develop manager skills. Managers will need both strategic and tactical skills to understand the organization's strategic direction and effectively translate it for the workgroup. They need partnership and leadership skills to put the progress of their employees first. They will also need new communication, interpersonal, and feedback skills. Interactions that facilitate progress should be joint, two-way discovery exercises where the messages to be communicated are constructed together by the employee and the manager during the conversation.
- Create a psychologically safe work environment. Progress is facilitated by a safe environment where employees feel comfortable being who they are, speaking up, and providing their input and ideas, where they can make mistakes and learn without fear of reprisal.[26]
- Leverage tools and technology. Finally, tools and technology are available to support progress. Progress checks and checklists, "snippets," progress rituals, "done lists," and daily journals can be used by individuals and teams to help process and reflect on the daily events, experiences, and circumstances they encounter. There are new technology applications to facilitate the capturing of this information, and these tools can also be embedded into formal processes to measure and track progress, feeding data back to managers, teams, and employees for problem-solving and idea generation.

Recognition

Think about the last time you put your heart and soul into a project or presentation, molded it into something you were proud of, and absolutely nailed the execution. That feeling of accomplishment is uplifting—but it is multiplied exponentially when others take notice.

The simple act of acknowledging achievement boosts employee morale and performance, which is why employee recognition is so critical.[27] When you recognize employees for their contributions, they feel ownership and pride—and are willing to work just as hard on their next project. Recognition connects them to the organization, elevates performance, and increases the likelihood they'll stay.

Reinforcement theory asserts that recognition is a powerful and natural reinforcer to improve performance.[28] This is because when a specific behavior is reinforced through recognition, it is more likely to be repeated in the future. A meta-analysis study demonstrated that recognition has a significant impact on performance in both the manufacturing and service industries.[29]

When employees feel valued for who they are and what they do—and are treated like they're more than cogs in the machine—they act differently, in ways that positively impact their teams and organizations. According to recent research from Gallup and Workhuman, only one in four employees report that they received recognition or praise for the work they had done in the past week.[30] If that figure doubled, the organization would see:

- 9% improvement in productivity
- 22% decrease in safety incidents
- 22% decrease in absenteeism

In Glassdoor's Employee Appreciation Survey, 53% of people said feeling more appreciation from their boss would help them stay longer at their company.[31] This is important because other research has shown that employee tenure (regardless of age) has a "significant positive and sometimes very sizable impact on financial performance and operational excellence."[32]

Some researchers have suggested that Social Cognitive Theory is a good explanation for the motivating factor of recognition.[33] This is because Social Cognitive Theory describes three dimensions to the motivational value of recognition: (1) the outcome utility (e.g., recognition from my boss will lead to a promotion), (2) its informative content (e.g., feedback on the specific behavior that is appreciated), and (3) its regulatory property in the ability to facilitate forethought in the employee that engaging in a specific behavior will lead to more positive outcomes.[34]

Recognition can be formal (e.g., such as an Employee of the Month program or Annual Sales Award) or it can be more informal, generally provided by either a manager or peer in recognition of a specific action (e.g., an exceptional effort that led to winning a new customer, or going beyond one's job to help out a teammate who needed assistance completing a business-critical task). Recognition can be given publicly or privately—and a best practice is to understand how the recipient would prefer to receive that recognition.

While having a formal Employee Recognition program is great, there are some things that managers can do to show appreciation for their employees that don't cost a thing:

1. Listen to them—put down your phone, turn away from the computer, and give them your full attention.
2. Tell your employees what you value about them—Acknowledge their human value. Managers can do this proactively, and it need not be tied

to a specific situation. However, as noted previously, recognition of a particular accomplishment in a way that is meaningful to the individual leaves a lasting impression.

3. Check-in to see how people are doing—When employees feel that you care about them, and that they matter, it enhances their self-esteem and their self-efficacy. Research shows that employees who feel cared for and valued demonstrate higher levels of customer satisfaction and productivity.[35]

It is interesting to note that most organizations have a recognition process that is separate from PM. We see this as an important element of the overall PE process. In fact, recognition is a very important element of this process because of the motivational value of personal recognition. Today, much of the focus on PM is tying pay to performance as a means of extrinsic motivation; however, knowledge workers are much more intrinsically motivated. Thus, pay may not be the most potent motivator for them. (A more detailed discussion of this topic is presented in Chapter 14.) In fact, recent surveys have shown that recognition from one's manager, peers, or customers is much more memorable than financial rewards.[36]

Regardless of whether a recognition program is separated from the PE process or designed as an integral aspect, we strongly support the use of non-financial rewards (or personalized gifts in lieu of money) as an important element of any PE process.

Coaching for Future Performance Achieves Results

Most people think about feedback as providing constructive advice about what someone has done that was wrong. However, there is growing support for positive feedback and strengths-based feedback as we discussed in Chapter 8. This type of feedback provides positive reinforcement of behaviors that achieve results and helps employees lean on their strengths to support their continued growth and performance.[37] We have no arguments with the value of reinforcing behaviors you wish to see repeated by recognizing them and encouraging employees to repeat those behaviors.

However, it is Marshall Goldsmith's work on feed*forward* vs. feed*back* that caught our attention.[38] Feedback looks in the rearview mirror and discusses what cannot be changed (although we can learn from the past). And as we discussed, feedback is often critical. Feedforward uses what we know from the past but focuses on how to provide information that will help a person to be successful in the future. Feedforward tends to be more positive and encouraging. This is the type of information that all employees, regardless of age, will be more receptive to because it is not negative or personal. When we move from feedback to feedforward, we shift from criticizing to coaching. While Marshall Goldsmith's work on feedforward provides a simplified management-style approach to it, we can learn a lot by reading some of the original research on the feedforward interview.[39] Subsequent research demonstrated that employees whose managers employed the feedforward interview technique significantly increased their performance in the following 4 months in comparison to those who were provided with traditional feedback.[40]

Table 11.2 provides some differences between feedback and feedforward. Here, you can see that feedforward provides constructive guidance to help improve future performance, whereas feedback is more evaluative and focused on past actions.

Leveraging our past experiences implementing PM processes, in combination with understanding the research on feedback, we hypothesized that companies that focused their process more on coaching for future performance would be more likely to achieve their intended outcomes than companies that strictly focused on feedback. Our hypothesis was supported in our research study; however, companies that both focused on coaching for performance *and* providing feedback performed just as well as the few

Table 11.2 Examples of the difference between feed*back* and feed*forward*

Feedback (past-oriented)	Feedforward (future-oriented)
"You missed the deadline last week, which impacted the team."	How might you manage your time better in the future so that you don't miss deadlines?"
"Your presentation lacked clarity, and the audience was confused."	"What are some strategies you could try to make your next presentation clearer? Could you try using more visual aids to clarify key points?"
"You did not collaborate well with the team during the project."	"If you think back to how your team collaborated last time, what could have helped strengthen the partnership? How might you gain input from others earlier in the process?"
"You didn't communicate your progress during the project."	"In future projects, consider giving weekly updates to keep everyone aligned." How could regular check-ins improve things?"

companies that strictly focused on coaching for future performance.[41] Providing advice/guidance/counsel for how to handle an upcoming situation can improve the outcome and leave the employee feeling supported.

We believe that this shift in perspective of why feedback (or feedforward) is provided is critical to improving the performance of both the individual and the organization at large. If prior research tells us that employees are resistant to any feedback that is critical in nature, then removing the value (positive or negative) of the feedback and instead turning to coaching for performance would be more likely to be well-received by the employee. Some coaching will inherently focus on the task at hand and how to successfully accomplish the task. For others, coaching may be focused more on the skills to navigate the organization to achieve outcomes. Regardless of the process, the intent is to coach on the progress toward a goal and what can be done differently to improve both the speed and likelihood of success. Coaching (both feedback and feedforward) should be tied directly to achieving goals.

Key Takeaways

- Feedback is essential for maintaining motivation and improving performance.
- Frequent and task-focused feedback is most effective.
- Adopting a growth-mindset culture is important as it encourages employees to embrace feedback as a tool for growth, innovation, and improved performance.
- Creating a feedback culture requires organizational support. Three organizational practices are critical:
  1. Enhance feedback quality by creating clear standards, training managers, and leveraging data when discussing performance.
  2. Emphasize the importance of feedback by having senior leaders role model providing feedback to others. In addition, senior leaders should recognize and reward others for providing feedback, and/or for performance improvement from acting on feedback.
  3. Provide support for using feedback through the use of skilled facilitators, access to development resources, and training for managers on how to coach their employees.
- Crowdsourced feedback is an important element of PE, given that many people work more closely with their peers than their direct manager.

- Recognition is a form of feedback that is critical to motivating employees. Personal recognition is more memorable than financial rewards.
- Feed*forward* and coaching for performance are the keys to creating a more positive and supportive feedback culture.

12
Focus on Development

As we discussed in Chapter 3, we view traditional performance management (PM) as part of an organization's coercive control processes. It is a part of an organization's pay for performance (P4P) practices to evaluate and differentiate performance and distribute rewards. However, if our goal is to enable, improve, and sustain individual and organizational performance, development must be a critical part of the process. According to research from Gallup, organizations that invest in employee development report 11% greater profitability and are twice as likely to retain their employees.[1]

This is one of the major ways our Performance Enablement (PE) process differs from traditional PM. PE has a larger frame that is focused on all of the elements necessary to enable performance. This leans more heavily on goals, progress, feedback, and development, and less on performance evaluation and tying ratings to rewards (because there are many ways to reward good performance).

In our experience, companies often relegate development planning to the bottom of the performance review form, both literally and metaphorically. Consequently, managers and employees are so exhausted by the process of setting new goals, reviewing past performance, and differentiating the performance of their employees that little effort is put into the development plan. But more importantly, if a development plan is created, it is often set and forgotten until the next year's review, with little follow-through. We argue that for PE, development planning is one of the most important parts of the process and deserves the time and attention it needs to be successful. Managers need to support employee development in the same way they support goal achievement. They need to be held accountable for facilitating employee growth and development.

There are important benefits to be gained from development planning in addition to improving an employee's performance. When PM is used more for development reasons—that is the emphasis is on development planning—employees are more satisfied with the process.[2] The overall lack of satisfaction with the PM process impacts employee engagement. This is exactly why so many high-profile companies such as Gap Inc., Eli Lilly, Microsoft, and

Performance Enablement. Edie Goldberg and Alan Colquitt, Oxford University Press. © Oxford University Press (2026).
DOI: 10.1093/9780197830642.003.0012

Accenture have shifted their programs to focus more on development than evaluation.

The research from the Institute for Corporate Productivity (i4cp) provides the most compelling reason for focusing on development planning and ensuring follow-through. In a study with over 1,000 respondents, they wanted to understand which human resources practices differentiated the best-performing companies from poorer-performing companies. They defined (market) performance based on revenue growth, market share, profitability, and customer satisfaction. They found that high-performing companies were twice as likely to use the PM process to create and follow-through on targeted development plans for the next performance period to help individuals achieve their objectives.[3]

This research is consistent with the research we presented in Chapter 11, which shows that companies with a performance feedback culture focused on helping employees improve are stronger performers.[4] These companies are clearly subscribing to the Growth Mindset ethos, that with the right support and hard work, intelligence can be *grown*. Employees can learn and grow, and when they do, they are capable of achieving more.

History of Development-Focus in Performance Management

Putting greater emphasis on development has strong historical roots. GE was experimenting with its PM process and the role of development planning as early as the 1960s. They conducted a study on the effectiveness of the traditional performance appraisal versus an alternative process they called "work-planning-and review" (WP&R), where they separated performance review and salary discussions from development planning.[5] Their results were very convincing. On every element they assessed, the WP&R group had more favorable attitudes about factors such as the value of the performance discussion, the extent to which their manager used their abilities and experience, and how much help their manager provided in improving their performance. Furthermore, 65% of employees who translated development areas into goals accomplished their objectives, while only 27% of employees who did not set development goals achieved desired performance improvement.

Over the decades since this innovation, companies have vacillated between thinking that two conversations took up too much time and that development gets lost unless it is its own conversation. Today, companies have increasingly recognized the wisdom of separating conversations about compensation from discussions focused on performance development.

There are some very good reasons why these two conversations should be separated. First, there is a very different focus between a performance review conversation and a development conversation. When managers engage in a performance review conversation, they are typically looking backward and discussing what has transpired over the prior performance period. This conversation becomes highly focused on external factors for motivation because the discussion about performance is often capped off with the consequences of performance, which for most companies is pay. Given what is at stake for the employee, this conversation can be stressful, as we learned from the NeuroLeadership research.

In contrast, in a development conversation, the focus is on looking forward, focusing on the future for growth and development and future performance. This conversation is very focused on the intrinsic motivation of helping the individual grow and develop so they can accomplish their goals in the future. It is a supportive and not an evaluative conversation. This allows performance development conversations to be more open and candid because both the manager and the employee are working together in the employees' best interests. Separating the "judging" sessions from the "coaching" sessions has been found to boost engagement and performance by not contaminating the development discussion with decisions about performance evaluation and rewards.[6] Gap, Inc., for example, moved from a traditional PM process focused on ratings and annual reviews to a process with more regular, ongoing conversations.[7] Their process included 12 performance conversations throughout the year, each with a separate focus (e.g., goals, development, performance, rewards, career), initiated primarily by employees as they need input, advice, and help with their work.

A few best practices have emerged for companies that are focused on P4P and strictly tying evaluations to compensation decisions. First, separate the development discussion from the evaluation discussion by at least one month. Some of our clients have managed this through the following routines:

- Development conversations happen mid-year, and evaluation conversations happen at the end of the year.
- Feedback and development are discussed on a regular basis (monthly or quarterly), and evaluation only happens at the end of the year or semiannually.
- Employees lead the development conversations, whereas the manager leads the performance evaluation conversation.

Progressive organizations that have already shifted their performance conversations to focus more on development with an emphasis on coaching and feedforward are ensuring that conversations about pay are separated from any conversation about performance and development. When pay is not directly tied to a discussion about performance, employees can focus on receiving and processing the feedback and planning for growth without the distraction of the potential financial implications of the conversation and the defensive response this is likely to foster.

We should note that some (although few) companies include development goals as part of the performance goals. In this case, employees are rated on their completion of their development objectives, similar to how they are rated on performance objectives. We do not recommend this approach. Individuals are already self-motivated to learn and grow. As we have discussed previously, attaching pay to these activities could diminish internal motivation. Furthermore, the benefit for employees of goal achievement is improved performance or new skills that make them eligible for promotions or an increase in base pay based on competence in the role. That is reward enough.

While the trend today is toward separating performance and pay conversations from development conversations, it is important to recognize that practices do vary based on company culture and management practices. It is common to find companies that stick with the annual review process to combine all conversations together. However, the benefits of separation are becoming increasingly recognized in modern PE practices.

Let's take a look at one HR executive who has focused on making development and individual growth a core feature of his process, rather than an afterthought. Dean Carter describes his new approach to managing performance as a journey: one that was many years and several companies in the making.

How Can a Company Make Development an Important Part of the PE Process?

From the Front Lines—Dean Carter

Back in 2000–2010, Dean Carter was the Chief HR Officer (CHRO) for the Fossil Group, Inc. He knew that PM was a universally hated practice, yet important. He called it "the Swiss army knife of HR." It does a lot of things, but none of them well. It has a bad screwdriver and a bad knife. It doesn't even cut things like it is supposed to. Dean set out to pull apart the PM process into its component parts and tried to make each element (goal-setting, development, evaluation, compensation) the best it could be.

His biggest aha moment was a meeting with David Rock, who shared with him the Neuroscience research on the human response to performance ratings and their impact on human beings. He immediately decided to remove ratings from his process—but that is a discussion for another chapter. He also decided that he really wanted to understand a person's skill level, and to better understand what their skill level means for their own personal development in both their current job and their future career. He shared that he "wanted to reward the individual who took a risk, and maybe failed, but learned a lot versus the individual who played it safe and did not learn at all."

Traditional compensation systems pay individuals in part, based on their level of expertise for a given role, from novice to expert. So, his goal was to understand how employees were "moving the needle" and becoming more expert. He accurately shared that "No one talks about the progression of novice to expert in terms of skills. That's not generally a conversation managers have with their employees, even though the compensation structure is designed around it."

Dean's solution was to provide employees and managers with a sliding scale from Novice to Expert and ask each to assess where the employee is currently performing along the continuum. They did provide managers with training on how pay is determined based on market rates and skill expectations. Amazingly, he saw very little variance from employee and manager ratings, although they were discussed. While you could think of this as a 100-point scale, employees are not labeled in any way. Employees whose skills increase earn base pay increases. (Note: Employees were paid a bonus based on the % of goal achievement.) At this time, it was one overall summary assessment of skill level. He implemented the same process when he was the CHRO of Sears, and began to refine it at Patagonia when he moved into that CHRO role in 2015. His refinement was to include specific skills (based on the company's core competency model).

Later in 2022, Dean became the Chief Purpose Officer at Guild. Once again, he wanted to reimplement this same PM process. Since Guild is an education company, they had a very sophisticated skills taxonomy. Each employee had skills assigned to them based on whether they were individual contributors or managers and some specific to the role they were in. Yet, he still implemented the same slider idea of assessing employees on their skills from Novice to Expert and using that information to determine merit pay increases. But rather than one summary skills assessment, employees were assessed on each of the critical skills for their role.

But it was outside of the PM process that Dean really leaned into his focus on skills and learning. He dissected the traditional Learning and Development Department

continued

continued

and created three new leadership positions: Mobility, Ability, and Agility. The leader of Internal Mobility was responsible for getting people promoted within the company. Their success was measured against the metric of the number of employees who moved up or into new roles that better leveraged their skills. The leader of Ability was focused on improving skills in current roles. So, this leader was measured against the extent to which the skills sliders moved in a positive direction for all employees. Finally, the leader of Agility was responsible for preparing employees for changing job requirements. They were responsible for communicating to employees when their current skills were of declining importance to the company, and which new skills were of growing importance. For example, as artificial intelligence rose in importance to the company's strategy, this individual was responsible for equipping employees with the new skills needed to advance the company's mission and goals.

This structure ensured a strong focus on employee development. The key for him was separating the skills and performance conversations (against goals), using a transparent skills progression model, and rewarding skill development alongside goal achievement. Putting in the infrastructure to support skill advancement was the crowning achievement on a long career journey to improve the PM process. His post-transformation survey results showed that employees thought the process was easier, took less time, and was fairer and more transparent. "This was the easiest performance process I've ever implemented." "I'm so excited about it. I would look forward to having a conversation." Clearly, Dean learned a lot over his career journey, and he continuously refined his process as he learned from each experience and discovered what was important to each organization at the time.

Dean provides us with an understanding of how an organization might make the transition over time to a process that is more focused on skills and development, rather than strictly focusing on goal achievement.

Recently, IBM overhauled its PM process with a focus on how to build a future-ready workforce. Their process has three core pillars: business results (performance goals), skill development, and behaviors.[8] After reviewing a three-year look back on the performance of top performers, they found that the performance of those individuals who failed to build new skills declined over time. Thus, they wanted to reinforce the need to become future-ready by continuously focusing on skill development. The addition of behaviors served to reinforce the company's culture and critical behaviors that drive the firm's success, such as curiosity, being able to move with speed, and the willingness to try new things and fail.

How Job and Career Development Fit Together

Employee development plans, often referred to as Individual Development Plans (IDPs), are often designed very similarly to business-focused goal-setting. The employee and the manager agree on a set of learning objectives or goals. Once goals are established, a specific action plan is created that may include special projects, internal or external courses, reading, etc. Generally, developmental goals focus on improving performance in one's current role, or more specifically, the development needed to achieve one or more of the agreed-upon business goals. Alternatively, development plans may also be created based on assessing skills or competencies needed for a role or a company-wide competency model—areas where the individual does not rate highly become the focus of these development plans.

In contrast, as was discussed in Chapter 8 on the importance of creating a supportive and positive PE process, the strengths-based movement encourages managers to focus employees on how they can leverage a strength to help them improve performance in another area, rather than focusing on developing weaknesses, which are more challenging to develop.[9] For example, an employee who is particularly strong in public speaking can leverage this skill to help them build their influencing skills. Public speaking often involves storytelling and persuasion, which are critical to gaining buy-in for any company initiative. This can help an employee rally support for a new project or be the spokesperson for the team on a request the team needs from management. Many organizations see the value of leveraging strengths, but also see the need to develop employees in areas that represent opportunities for professional growth.

Career management is the structured planning and focused attention to helping an individual achieve their career objectives. While many organizations will have a separate career management process that allows an individual to reflect on their personal motives and values to facilitate a career conversation, for other organizations, career management is part of the development planning process. According to research conducted by the employee engagement research firm Glint (now part of Microsoft Viva), over half of HR professionals indicated that the ability to grow one's career within the organization is one of the top factors impacting the employee experience.[10] A McKinsey research study pointed to a lack of career development and advancement as the number one reason stated why employees leave their existing jobs.[11] We believe addressing this need is critical to successful performance enablement. High turnover is a drag on organizational productivity.

When career development is synonymous with Development Planning, the development goals an individual sets may be related to their current job or may relate to building skills or acquiring new experiences that facilitate career progression. It is important for employees and managers to clarify what development planning should focus on. Is it to improve performance in the current role, to help the individual achieve current goals, or is it focused on development for future steps in their career? The decision regarding where to focus (current role vs. future role) may be driven by how proficient an individual is in their role or what is changing in the business environment. Those learning their role will have development focused on delivering on their key responsibilities. Those who already excel in execution in their current role may wish to focus on what is next in their career.

Organizations that have separate individual development planning focused on current jobs versus career development focused on future jobs need to demonstrate to employees how these two play together. A large, global healthcare company provided its employees with an illustration to explain how the individual development plan fits with their career plan and the company's Succession Planning process for senior leaders.

In Figure 12.1, the company depicted the three key Talent Management processes. Two applications apply to all employees: Performance Management and Career Management. The third is only for leadership, the Talent Review Process. The Performance Management process focuses on goals and key behaviors. In this case, a core set of company-wide behaviors was defined

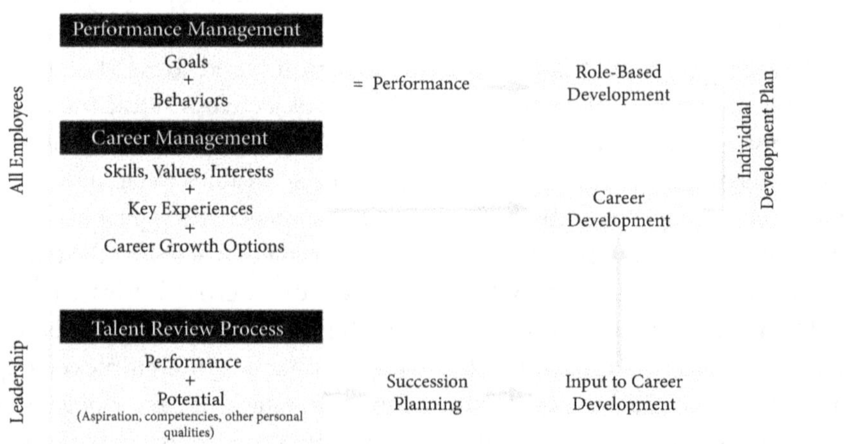

Figure 12.1 Talent management
Source: Authors

with behavioral expectations for individuals at different career stages. The input to the development plan from this process was focused on role-based development. This company also had a separate Career Management process that helped individuals assess their own skills, personal values, and interests. It gave them an opportunity to document their key experiences and to see what other growth experiences they might seek based on a career learning path that had been articulated for them. This process enabled the employee to add a few items to their IDP that were specific to their personal career development goals.

Leaders within the organization went through a separate Talent Review Process where they were assessed on performance and potential. While this informed their succession planning process, key points of feedback were shared with the employee to help inform their career development plan.

The Rise of Skill-Based Talent Management

While this topic is much broader than development alone, the skills-based movement leans heavily into the development conversation. A skills-based organization organizes work and talent around skills rather than traditional job titles, roles, functions, or hierarchies. This talent strategy realizes that skills—not job titles—are the currency of capability and performance in a rapidly changing and dynamic business environment. Thus, work is distributed dynamically based on the skills or interests of individuals, as well as the needs of the company.

And this is where development comes into play. Companies that create a skills-based talent management strategy not only allocate work based on people's skills but also connect employees to content and opportunities that help employees grow and develop new skills important to driving business success. Those opportunities may be new roles within a company that are a better fit for the employee, or help the employee to advance their career, or they are project-based opportunities that employees can take on to help learn new skills that will further their career. PE requires that employees continually focus on growing their skills to meet the needs of an evolving organization.

It is this latter strategy that has become critical as major talent shortages are impeding companies from achieving their strategic goals, and companies are realizing that they need to build, rather than buy, the skills they need to drive the future of the organization. If skills are the new currency of employees in a rapidly changing workplace, then companies need to leverage their PE process to align employee interests with business needs and help employees proactively build the skills that are of growing importance to the organization. With the recent invention of Generative AI, we can clearly see the importance of helping employees build new skills that will dramatically improve the performance of both individuals and the organization. In fact, in the 2025 Future of Jobs Report from the World Economic Forum, they predicted that on average, workers can expect that two-fifths (39%) of their existing skill sets will be transformed or become outdated over the 2025–2030 period.[12] Skills are shifting quickly and focusing on development is critical to driving company performance.

How Effective Development Happens

Effective development takes various forms and is a multifaceted activity. Based on research conducted in the 1980s at the Center for Creative Leadership (CCL), the most well-used guideline for how to develop an executive (or any employee) follows the 70-20-10 rule.[13] As you consider the Development element of our PE model, this is an important framework for thinking how employees should be developed. Adult learners achieve 70% of their most effective development through practical experience. Planned and intentional learning through on-the-job activities is the biggest opportunity for development. This may take the form of new tasks assigned to an employee, assigning employees to cross-functional projects or task forces, or through special project-based opportunities, what we call inside gigs, that expose employees to new skills or context in which to apply their skills.[14] Job rotations or internal job changes are also commonly used for on-the-job learning experiences.

Another 20% of effective development happens when adults learn from others. This includes ongoing feedback, coaching, mentoring, and other forms of guidance. Finally, formal training classes, workshops, and suggested reading account for around 10% of an employee's development. Formal learning must be practiced and reinforced for learning to take place truly. The support you give your employees in applying their learning on the job is critical to effective development (see Figure 12.2).

If you choose formal training as the mode of development, it is very important that you set the employee up for success. First, before the class, you should discuss what the employee plans to learn in the course. Then, after the course, you should have a specific discussion about what was learned and how it will be applied back on the job. Finally, after the learning has been applied,

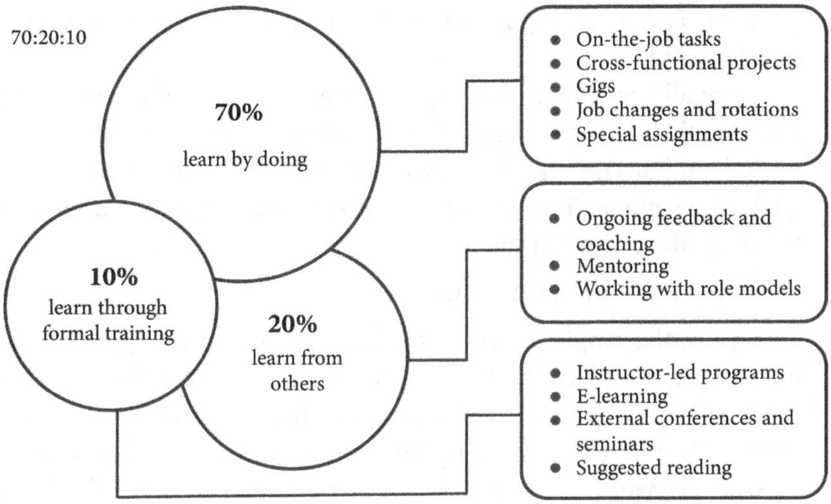

Figure 12.2 How effective development happens
Source: Authors

following up to find out what they learned by doing will further embed that learning experience.

Building an Effective Individual Development Plan

Managers can follow these five simple steps to build an effective development plan:

1. **Understand Company and Team Goals and Strategic Direction**:

   The first step is to ground yourself in the company and team goals so that there is clarity about what is important to the organization. Critical to this grounding is understanding the company's strategic direction. Are you moving into new areas of opportunity, planning on a transformation due to new technologies, moving into new markets, developing new products, etc.? Anything that might influence a change in skill sets and capabilities needed within the organization to drive the success of the business.

2. **Assess Employee Skills and Goals**:

   While some companies may engage in specific skill assessments, most have employees self-rate, and then managers rate employees on well-defined skills or performance against goals. This assessment sets the stage for either leveraging strengths or identifying opportunities for development.

Personally, we prefer flipping this conversation and having it at the outset of the year. Assessing skills and examining goals for the upcoming period, and discussing what development could build skills to enhance goal achievement. This is a more positive and supportive approach to thinking about development.

3. **Set Clear Development Goals:**

   Generally, the employee will take the lead in identifying 1–3 areas in which they would like to develop. For most employees, these goals will relate to improving their performance in their current role or learning new skills that are of growing importance to their role. Just like setting performance-based goals, it is important to set specific, difficult goals. The goals should be measurable and time-bound, with clear milestones and a timetable. Ideally, the individual development goals will be aligned with organizational objectives, and managers should strive to ensure this alignment. This way development both helps the employee and the company.

4. **Identify Development Action Plan:**

   Goals are a critical starting place, but breaking that goal into specific actions that will help achieve the goal is essential. This is the time that the manager plays a heavier role in the IDP by suggesting on-the-job experiences or relevant training that can facilitate personal growth. If your company has an internal talent marketplace that matches individuals to project-based opportunities based on the skills they want to grow, this is another avenue the employee can pursue. Managers are also more likely to be aware of mentors or a mentoring program that could connect the employee with someone who may be a role model and guide in their learning journey.

5. **Track Progress and Evaluate Results:**

   As we discussed previously, checking in and coaching employees on their development plan should not be a once-a-year activity but should be an ongoing dialogue about how the employee is progressing in their personal development. Where available, metrics should be used to measure progress against goals. Because much of an IDP may be focused on behaviors an individual is developing, gathering crowd-sourced feedback from peers can be very helpful in gauging progress. The manager and the employee should adjust the plan based on progress and what is being learned in the employee's learning journey.

Key Takeaways

- Shifting from evaluation-centric PM to development-focused PE drives better individual and organizational outcomes. Research demonstrates that companies investing in development experience higher profitability and retention rates.
- Separating development conversations from performance evaluations fosters a supportive, growth-oriented environment. This allows employees to focus on learning and improvement without the stress of compensation discussions. A case study from the career of Dean Carter shows how to focus on learning and improvement.
- The rise of skills-based organizations points to the fact that skills are the currency of capability and performance in a rapidly evolving workplace. Aligning employee development with the organization's evolving business strategy and need for new skills ensures that individuals and the company are ready for future challenges and strategic success.
- Effective development occurs through a mix of practical experience (70%), learning from others (20%), and formal training (10%), with managers playing a critical role in reinforcing and applying learning to ensure meaningful growth. Suggestions were provided for how to build an effective development plan.

SECTION IV

EVALUATION, REWARDS, TECHNOLOGY, AND IMPLEMENTATION

13
Performance Evaluation

As we discussed in Chapter 3, performance evaluation is central to a pay-for-performance (P4P) philosophy and is an important element of a coercive control paradigm. P4P requires a performance measure, and for most jobs, this means manager ratings of performance. In our study, 80% of companies used manager ratings of performance, and other studies put this number as high as 90%–95%. While companies use different formats, a five-point rating scale is the most popular.[1] Our survey showed that most organizations evaluate employees at the end of the year, but more frequent evaluations are becoming popular (semiannual or even quarterly).

Ratings under the Microscope

Organizations' commitment to performance ratings is surprising given the dissatisfaction with them. Only one in three companies say employees feel their performance is evaluated fairly.[2] The popularity of ratings is also surprising given the growing body of research critical of them.[3] There are several problems with manager ratings of performance.

Human Beings Can Be Unreliable Measuring Instruments

Anyone who has taken an introductory psychology has seen evidence of this. People see things that aren't there and don't see things that are. Extraneous factors influence their judgments, and they can't recall or tune out things they see and experience that affect their judgments.[4] Many biases affect people's judgments, including specific performance rating biases like central tendency, halo, leniency, severity, primacy, and recency.[5] And people come by many of these flaws honestly. Memories degrade quickly as we access them, and biases protect the brain from information overload.[6] Other research shows that rating errors result from imperfections in the way humans process information. We develop schemas and mental maps that help us organize

Performance Enablement. Edie Goldberg and Alan Colquitt, Oxford University Press. © Oxford University Press (2026).
DOI: 10.1093/9780197830642.003.0013

information about people and experiences. When we receive information that does not fit, it isn't as accessible to us when we need it to make an evaluation. Inconsistent information requires more attention to process, so if we are not paying close attention, that information becomes lost.

Manager Ratings Don't Account for Extraneous Factors That Affect Performance

Edward Deming famously said that 94% of individual performance outcomes are controlled by the system in which employees work.[7] Performance varies for reasons that have little to do with employee talent, ability, and hard work, including luck, circumstance, technology, the efforts of other people, and the like.[8] It is a lot to expect of managers to account for these factors when making their ratings. Employees understand this issue as well. In a study conducted by one of the authors, only 30% of employees felt they had significant control over their final PM rating through their own efforts.

Managers Use Criteria Other Than Current Performance to Make Their Ratings

In our research, nearly two-thirds of respondents said factors other than current performance had at least some effect on a manager's rating (e.g., prior performance, performance distribution requirements, leadership potential, retention risk). In a study by one of the authors, half of managers admitted that these nonperformance factors had at least a moderate impact on their ratings.

Managers Are Not Always Motivated to Make Accurate Ratings

Traditional PM processes are designed to give most employees bad news. In most companies, PM is a zero-sum game with fixed reward budgets and a limited number of top ratings and rewards. Since most employees believe they are above average, anyone who doesn't receive top ratings and rewards will likely be disappointed.[9] Managers don't like delivering bad news and tend to assign employees ratings that will give them the reward outcomes they want. To quote psychologist Steve Kozlowski and his colleagues:

> Rating an employee's performance is best viewed as a discretionary, motivational and political process that managers use to reward and punish subordinates and influence organizational decision making.[10]

These factors add noise (error) to an employee's rating. Many experts agree that manager ratings of employee performance say more about the managers making them than the employee's achievements being rated. Across a large number of employees rated by their managers, only about a quarter of the variation in manager ratings is attributable to employee performance, and some studies put it as low as 8% or 9%.[11] Some practitioners aren't ready to give up on ratings, however suggesting they are reliable enough to be useful, and they can be improved.[12]

Why Do Ratings Persist?

Given these problems, why do organizations continue to use them? In the words of psychologist Kevin Murphy, "Why do they refuse to die?"[13] There are three primary reasons.

Organizations Need Them

Organizations have HR processes that require performance input. As we discussed in Chapter 3, PM has become an administrative process to allocate rewards, a key part of a company's P4P philosophy. This purpose is deeply embedded in organizations and isn't questioned.

In a project one of the authors participated in, the project team identified 31 processes and decisions where performance ratings were used as input. It is easy to see how companies throw up their hands and decide to keep them despite the noise they are hearing from employees and managers.

Companies also believe they need ratings to defend against litigation. While this is a concern, this risk may be exaggerated. Few employees get the lowest ratings and fewer of these are likely to be discharged. And few discharges lead to complaints or litigation, or ultimately to settlements or unfavorable judgments.[14] In addition, in cases involving performance ratings, courts don't pay as much attention to the reliability and validity evidence for ratings as they do due process issues related to the PM process itself (we will discuss these issues in Chapter 16).[15] Finally, research shows that ratings and performance documentation may not actually give the company an advantage in litigation and may more often benefit the plaintiff.[16]

Organizations Believe Ratings Motivate

As we discussed in Chapter 3, Tournament Theory principles are central to traditional PM processes. These principles emphasize ratings (especially relative ratings), differentiation, and competition to motivate employees. Research, however, shows that this kind of feedback can have the opposite effect, negatively affecting performance and leading to counter-productive behavior like sabotaging others and artificially inflating their own output.[17] Poorer performers can also get demoralized by their ratings and give up while high performers "let off the gas" and reduce their efforts.[18] Relative ratings can also create problems where strong norms of collaboration, collegiality, and reciprocity exist.[19]

From the Front Lines—Eli Lilly

Eli Lilly & Company discovered these problems when they were studying their PM process. They tracked employee engagement results monthly and saw a significant drop in engagement following the year-end performance process.[20] Their research showed that immediately following the year-end process and for 5–6 months afterward, engagement went down significantly for 85% of their employee population (see Figure 13.1). Their research indicated that employee engagement was a critical driver of business performance, so the company sought ways to eliminate this drop in engagement—and eliminating ratings was part of their strategy.

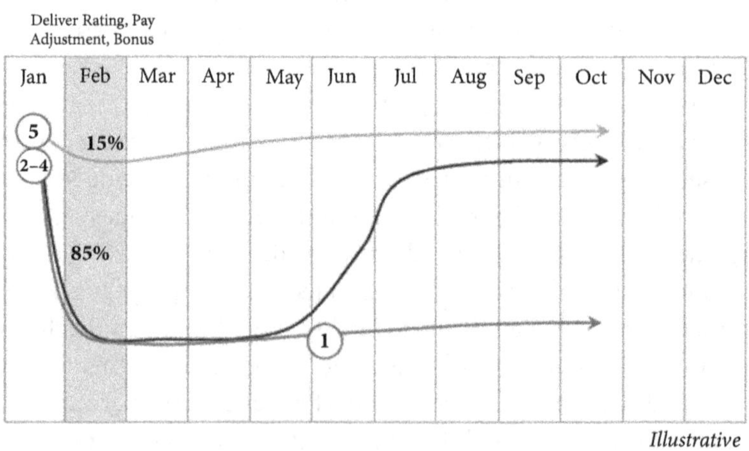

Figure 13.1 Monthly employee engagement following performance reviews

Source: Rock, D., & Ferrara, M. (2015). *Transforming performance management: An Eli Lilly case study*. NeuroLeadership Institute Webinar, September 21, 2015.

Making matters even more difficult, employees themselves believe ratings are necessary. And why wouldn't they? They have been rated, graded, and compared with others for most of their lives. How else would their rewards be determined, if not based on "performance?" And given people's biases, most employees believe they will get high ratings. This "illusory superiority" bias is well-documented.[21] Although employees *say* they want to be rated, evidence suggests they really don't. One study showed that 74% of people said they want to be rated, but when given the choice of two jobs, one where they would be rated and one where they wouldn't, most chose the job where they weren't rated. Even more damaging, those who chose the job where they were rated were less likely to return for more work and performed more poorly when they did return, even if they received high ratings initially.[22]

They Don't See an Alternative

Most organizations aspire to be meritocracies where employees are rewarded and advanced based on merit. Well over 90% of companies have a P4P culture.[23] This requires some way to determine "merit" which requires some form of performance measure.

The Path Forward

There are three general paths for companies to take regarding performance evaluation and ratings:

- Keep them and try to improve them.
- Abandon ratings (and either keep P4P or abandon P4P as well).
- Use objective data to substitute for ratings.

Keep Ratings and Try to Improve Them

Most companies have chosen this path, and several approaches have been taken to improve the reliability and accuracy of ratings.

Improve rating scales

There has been a lot of research experimenting with different types of rating scales. Researchers Frank Landy and James Farr suggested a moratorium on these efforts more than 40 years ago after their comprehensive review showed little progress.[24] While a five-point rating scale has won popular favor because it can produce a more normal distribution curve (which fits people's assumptions about how performance should be distributed), research suggests a three-point rating scale is more effective. Three segments of employees are more reliably differentiated, and employees feel this scale is fairer with fewer deficiencies than a five-point scale.[25] We share research in this area by David Futrell in the case below: "Building a Better Ratings Mousetrap." Furthermore, as we discussed in Chapter 9 on the importance of simplifying the process, a three-point scale tells us who needs attention (the top—who needs to feel appreciated, valued, and rewarded; and the bottom—who needs to be coached more aggressively, put on a performance improvement plan, or who needs to be separated). Finally, recent research goes further, suggesting that a two-point scale may reduce some of the racial biases in ratings. This research looked at customer ratings of online offerings (e.g., of a person, goods, or services) and shows that moving from a five-star rating to a simple dichotomous rating can reduce customers' subtle racial discrimination in these ratings.[26]

When it comes to clarifying and measuring expectations, behaviorally anchored rating scales (BARS) are the standard for defining performance at various levels of performance (e.g., below expectations, at expectations, exceeds expectations).[27] This format has the advantage of providing a detailed, objective, and behavior-specific framework for defining different levels of performance. This is in contrast to processes that either have no behavioral definition, just labels or names of behaviors, or single definition that only describes a general standard of performance that is expected. While this latter format is helpful, it does not provide managers with the standards or a framework to differentiate people who are not meeting or exceeding expectations to facilitate coaching the individual to improve performance.

Is a Three-Point Rating Scale Better than a Five-Point Rating Scale?

From the Front Lines: Walmart—Keeping Ratings: Building a Better Ratings "Mousetrap"

In 2021, Walmart redesigned their PM process. David A. Futrell, PhD describes their learnings regarding performance ratings.[28] One of their goals was to simplify the process. To this end, they streamlined their performance ratings and changed their overall rating (which affected rewards) from a five-point to a three-point scale. The scales and distribution guidance are listed below.

Original Scale

- Below expectations (5%)
- Needs improvement (5%)
- Meets expectations (65%)
- Exceeds expectations (20%)
- Top performer (5%)

New Scale

- Opportunity (5%)
- Successful (85%)
- Exemplary (10%)

Leadership challenged this change because it reduced the number of high ratings (ratings above the midpoint) from 25% to 10%. They worried this would disengage employees. However, the team felt the three-point scale may be better since a five-point scale would allow for higher expectations since more employees would feel they deserved to be rated above the midpoint with more employees feeling disappointed in their final rating.

Employees who receive a different rating than they *expect* are, by definition, *surprised*. These surprises can be either good (a *better* rating than expected) or bad (a *worse* rating than expected). Employees who receive a different rating than they *believe they deserve*, perceive this inequity as *unfair*. This perceived inequity can be either good (a *better* rating than deserved) or bad (a *worse* rating than deserved). The team decided to conduct a study to see which ratings scale was best. They hypothesized:

- A lower percentage of employees will experience a "bad surprise" (receiving a lower rating than they expected) with the three-point scale than with the five-point scale.
- A lower percentage of employees will experience a perceived "unfair" rating (receiving a lower rating than they believe they deserved) with the three-point scale than with the five-point scale.

Surveys were sent to employees before any rating changes were announced, and again the following year, after the new rating had been implemented. Surveys were sent three weeks after learning of their final rating that year. Employees answered three questions in both surveys:

1. What performance rating did you *receive*?
2. What performance rating did you *expect* to receive?
3. What performance rating do you believe you *deserved*?

continued

continued

By comparing the rating they *received* vs the rating they *expected*, they calculated whether the employee was *surprised*. Similarly, by comparing the rating they *received* to the rating they *believed they deserved*, they calculated whether they believed their rating was *fair*.

As hypothesized, the proportion of employees who experienced a bad surprise decreased significantly with the move to a three-point scale, from 26% to 17%. The proportion of those who received the rating they expected increased by a similar magnitude from 64% to 75%. The second hypothesis was also supported. The proportion of employees who experienced a lower rating than they believed they *deserved* also decreased significantly from 38% to 26%. The percentage who received the rating they deserved increased from 59% to 72%. These results clearly show that the three-point scale reduces surprises and perceived unfairness (see Figure 13.2).

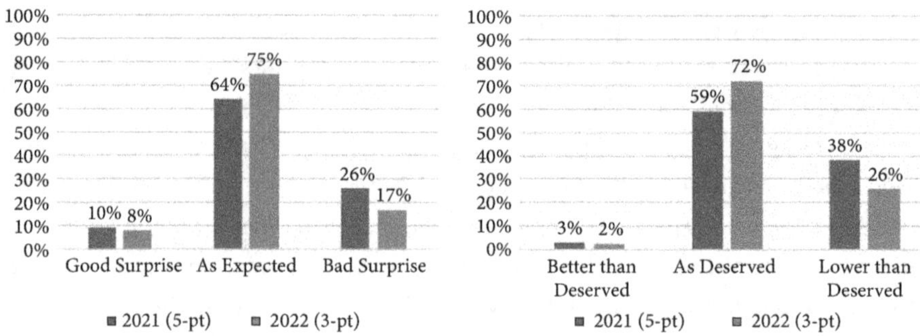

Figure 13.2 Comparison of results for old and new rating scale

Source: Futrell, D. (2022). *It's about the conversation! Having high quality performance discussions*. Society for Industrial and Organizational Psychology 2022 Conference, Seattle, WA.

They also asked employees to compare the old and new processes. While the rating was only one of the changes made, the overall evaluation was positive, with 31% rating the new system as better while only 17% rated it worse.

Another benefit of the three-point scale is it allows for more differentiation in compensation. Since only 10% will be in the "exemplary" category with its higher payout, the difference vs. the midpoint can be substantially greater than when 25% of ratings are above the scale midpoint. Finally, managers also reported that the three-point scale made the rating and calibration processes easier and more efficient.

It is clear from this research that if you decide to keep ratings and want to minimize the perceived unfairness of those ratings in the eyes of employees, a three-point scale is a better choice.

Alternative ratings

Companies are also experimenting with different rating strategies. Deloitte, for example, replaced overall performance ratings with four questions asking managers about future actions they might take with an employee:

1. "Given what I know of this person's performance, and if it were my money, I would award this person the highest possible compensation increase and bonus."
2. "Given what I know of this person's performance, I would always want him or her on my team."
3. "This person is at risk for low performance."
4. "This person is ready for promotion today."

Managers answered the first two questions along a five-point scale ranging from strongly agree to strongly disagree. The last two questions are simple yes/no questions. They thought managers would be better at rating future-focused questions regarding their feelings and intentions about each employee. Managers complete these assessments quarterly and the data are aggregated to provide an annual "performance snapshot" which is used for rewards and other decisions.[29]

Manager training

Other companies are trying to improve ratings by training managers to be better raters. Nearly 80% of companies we surveyed provide manager training. Despite the pervasiveness of training, fewer than half of companies feel their managers are effective in assessing the performance of their employees.[30] Research suggests that these efforts have led to, at best, modest improvements in the quality of performance ratings.[31] Even professional judges in competitions from athletics and music to wine-tasting struggle to make accurate and reliable ratings or simply have other motives for the ratings they make, other than accuracy.[32] The stakes are high in these competitions, and they are high in organizations as well, which may explain the intentional distortion in ratings. Companies spend an estimated $345 million in merit and bonuses each year in the United States alone, much of it based on performance ratings made by "amateur" raters who make these ratings once a year.[33] These ratings affect the careers of millions of employees. Given what is at stake, companies should make a significant investment in training for managers, not just in how the process works and how to avoid rating errors, but to develop all of the skills necessary to enable employee performance.

Forced and guided distribution processes

Most companies are also putting in place policies to force (or guide) managers in distributing their ratings across the rating categories (typically in a normal distribution) in the hopes of making them more accurate. This practice was popularized by Jack Welch and GE in the early 1990s. It is still popular among companies using ratings (70% have such policies in our study). There have been many proponents of this strategy.[34] It *can* be effective in addressing certain rating biases like leniency, but it can also foster a competitive, zero-sum atmosphere and interfere with collaboration and innovation.[35] Given the increasing importance of teams and collaboration among today's organizations, this practice might create problems in organizations with more collaborative cultures.

Calibration meetings and processes

Many organizations are getting managers together to publicly present, discuss, and review the ratings of their employees. These meetings have become more popular as concerns about bias and fairness have increased.[36] Over 70% of companies we surveyed conduct these meetings. Some research shows that these processes can be effective in reducing error and increasing the quality of ratings in some situations.[37] Other research suggests that these practices can actually make rating quality worse.[38] Our experience suggests that these sessions can have multiple, competing purposes: improving rating quality by reinforcing standards and criteria, holding raters accountable by making them explain their ratings publicly, and policing bias, but also to enforce rating quotas, especially for those with top ratings. Research by one of the authors showed that as many as 80% of managers reported they were forced to change performance ratings of their employees as a result of these sessions. One can imagine what this "politicization" of ratings does to a manager's motivation to make accurate ratings.

If you decide to keep ratings, here are some suggestions based on research and our experience:

- If you use ratings, conduct calibration meetings. Managers and employees (and regulators) will see the process as fairer, and managers will be held accountable for the quality of their ratings. The feedback generated in these sessions will also be helpful for managers to use with their employees.
- Conduct higher-level calibration/roll-up meetings to review rating distributions. This will also increase manager accountability.

- Be clear about the objective of these meetings: enforcing ratings targets; bias reduction; policing standards; and ensuring appropriate criteria are used to make ratings.
- Conduct a precalibration exercise with participants in advance to examining rating distributions and surface disagreements about ratings ahead of the meeting. Have managers rank order all employees being rated as part of this process. This rank ordering may be a less-biased starting point for ratings. There are good technology tools available today to facilitate this process.
- If there are strong guidelines on rating distributions, make sure rating distributions conform to guidance before going into calibration meetings. Make every effort to ensure that managers don't have to change their ratings because of higher-level reviews of rating distributions.
- Integrate training into both the precalibration process and calibration meetings to sharpen managers' skills and remind them of the rating criteria and standards.
- Train HR business partners to facilitate these meetings.

Taking these steps will increase the complexity of the process and the time commitment for managers and HR, but these steps are necessary to maximize fairness and quality.

360-reviews

Less popular are efforts to include more rating sources to improve the accuracy, reliability, and validity of ratings. Only about 30% of companies we surveyed include a 360-degree or "crowdsourced" feedback component to their PM processes. Some researchers have suggested that ratings from multiple sources can increase reliability, reduce bias, and reduce leniency by pooling ratings across raters.[39] As we discussed in Chapter 11, however, other research suggests that this may not be the case. Each rater has their own biases and own unique experiences with the employee that influence their ratings. Another drawback of a 360-degree rating process is the additional time and resources required for managers and employees. However, as we suggested in Chapter 11, we believe crowdsourced feedback done well may be helpful in both providing well-rounded feedback and providing more fact-based information for the manager to draw upon in their final evaluation.

Abandon Ratings

A more radical approach to pursue is to get rid of ratings altogether. While the research discussed above suggests that this may be the best option, few companies are taking this step. Only 25% of the companies we surveyed considered it, and the number actually eliminating ratings is as low as 5%–10%.[40] Companies considering this possibility have two primary options to move forward: get rid of ratings but keep the current coercive control paradigm; or abandon the paradigm altogether.

Maintain an individual pay for performance and coercive control philosophy

Companies can eliminate ratings but continue to tie PM to reward distribution. They simply have managers make reward decisions without the intermediate step of a formal performance rating. Our experience suggests most companies that have eliminated ratings are pursuing this path. It is a straightforward exercise to ask managers to make merit pay and bonus decisions considering several criteria, one of which is performance. Removing the hardwired connection between ratings and rewards also acknowledges what many managers already do today, namely, factor many things into their reward decisions (current performance, historical performance, retention risk, potential level, market factors, skills, position in the salary range, tenure, etc.).

It remains to be seen if this path will be effective in the long run. Companies like Eli Lilly and Company, Adobe, and Kelly Services, for example, have successfully done without ratings for many years. At the same time, other companies (e.g., Medtronics, Microsoft) eliminated ratings and then reinstituted them later. Some research suggests that eliminating ratings doesn't necessarily improve outcomes.[41] Our research showed that companies that had abandoned ratings seemed to be no better (or worse) than those that still had them. Simply eliminating ratings is not enough; companies need to put in place other practices like more feedback, more development, more coaching, and so on to improve their PM processes. But eliminating ratings can send a strong signal that the company is approaching this process differently.

Abandon the individual Pay for Performance and the coercive control paradigm

We will discuss this strategy in the next chapter. It requires abandoning individual P4P and separately considering the best way to accomplish the tasks of "motivating employees" and "managing their compensation." It involves motivating employees with less reliance on money and managing compensation with less (or no) reliance on individual P4P programs with high levels of pay differentiation. It also means investing in more enabling control practices like continuous feedback and progress, purpose/meaning, belonging, team and organizational rewards, and investing more in managers.

Objective Performance Evaluations

To close this chapter, it is worth mentioning that some are suggesting there is a third option to deal with the problems of manager ratings of performance. Some argue that they can be replaced by objective measures of performance that are now available as new technologies are implemented in organizations. The use of advanced technologies (artificial intelligence, machine learning, natural language processing) has gained momentum in recent years as technical capabilities have improved. The digital revolution has also dramatically increased the information available about employees both inside and outside of work. Employees leave a "digital wake or footprint" wherever they go online, and new technology can track, scrape, and mine this data which may reflect different aspects of employee behavior and performance. Some believe we will soon be able to measure performance more completely using this information. We remain skeptical and will discuss this trend in Chapter 15.

Key Takeaways

- Despite widespread dissatisfaction and significant research criticizing their accuracy, most companies continue to use manager ratings to evaluate employee performance.
- Human biases, memory limitations, and external factors unrelated to employee effort (e.g., luck, circumstances, and team contributions) all contribute to the inaccuracy of performance ratings.
- Companies rely on ratings for HR decisions like pay, promotions, and legal defense. Many believe performance differentiation is necessary to maintain a meritocratic culture.
- Some companies are exploring alternatives, such as simplified three-point scales, future-focused rating questions (like Deloitte's approach), and use of calibration meetings to reduce bias.

- While most organizations invest in manager training to improve rating accuracy, studies show only modest improvements, as biases and motivation issues, persist.
- While forced ranking can reduce leniency bias, it may also harm collaboration and morale. Similarly, 360-degree feedback may not significantly improve accuracy due to individual rater biases.
- A small but growing number of organizations are moving away from formal ratings, opting instead for manager-driven reward decisions based on multiple factors, though long-term effectiveness remains uncertain.

14
The Performance Management–Reward Connection

As we discussed in Chapter 3, traditional performance management (PM) is an essential part of an organization's pay-for-performance (P4P) philosophy. In fact, we would argue that compensation is the primary driver of the design of most companies' PM processes. If organizations are to move toward Performance Enablement (PE) and more enabling control mechanisms, they will need to make significant changes to their reward practices. In this chapter, we make the case for questioning our commitment to P4P and discuss alternative solutions. We also share a case study of a company that has reinvented its approach to rewards with a Performance Enablement (PE) mindset.

There are three important aspects of any company's traditional approach to compensation and P4P that will be the focus of our discussion:

- A strong emphasis on *financial rewards*
- A focus on individual rewards that are *contingent* on individual performance (in contrast to rewards that are contingent on team, unit, or organizational performance)
- *Differentiation* of rewards based on individual performance. The goal is typically to maximize the differences in rewards for top performers relative to others

Financial rewards are a central feature in talent management practices, from attraction and hiring to engagement and retention. As we discussed in Chapter 1, nearly all companies link pay to performance in some way.[1] Since the 1980s, variable pay has become a larger percentage of total compensation in the United States, for a larger percentage of the workforce.[2] With the rise of P4P, financial rewards and incentives have become the primary strategy for driving change in organizations. For example, if an organization is driving culture change, the strategy is to distill the change down to the new behaviors, reward employees for displaying those behaviors, and punish those who don't. If an organization is driving innovation, identify the key metrics and behaviors and build them into the reward system. In the past, incentives

Performance Enablement. Edie Goldberg and Alan Colquitt, Oxford University Press. © Oxford University Press (2026).
DOI: 10.1093/9780197830642.003.0014

were seen as *necessary but not sufficient* for change; today, they are seen as *sufficient*. Driving and supporting organizational change of virtually any kind (structural, cultural, or process) has become a matter of "getting the incentives right."[3]

As we discussed in Chapter 1, the popularity of these practices is surprising given the dissatisfaction with them. A report by Mercer, 2019, shows that only 22% of employees give their company an "A" grade for ensuring equity in pay and promotion decisions.[4] Companies lay the blame in many places. Most blame managers first. Nearly three-quarters of companies said they needed more training, skills, and courage to differentiate performance and rewards. Companies also blamed budgets, with nearly two-thirds saying they need more money to increase differentiation. Some suggest that a merit increase of at least 5%–7% is needed to motivate employees.[5] Most organizations fall far short of this number, with the average merit budget now below 3%. And, as we discussed in Chapter 3, these budgets have been shrinking since the late 1980s. Other problems include inconsistent administration and poor execution. Nearly three-quarters of the companies we surveyed said factors other than performance affect reward decisions (potential, critical skills, historical performance, retention risk, position in range, tenure, etc.). Companies *say* they pay for performance, but we would argue that most companies are paying for many things, but performance is probably not one of them. Finally, nearly half of the companies in the Mercer report cited problems of the fit of their P4P programs with their company culture (45%).

Effectiveness of Pay for Performance

There is a rich research literature across multiple disciplines on the impact of these reward practices on employee and organizational outcomes.[6] Overall, the findings suggest that these practices are not the panacea most assume. There have been hundreds of studies and several meta-analysis studies looking at the impact of individually focused P4P programs on performance and productivity.[7] These results suggest that financial rewards, P4P, and differentiation of rewards *can* work, but there are several important caveats.

- When they work, improvements are modest (in the 5%–10% range).
- These programs have been most effective in laboratory experiments and for low-complexity jobs (e.g., production, warehouse, retail). They also work best for jobs that are boring or that contain noxious tasks where it may be difficult to get people to perform them, and for jobs where paying closer attention and working harder can improve performance.

- Piece-rate reward programs and quantitative performance measures are disproportionately over-represented in this research which limits generalizability of results. There are relatively few jobs in most organizations today where piece-rate reward systems can be implemented and where good (reliable, valid) quantitative performance measures are available (sales is often an exception although many sales measures, while quantitative, can be problematic for many other reasons).
- This research can be very messy which limits the conclusions that can be drawn about the effectiveness of these programs. For example, many of the institutional research studies (examining practices across large numbers of companies) examining the impact of P4P programs don't distinguish between individually based and organizationally based programs; they lump them together.

Research on the impact of the amount of differentiation of rewards on performance and productivity reaches similar conclusions. It shows that more differentiation isn't necessarily better, especially in organizations with more collaborative cultures.[8] The effectiveness of differentiation also depends on how much there is. Research shows there is a threshold or "sweet spot" for how much differentiation is effective and this threshold tends to be at a relatively low level of differentiation, based on more legitimate factors. Above this point, more differentiation isn't more effective. The effectiveness of the amount of differentiation of rewards also depends on the legitimacy of the factors companies are using to differentiate (e.g., performance, qualifications, level, education). Companies basing reward differentiation on more "legitimate" factors are more effective on many outcome metrics, while companies basing reward differentiation on less legitimate factors are less effective.[9] It is important to reinforce that differentiation of rewards (produced by P4P programs) *causes* pay inequality. Many researchers (especially economists) assume that pay inequality is based on performance, so is seen as legitimate and desirable. Based on our discussion in Chapter 13, it should be clear that this isn't necessarily the case since the primary performance measure used in organizations is manager ratings of employee performance.

Harvard professor Ethan Rouen challenged the conventional economic wisdom that pay differences are mostly caused by legitimate factors. In his study of nearly 300 companies, 39% of the variation in CEO pay and 42% of the variation in employee pay could not be explained by legitimate factors.[10] While several nonlegitimate factors can influence pay inequality in organizations (for example, gender has received a lot of attention recently), ineffective and unfair variable pay programs are almost certainly a key contributor.

Pay inequality is increasing rapidly, and research shows that variable pay programs account for a significant amount of this increase, especially for higher wage earners, where it can account for up to 70% or even 80% of total pay.[11] From our discussion above and in Chapter 13, it is clear that the way these programs create pay inequality is not always fair (e.g., flawed performance ratings, poor program designs, poor or inconsistent execution, manager skills and bias, and discrimination based on factors like gender, age, or ethnicity).

Research has also looked at the impact of financial rewards, P4P, and differentiation of rewards on other outcomes.

- **Attraction**: There is strong support for the notion that financial rewards and P4P programs drive attraction and job choice.[12]
- **Retention**: Pay and satisfaction with pay are only weakly related to turnover.[13] Having pay tied to individual performance does not reduce voluntary turnover, controlling for other important factors.[14] Research on pay differentiation shows similar results: more differentiation does not decrease turnover and, in some cases, may actually have the opposite effect.[15]
- **Creativity/Innovation**: Research shows that several traditional PM and reward practices like strong focus on evaluation, surveillance and monitoring, contracted-for reward, competition, and extrinsic reward orientation are negatively related to creativity and innovation.[16] Research also shows that creativity and innovation is higher with lower levels of pay differentiation and suffers when differentiation goes above a certain threshold.[17]
- **Satisfaction/Happiness:** While the impact of financial rewards on satisfaction is deceptively complex to disentangle, there is little support for the hypothesis that money makes people happy at work or in life. The relationship between pay and job satisfaction is modest at best.[18] Other things (e.g., social factors, education, and personality) are more important and factors like adaptation, status, and external comparisons conspire to severely limit the power of additional money to increase happiness.[19]

Unintended Consequences of P4P Programs

Even when they work, many of these practices have side effects and unintended consequences that significantly reduce or eliminate any value they provide. In Steve Kerr's classic article "On the folly of rewarding A, while hoping for B," he describes examples from many sectors, including medicine, universities, politics, and business where organizations end up rewarding behaviors they wanted to discourage and not rewarding behaviors they wanted to encourage.[20] The research literature and popular press are full of examples of these consequences, especially in business, education, and healthcare contexts (e.g., Wells Fargo, Enron, Tyco, WorldCom, the Atlanta teacher's crisis, the Financial Crisis in 2009).[21] Other research shows that P4P practices can negatively affect employee health by increasing stress, blood pressure, anxiety, depression, somatic complaints, and other physiological risk factors for cardiovascular heart disease.[22] Finally, as we have shared in other chapters, in contrast to assumptions underlying traditional PM processes and coercive control philosophies, employees want to do a good job and are motivated by intrinsic factors (e.g., purpose, meaning, belonging, mastery, autonomy). One consequence of relying on extrinsic rewards to motivate is this practice can "crowd out" employees' natural intrinsic motivation.[23]

There is also a more troubling consequence of reliance on these practices—they may be changing the value systems of our leaders and employees. Research shows that focusing people on money changes them, making them more financially and economically minded, instrumentally focused, less cooperative, and more self-interested.[24] And research shows this effect is causal. Putting otherwise cooperative people into organizations using P4P systems *causes* them to become less cooperative, and it does so very quickly, with lasting consequences. These practices can also make financial rewards more important to people, making their use more necessary, creating a vicious cycle of increased reliance on them.[25] Some researchers compare money to drugs in terms of its effects.[26] It has addictive qualities and attraction to it can have negative consequences. It tends to focus people on more immediate reward gratification at the expense of longer-term goals and activates the brain's reward center. It also acts as a salve, making things temporarily less painful. Practitioners who have tried to change or get rid of P4P practices in organizations can testify to the strong attachment to financial rewards. Finally, people are also biased to believe money and extrinsic rewards motivate.[27] These biases, along with the effects of benchmarking, institutional envy, and competitive labor market dynamics, may go a long way toward explaining the use of these programs, despite unhappiness with them, reservations about how well they work, and negative side effects associated with their use.

Solutions for Moving Forward

There are two general paths companies can take to deal with the problems associated with over-reliance on financial rewards, individual P4P programs and high levels of differentiation of rewards.

Tactical Changes to Reward Practices

There are several trending solutions companies are adopting to address the challenges they are reporting (cost pressures, dissatisfaction with reward practices, poor execution, ineffective managers, lack of fairness, lack of transparency).[28] It is important to emphasize most if not all of these changes maintain a more coercive approach to control in organizations and retain a heavy focus on financial rewards, individual P4P, and differentiation of rewards. Many of these solutions attempt to reduce the noise, pain, and dissatisfaction with current practices.

- **Shift money from merit to variable pay**: This solution responds to the complaints about small merit increases not being motivational. Giving rewards all at one time in a bonus (vs. buried in a regular paycheck and spread out over multiple pay periods) makes it seem bigger, suggesting it will be more motivational to employees. There is also a cost savings with this strategy since merit increases are permanent and compound year-over-year while bonuses are not and may fluctuate with performance.
- **Spot bonuses**: Some companies are reallocating money from annual merit pay and variable pay budgets so they can provide smaller more frequent bonuses delivered closer to the time of the performance as more immediate recognition for good work. This trend assumes a closer alignment in time between performance and reward will increase motivation and satisfaction.
- **Non-cash rewards, recognition**: Many companies are supplementing cash programs with noncash programs like recognition, experiences, time off, merchandise, gift cards, etc. The assumption is that employees value things other than cash and providing them will improve motivation and performance. This also enables managers to personalize recognition based on an individual's preferences.
- **Differentiation**: Other companies are dealing with cost pressures and shrinking reward budgets by doubling down on differentiation, giving an even larger share of smaller budgets to top performers.

Other companies are actually reducing differentiation by changing the reward mix. For example, they are reducing rewards based on individual performance and increasing rewards based on organizational performance. Some companies are differentiating rewards by delivering special bonuses ("bonus kicker") at the end of the year to top performers.

- **"Total rewards"**: Many organizations are emphasizing nonfinancial elements of their value proposition (e.g., job itself, work environment, colleagues, learning opportunities, PTO, benefits). For the past 30 years, companies have marketed these other elements of total compensation more aggressively to employees to improve their engagement and satisfaction levels.
- **Transparency and communication**: Other organizations are becoming more transparent with salary ranges and market data to defend reward decisions and to market the competitive value of their programs. This is also a reaction to the trend of outside employment firms providing this data directly from current and former employees (e.g., Glassdoor). Furthermore, both the EU and several states within the United States (e.g., California, Colorado, New York, and Washington) have enacted pay transparency laws that require employers to disclose salary ranges.

Strategic Changes to Reward Practices

This second strategy is more transformational and requires that organizations separate the task of *managing employees' compensation* from the task of *motivating employees* and aligning their efforts with company priorities. It means motivating employees without relying heavily on money, P4P, and differentiation. It embraces a more enabling control paradigm by leveraging nonfinancial strategies to motivate, appealing to the deeper needs of employees discussed in Chapter 3. We discussed the principles embodied in this shift in Chapters 6–8 and the practices that reflect these principles in Chapter 6 and 10–13. What we haven't discussed to this point is how companies moving to PE and enabling control principles should manage compensation without over-relying on financial rewards, individual P4P programs, and aggressive differentiation of rewards. Organizations making the shift should focus on four broad compensation objectives:

- Pay employees competitively
- Increase their pay over time

- Share the wealth
- Leverage other nonfinancial rewards

Pay employees competitively

Paying employees well relative to the market helps attract employees and prevents them from being attracted away by competitors. Treat compensation as a hygiene factor instead of a motivating factor.[29] As writer Dan Pink writes, "pay people enough to take the issue of pay off the table."[30] Companies should put more emphasis on base pay, which employees prefer.[31] Organizations should change to a market frame (vs. an internal relativity frame). They should strive to pay employees well relative to the market and to focus on narrower, job-related markets as jobs become more specialized.[32] Organizations should also consider paying employees with critical skills above market.

Increase employee pay over time

Organizations have traditionally used annual merit increases to boost pay. As organizations reduce these budgets in favor of more variable pay, employees are more vulnerable to being attracted away.[33] Merit budgets today have become more focused on maintaining market competitiveness (vs. rewarding high performance) anyway.[34] Many companies that have disconnected performance ratings from compensation have used cost-of-living and market adjustments to increase base pay in lieu of "merit" increases. This keeps employees whole with the market and prevents them from being attracted away by an opportunity that pays them market wages. Compensation experts are increasingly conducting job-based market studies, which enables organizations to make more targeted adjustments to salaries as needed.[35] Companies have also begun to promote employees more often. A robust internal labor market with opportunities for promotion is a powerful motivator.[36] Movement away from broad-banded job structures to narrower structures will make more frequent promotions easier to manage administratively.[37] However, it can also result in "title inflation" if not designed appropriately. If an employee has skills or capabilities that are worth more in the market, consider increasing their pay.

Share the wealth

A third strategy is to implement organization-based reward practices like profit-sharing, gainsharing, and employee stock ownership programs. These programs typically base employee rewards on organization, department, or team performance. Research shows that these programs drive higher levels of company performance and productivity, lower turnover, and greater loyalty and willingness to work hard.[38] These programs also cause employees to identify more strongly with the broader groups of which they are a part (workgroup, team, or organization) and they have fewer negative unintended consequences than individual P4P programs. As we discussed in Chapter 4, this strategy is particularly well-aligned with the move toward more collaborative work environments that are increasingly more common today.

Invest in other nonfinancial rewards

Finally, there are many things other than money that motivate employees (e.g., time off, public recognition, experiences, special assignments, food, entertainment, etc.). Organizations should implement nonfinancial recognition programs to allow managers and employees to show their appreciation for the efforts of their colleagues. Organizations should also use opportunities for learning and development to motivate employees. These opportunities can take the form of formal training and development programs, or they can be special projects or short-term assignments.

This discussion shows that it is possible to manage compensation effectively to meet employee and organizational needs without the problems associated with individual P4P programs and high levels of pay differentiation. And many of these programs and practices are already being used in organizations today, with very good results. Some of these changes, however, might create the need for a greater partnership between HR and Finance, with more flexible reward budgets that can be adjusted as conditions and priorities change. Companies embracing agile methodologies are already forcing this new approach as project and funding decisions are made throughout the year instead of just at the beginning of the year.

How Can a Company Manage Compensation without Rating Employee Performance?

From the Front Lines—MidPen Housing

MidPen Housing was founded in 1970 and today is one of the largest nonprofit developers, owners, and managers of high-quality affordable housing in Northern California. MidPen Housing is a mission-driven organization. Their mission is:

> **To provide safe, affordable housing of high quality to those in need; establish stability and opportunity in the lives of residents; and foster diverse communities**

continued

continued

that allow people from all ethnic, social, and economic backgrounds to live in dignity, harmony, and mutual respect.

With 550 employees and assets totaling $2.9 billion, they fulfill this mission through three highly integrated nonprofit companies:

MidPen Housing: Drives the company's operations and development efforts, including property acquisition, planning, design, construction, and renovation.

MidPen Property Management: Provides professional property management for all their properties.

MidPen Services: Provides on-site support programs to advance residents' physical, economic, and educational well-being and helps them move toward their personal goals.

In 2019, they knew that their current PM process was not working. Their business was dynamic, but goal-setting was not. Employees did not get enough feedback. The organization wanted to be a learning organization, but its practices did not support this. Finally, small merit pools led employees to perceive that ratings do not impact their pay, and most people were unhappy with ratings because everyone thought they deserved an "exceeds" rating. One of the authors was asked to help redesign their process.

They began by creating a set of Design Principles that guided the development of their new process, consistent with the principles in our PE framework. Some examples of their design principles include:

- Create a workplace environment where employees can reach their full potential.
- Challenging goals, development, and on-going coaching and feedback bring out the best performance.
- Goal alignment is important to provide employees with context regarding what the organization is trying to accomplish.
- Setting goals helps to focus effort, clarify expectations, and motivate performance.
- Development is critical to improving individual and company performance.
- We need to clearly define behaviors for success so employees understand why and how to improve.
- Pay employees a fair and competitive compensation and reward exceptional performance through a spot bonus program.

Based on these design principles, they set out to design a new process that focused on:

- Setting a few challenging (SMART) goals that would be reassessed each quarter.
- Ongoing coaching and feedback (at least quarterly), including peer recognition.
- A greater focus on development planning to support the company's growth mindset.
- The elimination of performance ratings.
- Training for all managers to improve their skills at setting OKRs, development planning, and providing meaningful feedback.

As a result, they had to change their approach to compensation. The senior leadership team took a step back to consider their competitive talent market and what attracts people to MidPen. MidPen operates in Northern California's highly competitive talent market, with its company headquarters near Silicon Valley. They do not offer stock incentives, which puts them at a competitive disadvantage in the region relative to for-profit companies. Thus, they knew they had to compete on mission alignment, employee experience, and total compensation.

Employees joined MidPen to make a difference in people's lives. Creating a bonus plan that tried to incentivize goal achievement felt tone-deaf to their larger mission. Employees wanted to have an impact. Employees also wanted a flexible work environment (even pre-COVID), working with like-minded professionals who cared about the mission and embraced the values-driven behaviors at the core of the company's mission.

The senior leadership team knew that the "merit pay" concept did not work given small budgets. They wanted to move away from the demoralizing process of rating employees and create a new approach to pay people fairly and competitively against their nonprofit peers.

As a result, their approach to compensation followed these guidelines:

- Understand the local market rate for each role based on comparable rates for their nonprofit peers. Target paying employees at the 62.5th percentile. Fully proficient employees would be paid at the midpoint of their range.
- Base pay would increase based on:
  - Annual Cost of Living (COLA) increase
  - Changes in market rate
  - Increased proficiency in the role
  - Change in role (promotion or lateral move).
- To recognize and reward exceptional performance, the organization set aside 3% of salary as a potential pool for this type of recognition, which could be

continued

continued

a monetary or nonmonetary reward (e.g., cash, gift card, learning experience, etc.).

- Other rewards were also offered as part of their total compensation for all employees (e.g., time off to volunteer, wellness days, tuition support, etc.).

The company administered an Engagement Survey in Q1, just after completing their annual reviews in their old system. This survey was repeated in Q4 after they had launched the new process and completed two quarterly check-ins. Table 14.1 shows the changes in scores for items related to the PM process.

Table 14.1 Engagement survey feedback: Performance management

Survey Item	Favorability Q1	Favorability Q4	Change
I like our process for reviews, feedback, and goal-setting	38	54	+16
I understand how my work is evaluated	63	72	+9
I know how to do well in my job	89	94	+5
The feedback I receive helps me improve	70	82	+12
I get meaningful recognition when I perform well	60	66	+6
I am developing important skills through the work I do every day	80	87	+7
My manager helps me to develop key skills	68	82	+14
My manager sets a high standard of excellence for the team	80	90	+10
I understand how to grow my career at MidPen Housing Corporation	59	64	+5

Based on these results, the changes had their intended impact. As can be seen, the elimination of ratings did not negatively impact factors such as understanding how their work was evaluated or the perception that they were recognized for good work. The conversations managers had with employees helped employees feel valued. Furthermore, the shift to a greater focus on development resulted in positive experiences for employees that improved their performance.

Key Takeaways

- P4P programs are deeply embedded in organizations but are often ineffective, leading to unintended consequences such as pay inequity, decreased motivation, and a misalignment with company culture. Research suggests that financial incentives yield at best modest performance improvements and work best in low-complexity jobs.
- While organizations aim to differentiate pay based on individual performance, research shows that excessive differentiation can be counterproductive, especially in collaborative work environments. Many companies unknowingly base reward differentiation on nonlegitimate factors, worsening pay inequality.
- Organizations can move beyond individual P4P by adopting a compensation model that focuses on competitive base pay, consistent pay increases, and organization-based rewards like profit-sharing. This approach aligns better with PE and supports a more sustainable workforce strategy.
- Employees are motivated by more than just money—recognition, career development, meaningful work, autonomy, and purpose play significant roles. HR professionals should leverage nonfinancial rewards such as learning opportunities, flexible work arrangements, and public recognition to drive engagement and retention.

15
Technology and Innovations in Performance Enablement

Technology holds great potential to help truly transform performance management (PM). But today, most companies use it merely to automate a fairly traditional PM process and to track compliance. The original promise of technology was to automate and standardize HR processes, as well as integrate them with one another. Some of the specific advantages cited for PM applications specifically include:[1]

- **Integration**: Performance ratings, strengths, and development needs can be shared with other applications (e.g., staffing, HR planning, succession management, and learning and development).
- **Access**: Performance information is easier to access, especially when needed for decision-making.
- **Standardization**: Performance management forms and processes can be standardized, allowing more control over templates and workflow.
- **Control**: Access to data and information can be strictly controlled via permissions.
- **Flexibility**: Processes and forms can be changed quickly. If needed, multiple versions of forms and processes can be allowed by the organization.
- **Efficiency**: Eliminates the movement of paper forms back and forth, saving time for both employees and managers.
- **Training**: Training can be pushed out to employees and managers to ensure that they are current in their knowledge and skills.
- **Legal Risk**: Forms and databases can be scanned for problems; error and risk checks can be conducted.
- **Feedback**: Special feedback tools can be incorporated that can facilitate employees or managers in collecting feedback.
- **Reporting and Analysis**: All manner of data and information are captured in structured ways, allowing for better analysis and reporting to enhance accountability.

Performance Enablement. Edie Goldberg and Alan Colquitt, Oxford University Press. © Oxford University Press (2026).
DOI: 10.1093/9780197830642.003.0015

These solutions are not a panacea. They have disadvantages, and many of the advantages of these solutions can fail to materialize. For example, 40% of respondents to an Institute for Corporate Productivity (i4cp) survey reported that solutions did not meet their expectations around integration, and more than half said the same about reporting.[2] Many of these HR technology firms grew by acquisition, buying up firms that were niche players. The modules and solutions that are available may not integrate well because they came from different companies originally. Other disadvantages of technology solutions include that they are always difficult to implement, and data privacy needs to be very carefully managed because they will contain sensitive information about employees.

Simply automating existing processes does not improve them, although it can make them more efficient. While several nimbler technologies have emerged in the past decade (e.g., mobile-first, crowdsourced recognition, focus on coaching for performance), most companies are still utilizing a more integrated talent management suite (e.g., Workday, Oracle, SAP/SuccessFactors, etc.). Industrial and Organizational Psychology has been at the forefront of demonstrating that integrated talent management systems are more impactful than disconnected systems.[3] An integrated talent management system is where all HR talent management programs share a common set of data sources and are aligned and integrated based on a common set of competencies or behaviors. The inputs from PM feed into learning and development, succession planning, and compensation. However, too often, compensation drives PM design as opposed to managing employee performance for improved business outcomes.

This leads us to the most important question for PE design, as we articulated at the beginning of this book. "What is the main purpose of your performance enablement process?" Ensure that the design of your PE process is addressing this question, and that you are not allowing the vendor's standard configuration dictate how you design your process. It is often the case that well-established Human Resources Information Systems (HRIS) come with their own templates for you to use in your PM process. If your process does not align with their template, it is very costly and time-consuming to adapt their system to your needs, and often, that's not even an option. First, design the process you need to drive performance within your organization, then seek out a technology that can help you enable that process. In many of the case studies in this book, companies have built their own systems because nothing available on the market met their needs, or they have bought additional "fit for purpose" applications to close the gaps of the larger applications or to add functionality not provided by existing applications.

While tailoring the technology to your process may not work for some organizations, we encourage you to find a solution that makes your PE process drive business results.

How Technology Is Supporting Performance Enablement

While we have seen the negative impact of rigid technology systems that make HR conform to a more traditional PM process, we have also seen a great deal of innovation in this space, bringing organizations new technologies that enable a Performance Enablement (PE) framework. In this chapter, we will highlight the innovations, benefits, and downsides, as well as the new energy and excitement that new technologies are bringing to PE. We will discuss how companies transform old processes that were labor-intensive, solely dependent on manager feedback, and too slow to be meaningful into agile PE processes tied to business outcomes.

Real-Time Performance Feedback

In 2014, one of the authors published an article called "Performance Management Gets Social," which discussed a new emerging trend: the technology-driven capability to capture crowdsourced feedback in the PM system.[4] Social performance management (SPM) systems allow employees to request and receive feedback from anyone at any time, facilitating real-time feedback and recognition. Similar to social media platforms like Facebook or LinkedIn, SPM systems allow employees to share their goals with co-workers and get and give feedback to others on an ongoing basis. These systems create a performance dialogue rather than a performance review. While feedback most often comes from peers or other managers with whom the employee works, it could also include customer feedback. The most important feature of SPM systems is that they're always on; they solicit feedback continuously and not just at the end of a performance cycle. Employees can ask for feedback anytime, and work partners can provide real-time feedback to help recognize strong performance or to help improve individual and team performance.

With the recent advances in Artificial Intelligence (AI), companies have new ways of passively collecting and analyzing data on behavior and actively collecting performance data and feedback that are easier and more inclusive than ever before. For example, if your company uses email, Slack, Teams, or other communication platforms for internal communications, AI can recognize the feedback in day-to-day conversations and pull that information into your PE process. From the various sources of feedback or information an individual may get, either seeking out specific feedback through daily electronic communications or performance data that can be shared transparently, an employee can get real-time feedback that helps them to improve their performance. This real-time performance information enables managers to recognize and act upon employee feedback in the moment rather than waiting for a specific formal performance discussion. Before a manager meets with their employee for a formal discussion, they can have an AI-enabled system summarize the information received to date, so that the discussion is based not only on the most recent event to occur but also on the employee's entire record over time.

Automation, Streamlining, and Nudge Technology

Some of the most obvious ways technology can improve the PE process are by reducing the administrative burden. Automated PE systems can schedule meetings automatically, summarize feedback, and provide managers with a list of questions for 1:1s or performance discussions. These tools can personalize these discussions for the individual based on their role, goals, and the feedback and performance information gathered by the PE system. By reducing the administrative burden, managers have more time to spend coaching individual and team performance.

To streamline the process, these systems may also connect individual goals electronically to higher-level goals so that management can see how employees' collective actions are helping them succeed. Furthermore, AI can capture the goals and development needs of all employees across the organization to identify strategic capabilities that need to be developed to help the company achieve its goals.

Information from one system can automatically populate others, eliminating the need to copy and paste information between them. Such systems can also track goals automatically by connecting data feeds into the PM platform. For example, in a call center, a data system automatically tracks the number of calls, the amount of time it takes to resolve each call, how many calls need to get escalated, and customer satisfaction at the end of the call. Automated systems can connect this dashboard to the employee's profile and provide a real-time assessment of performance against goals.

Some new technologies are game-changers for making it easier for managers to engage in the behaviors that drive performance. These technologies leverage electronic nudges to change manager behavior.[5] For example, before a meeting with an employee, the system might remind the manager to follow-up on a development activity the employee has engaged in and how they are applying what they learned on the job. Or it might remind a manager to ask what assistance is needed in making progress against goals. While only 18% of our survey participants had already employed nudges to remind managers and employees to engage in PM activities, this is a growing capability in both leadership development and PM software. The ability to remind managers to engage with their direct reports helps to improve manager performance.

AI and Data Analytics

Companies are now leveraging AI and data analytics to create deeper insights into employee performance. AI-powered tools can collect and analyze large amounts of data to provide real-time performance information. They can identify trends in performance data and draw conclusions on opportunities for improvement. Imagine a system that can analyze the code that a software developer is writing daily and then identify inefficiencies in the code or how training in a new area could help improve the performance of the individual.

The new developments with Generative AI (GenAI) help managers to review the performance data currently available for the year to date and draft an initial performance review, to which the manager can add additional commentary and provide more specific feedback. This ability to create a first draft of goals, development plans, or performance reviews is a game-changer. However, managers should *not* rely on the AI-written draft for their final employee-facing review. Employees can often tell when text is composed by AI, and the use of automation in such cases may break trust with management. The prospect of "hallucinations," e.g., where the machine conflates performance between two employees who work together, is enough reason for managers to use caution. Be sure to read and edit any first drafts written by AI.

If employees enter their career goals into the system, AI tools can track their performance against these goals over time. AI can also recommend development activities designed to improve current performance or to help an employee to achieve their goals and identify steps that could further their career. GenAI can draw on vast amounts of data to understand the profile of successful individuals in different roles and can leverage this information to develop highly personalized development plans. Both managers and employees benefit from the assistance of AI in development planning. Furthermore, today, we are seeing an explosion of AI-coaching tools that can be used to help individuals improve their performance.

In Chapter 13, we discussed research showing that manager ratings, intentionally or not, are often flawed. With technology that supports collecting multiple sources of performance information, organizations are now able to combine multiple methods of assessing an employee's performance from several perspectives to improve their accuracy and completeness. Organizations may gather feedback not only from an employee's manager but also from co-workers, peers, or other managers. Performance data may also include employee survey feedback or other available assessment data. By leveraging multiple and diverse inputs, a manager can obtain a more complete and less biased view of the individual. Furthermore, Electronic Performance Monitoring (EPM) systems enable performance assessments based on objective data as opposed to the subjective opinion of a manager. EPM can track measurable performance outcomes (time to resolve a call, customer satisfaction, speeding) and it can also track behavior (e.g., time away from the computer).

Measuring Employee Performance via Technology—The Good and the Bad

EPM refers to an array of methodologies for capturing performance information—keystroke analysis, screen capture, voice monitoring, location tracking, and data from systems that record anything from the speed of a vehicle to the amount of time on a call, to customer satisfaction at the end of a call. Only 20% of our study participants in 2020 were currently using technology to track performance or behavior to provide real-time performance feedback. However, recent research shows that use of this type of surveillance has gone up over 600%.[6] A recent New York Times article reported that "eight of the 10 largest private US employers track productivity metrics of individual workers."[7] This technology has the greatest possibility for fundamentally changing PM. For decades, much of the discussion has been on the inaccuracy of employee ratings. If we had systems that could automatically track objective performance metrics, organizations would have a fairer and more objective process. Today's technology is finally allowing companies to fulfill this promise.

One example of a role that is well-suited for EPM is that of a call center agent. Call centers have detailed performance-tracking systems regarding how many calls are received within a performance period, the success rate in resolving those calls, customer feedback on the quality of service, speed of call resolution, and the amount of time not on the phone. Today, they can even analyze the tone of an agent's voice, as well as their speed and rate of talking during a customer call. Performance metrics on these systems can provide real-time performance feedback on how an individual is performing, alert a manager when coaching is needed, and even provide the coaching directly.

MetLife Inc. uses an AI solution to provide real-time feedback to call center agents on their voice tone. Voice tone can communicate empathy or confidence. When an agent speaks too fast or cuts the customer off, that can be frustrating to a customer. When the agent is tired, their voice might indicate a lack of confidence or interest in solving the customer's problem. MetLife's system detects when employees sound tired and they are prompted to sound more lively when an icon of a coffee cup appears on their screen. This real-time feedback to agents has had a positive impact, as they have seen an improvement in customer-experience scores.[8]

Other performance-monitoring technology exists to help track and improve performance. For example, transportation companies have technology that tracks the speed of a vehicle, the route taken, whether full stops are completed, and how often left turns are used vs. right turns, to improve safety and productivity. Some companies employ technology to identify when an employee is engaged in task-driven behavior or when they are on websites for personal use. Freelance platform Upwork employs technology that provides a screenshot of the worker's computer activity to provide evidence that they are working while billing customers on an hourly basis. While this type of EPM may be very desirable from the organization's perspective, its utility is limited to a relatively small number of roles and situations. It is inherently more difficult to use technology to track and quantify the performance of knowledge workers.

Agency theory suggests that when employees are provided with more information on their performance, they can better align their own behaviors to meet the expectations of the organization. However, while this same theory suggests that EPM may increase task-focused behavior, it may also lead to a decrease in organizational citizenship behaviors (OCBs), such as going above and beyond one's role to achieve positive organizational outcomes.[9] As we discussed in Chapter 7, it is the OCBs that lead to extraordinary performance as employees think beyond their required tasks or projects to other actions that will drive performance.

Some research has shown that technology-enabled monitoring positively impacts performance. Research from a call center study demonstrated that the more frequently managers shared performance information with their employees, the greater the performance improvement.[10] Contrary to the expectations from agency theory, this study found that EPM increased OCBs. Thus, the willingness of the manager to help the employee improve their own performance was rewarded; not only did employees act on that performance information but EPM also helped to create a context that encouraged employees to go above and beyond their role and to extend themselves to help others.

Interestingly, more recent research points to the fact that EPM may have a negative impact on the employee–manager relationship.[11] Through the lens of leader–member social exchange theory (LMSX), we know that managers build positive relationships with their subordinates not only by supporting them but also by giving them agency through delegation and greater autonomy.[12] Such relationships foster trust and create a positive work experience, which leads to better individual performance. However, EPM may become an organizational control tactic that often leads to a loss of autonomy and perceived trust between the manager and the employee. However, when the performance feedback is positioned as developmental, it buffers the negative consequences of being monitored.[13]

Some research does not support the view that EPM has a positive effect on individual performance. A meta-analysis of the effects of EPM on work outcomes suggested that there is no evidence that this more objective way of assessing employees has any positive outcomes on worker performance. In fact, this research points to increasing stress levels as a negative impact of performance monitoring. However, the researchers did find that when organizations were transparent about how managers were monitoring performance and why, workers had more positive attitudes about being surveilled.[14] A good rule of thumb is to be transparent that performance is being monitored, clarify how it is job-related, specify what behavior is being monitored, and how the information is being used.

Since COVID, there has been an increase in surveillance technology aimed at ensuring that employees are being productive and not goofing off. This is often done by ensuring that employees are making keystrokes or moving their mouse. But be advised, an entire industry has been created to thwart this type of surveillance. From mouse wigglers to USB sticks that simulate movement, this has devolved into little more than "productivity theater" and a company would be wise to stop this type of performance monitoring. It breaks employee trust and is easily gamed. Furthermore, this idea of productivity tracking does not take into account thinking time, collaboration with others offline, or providing customer support that is not online, all activities that are highly important for knowledge workers.

Enabling Deeper Dives into Understanding Employee Behavior

Two innovations in PM are specifically designed to understand behavior that optimizes performance, rather than tracking outcomes. These two innovations include sociometric badges and the use of organization network analysis (ONA) for PE. These technologies are not designed to replace manager ratings; their purpose is to understand how individuals interact and the impact of those interactions on outcomes.

While this capability goes beyond the traditional notion of PM, sociometric badges enable companies to track real-time human behavior. These wearable badges contain electronic sensors, developed from research at MIT's Human Dynamics Lab. The badges track how individuals interact with each other to optimize talent within the organization.[15] Sociometric (RFID) badges track individual behavior to help the organization understand which actions make the biggest impact on organizational performance. Companies can then provide feedback to employees that leads to better performance.

For example, their initial research found that employees who met with people outside of their team increased their performance compared to individuals who stuck to their group. While sociometric badges track physical interactions, the next innovation we discuss tracks individual digital interactions.

Employing ONA in the PE process leverages the power of data analytics to help managers better understand organizational behavior. ONA examines the informal networks between employees in a company. It identifies who employees interact with, how frequently they interact, and the nature of the interactions. It generates networking data based on employee surveys that ask respondents to identify their key contacts across the organization, who they seek out for advice, help, motivation, or energy. ONA technology can also analyze email traffic, communications on internal communication platforms (e.g., Slack, Teams), and phone logs to track who is communicating with whom and who is initiating the contact.

As we discussed in Chapter 4, collaboration in organizations is becoming more important. To succeed, individuals need to collaborate with people on their team and with people across the organization. In fact, the second biggest predictor of high performance is building relationships that span the boundaries of geography, function, and expertise.[16] Highly connected employees are far more valuable than individuals who stick to their own set of tasks and do not reach out to others for collaboration and support. However, the biggest predictor of success is being sought out by others. Employees who are the most connected and helpful across the organization are in the best position to influence any type of change needed within the company. Thus, by adding ONA to a PE system, managers can not only understand how the employee has performed against key behaviors and goals but also understand what role the individual plays in facilitating work across the organization. This type of information is invaluable when managers use performance information to determine not only compensation but also promotion.

Key Takeaways

- Design PE processes to fit your objectives and the design principles for your intended process, rather than conforming to vendor-imposed templates.
- Leverage tools like SPM systems and AI for continuous, crowdsourced feedback from the people employees work with on a regular basis. Leverage AI and automated system reminders, automated meeting scheduling, and goal tracking to reduce the administrative burden on managers. This will free managers to focus more on coaching employees rather than spending time managing the process.
- Enhance objectivity and reduce bias by integrating diverse feedback sources and objective performance metrics to create more accurate and fair assessments.
- Use AI, Generative AI, and tools like sociometric badges and ONA to identify key contributors, improve collaboration, gain deeper performance insights, and personalize development plans.
- Balance technology with trust and human oversight. Apply technology thoughtfully to enhance, not undermine, trust, and autonomy. Ensure EPM is used transparently and with the intention to support performance improvement.

16

Effective Practices in Designing and Implementing Performance Enablement

Companies change their performance management (PM) process regularly. In our study, 40% of participating companies had modified their process in the past 1–2 years, and 46% were contemplating or getting ready to make changes. Each change comes with the hope that this technology or that new rating scale will make all of the difference in the world and will result in managers and employees being more satisfied with the process. Unfortunately, these incremental changes have not always made the desired impact. While some blame may be in not making big enough changes (automating a bad process does not make it any better), too often, companies do not invest enough time in the change management required for success.

In our experience, a company should invest as much time and effort—if not more—on their implementation effort as they did on the design of their process. We want to highlight a few aspects of change management that are particularly important for an effective Performance Enablement (PE) design and implementation process.

Engage Key Stakeholders Early and Often

HR may "own" the PE process, but managers have to live with it both from a manager's perspective and an employee's perspective. They should play a significant role in vetting potential design criteria and options. Employees are a good source of feedback regarding what does not work in terms of the current process, as well as what they need to help them be more successful. Different parts of the business (i.e., Sales, IT, Engineering, Finance) may have different needs, so perspectives from across the organization regarding whether there should be one process or different processes (by level or function) need to be considered. In our experience, most companies create one company-wide process, although it is not uncommon for decentralized organizations to allow each division to make modifications to this overall design.

Performance Enablement. Edie Goldberg and Alan Colquitt, Oxford University Press. © Oxford University Press (2026).
DOI: 10.1093/9780197830642.003.0016

If the PE process plays a key role in informing other HR processes (e.g., Learning and Development, Succession Planning, Compensation, etc.), then collaborating with these leaders early in the design process would be important as well. It is critical to understand how changes to one process may impact another.

Our key message is that you need to not only engage all of your potential stakeholders early, but as you move through the process, you need to test ideas or process design with the people who will be most impacted.

Design Thinking

Engaging with your stakeholders brings us to the concept of Design Thinking. Design Thinking is a user-centered approach to problem-solving or process design.[1] The classic process flow of Design Thinking is based on a five-step process.

1. **Empathize**: Immerse yourself in understanding the needs of the end-user. Interview prospective users or conduct job shadowing to understand their needs (similar to what you would do for a job analysis). This is exactly what we mean by engage your stakeholders early.
2. **Define**: Develop rich stories of different personas that explain how and why people need a solution. What pain points do they have today? Often, the activities conducted in the first step provide new insights that help to frame the problem.
3. **Ideate**: Similar to a classic brainstorming exercise, the team generates as many ideas as possible. There is an emphasis on getting the standard ideas out quickly and then spending time thinking differently. Use "yes and" thinking to broaden ideas and facilitate divergent thinking. Once all of the ideas are on the table, the team can prioritize and converge on a solution that seems to be the best fit.
4. **Prototype**: In HR, there is a tendency not to roll out a solution until it is 100% perfect (which slows down innovation). The idea here is to prototype ideas in physical form or by storyboarding. Try something new, fail fast, and iterate.
5. **Test**: Finally, rather than going out to the entire organization, the idea is to test or pilot the solution with a small group and then learn from the feedback, iterate, and improve as you gain more experience with the product or process.

IBM was one of the first organizations to intentionally use Design Thinking to develop its PM process. This experience has been widely shared in various conferences and articles.[2] When we asked participants in our study what research they used when deciding how to design their PM process, 46% of participants indicated that Design Thinking was a source of influence for them. This was more popular than any other body of research, including Agile Methodology (40%), Pay for Performance (36%), Growth Mindset (35%), and Neuroscience (28%).

In a world increasingly calling for human-centered design, PE needs to be created with employees at the center. While the ultimate goal of PE is to drive individual and company performance, we must recognize that achieving these outcomes requires systems and processes that truly resonate with the employees expected to engage with them.

Consider this: traditional PM systems often feel like an administrative burden—more about compliance than connection. These systems can disengage employees, leading to a check-the-box mentality that stifles innovation and growth. In contrast, a human-centered design focuses on creating empowering experiences for employees. It ensures that the tools and processes you implement are meaningful to them, encourages two-way dialogue, and makes performance conversations something they look forward to rather than dread.

Human-centered design also acknowledges the diverse needs of your workforce. It enables you to craft solutions that account for different roles, career stages, and working styles, ensuring that the PE process feels inclusive for everyone.

Human-centered design bridges the gap between organizational goals and employees' needs. It transforms PE from a rigid, coercive process into a dynamic, people-focused process that drives outcomes by fostering an engaged, motivated, and high-performing workforce.

Communicate Key Messages Frequently

Bring the organization along on the journey with you. It is a good practice to let employees and managers know what is coming and to begin to communicate key messages about the new process early. Organizations have a lot to communicate with their employees and managers on a regular basis. Ensuring that communication messages are timely, appropriate, and aligned is very important. If the company is changing both the PE and the compensation process at the same time, these should not be communicated as separate projects but as one thoughtful, integrated approach to designing HR processes.

Identifying key communication messages that describe your ultimate goals is important (e.g., we want to become a learning organization, we want to facilitate a culture of collaboration, we want to become more agile, managers provide supportive coaching and feedforward to help employees be successful, etc.). These key messages can then be interwoven into communications from different sources (leaders, managers, and HR) and can demonstrate consistency and commitment to a new direction.

Identifying key communication messages that describe your ultimate goals is important.

A critical step in defining your key messages is thinking through and articulating the design principles for your process. These are the guidelines that set the stage for the way the company thinks about performance, how best to inspire great performance, the role of feedback and development in your process, and what emphasis you want to put on evaluation—and why. It can also articulate your thinking on what you want to reward. We find that when organizations argue about practices during the design process, it is because design principles aren't clear or haven't been agreed upon.

Align Your Implementation with Connected HR Processes

While we have argued in this book that PE (and its predecessor PM) cannot serve many different processes and do justice to them all (e.g., compensation, development, goal alignment, promotions, etc.), your company may be rolling out a new competency model at the exact time there is a new PE system. More importantly, you may want to assess the impact of your redesigned process during your employee opinion survey process. Working on a calendar that shows the alignment of various communication efforts, training being offered, systems implementations, and surveys to be completed will help the HR organization deliver on a unified talent management strategy.

It's important to create a one- to two-year communications plan where key messages will be shared with employees and managers at different points during the year. These messages need to be built into leadership and management communications and connect all related programs being communicated during the year. It cannot be a once-and-done communication strategy.

People have short memories and lots of competing priorities. If your key messages are not reiterated in different forums and at different times, they will not have a lasting impact on the company culture. Exactly how PE connects to other HR processes (e.g., compensation, succession planning) is important to provide the big picture of how talent is managed within your company.

The Role of Senior Leadership

Most HR leaders understand the importance of senior leadership support of the changes made to the PE process. Senior leadership sponsorship, in terms of role modeling desired behaviors and advocating the importance of the process, is more essential. This type of sponsorship had the strongest relationship with desired outcomes than any other practice in our study. In fact, we found a linear relationship between senior leadership sponsorship and outcomes (see Figure 16.1).

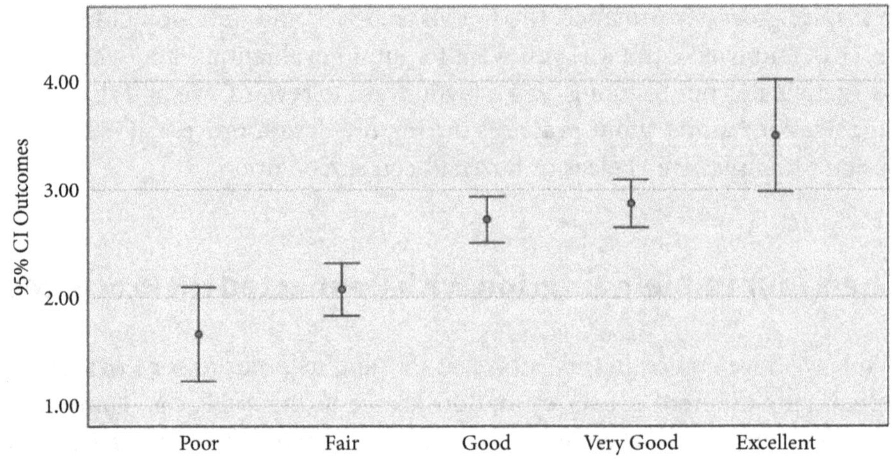

Figure 16.1 Impact of senior leadership sponsorship on outcomes

Source: Colquitt, A. L., & Goldberg, E. L. (December, 2020). *Designing performance management for impact: Practices that make a difference.* Unpublished Participant Research Report.

This result supports prior research that the most effective programs are more than three times as likely to have leadership sponsorship.[3]

The Importance of Training

Training is important not only to clearly communicate the expectations for how the process is to be executed but also to educate participants on the elements of the process and technology and the skills needed to execute it successfully. Unfortunately, in practice, most training programs focus most of their time on how to navigate the technology system. This clearly misses an opportunity to instill the mental model and skills needed to be successful in PE.

As was stated previously, most managers lack the skills to provide effective feedback and coaching. This type of training is essential. In our study, we asked HR professionals to rate the skills of their managers in providing honest, effective performance feedback and coaching to employees. Sadly, only 26.9% thought managers were good at this skill. Clearly, managers need more development. In fact, research has found that manager capability was the second most critical factor that drives program effectiveness, following leadership sponsorship.[4] Companies that focus their manager training on how to coach and develop employees and how to navigate difficult performance conversations effectively were significantly more likely to achieve the desired outcomes of the process than those that did not.

If companies continue to have ratings as a part of their process, the Industrial/ Organizational Psychology literature points out the importance of training in biases and rater errors and Frame of Reference Training—based on the use of behaviorally anchored rating scales.[5]

Our recent study had one somewhat surprising result. While most organizations provide some PM training for managers, only about half of our survey participants indicated that their companies provide employee training. But those companies that did were significantly more likely to achieve their desired outcomes. We believe that when companies use the PM process to introduce a significant change (possibly to reinforce a culture element), they include employees in training as well. For example, in our practice, when we have helped companies focus more on supportive coaching and continuous learning, and ratings were removed to communicate an emphasis on the conversation, these companies always included employees in some training element. The training aimed to help employees understand the new process, how their performance will be evaluated, and what tools will be available to help them improve their performance.

The model we have presented for PE is a significant departure from the traditional PM process. To implement this process, managers will need to develop new skills in coaching and supporting employees and providing feedforward to sustain and improve their performance. They will need to be educated on how the company plans to support the development of employees when skills are shifting so quickly. Managers need to understand how their objectives align with company priorities so that they can help engage and align their employees and teams and set goals that are supportive as well. Furthermore, employees need to learn how to enable, support, and provide feedback to others (peers, their manager, etc.), how to ask for feedback and support when needed, and how to write both performance and development goals.

Evaluating the Effectiveness of Your Process

Ensuring the effectiveness of your PE process involves assessing how well it achieves your intended outcomes, such as motivating employees, improving individual and organizational performance, enhancing employee engagement, and supporting talent development. Here are some of the key approaches we have used in our experience to assess effectiveness.

Define Clear Objectives

Begin with the end in mind. At the outset of any design process, it is essential to be clear about the objectives of your process and your design/redesign project. Is your sole purpose to drive individual and organizational performance, or are you trying to create a process that equitably distributes compensation? Should the process be supportive of your goal to be a learning organization, or are you focused on compliance due to a highly litigious environment? Is your main objective to align goals to ensure that the organization is focused on its most critical business priorities, or do you want to support innovation and improve the company's agility to shift business priorities? All of these are admirable objectives, but one system cannot do it all.

Since we discussed Design Thinking and the importance of human-centered design, maybe a core design principle should be to create a process that managers and employees love rather than loathe.

Use Key Metrics

It is impossible to understand if your PE process has met its objectives unless you establish clear performance metrics. Success does not need to be defined as a singular objective. It can be multifaceted. Some common metrics we have used in our own work include the following:

- **Employee productivity**: Assess changes in output, quality, or efficiency.
- **Company performance**: Measure the impact of the new process on important business metrics such as revenue growth, profitability, Net Promoter Score (NPS), customer churn, or new product development.

- **Engagement or satisfaction scores**: Use employee surveys, or pulse surveys, to measure how the process impacts engagement and motivation.
- **Turnover rates**: Analyze if your new process leads to better retention, especially among your high performers.
- **Skill acquisition**: Determine if the new process is helping you to build the skills of your employees.
- **Promotions or internal mobility**: Assess if employees are developing themselves and either getting promoted or moving into new roles.
- **Time spent in PE activities**: With today's technological innovations, we are hoping that less time can be spent on the administrative parts of the PE process and more time be spent having quality conversations that drive performance. We would not be strong proponents to say managers should be spending less time on the process; after all, managing their employees is their job. However, how the time is spent and the perceived value for that time spent is absolutely something you will want to assess.

Obtain Manager and Employee Feedback

While one of the metrics mentioned is engagement or satisfaction scores, short pulse surveys that assess the quality and timeliness of feedback and whether the feedback they are getting is actionable are great areas to assess through one or two pulse survey items. *We must hold managers accountable for having regular, meaningful performance conversations.* This is often accomplished by having managers rated on key behaviors that are being targeted for change. You can also ask managers if they are spending time on the tasks that matter (dialogue) vs. administration. Beyond surveys, we find that it is incredibly helpful to conduct 1:1 interviews or focus groups with employees and managers to gain insights about the user experience. If you have prioritized development, do employees feel that this new process supports their personal growth more?

Evaluate Goal Alignment and Achievement

Critical to understanding if your process is working is whether or not employees are achieving their personal goals and if the company is achieving its collective goals. Multiple measurements can be helpful. First, what percentage of individual and team goals aligns with company goals (we hope this is 100%)? Second, what percentage of goals is being achieved? Third, if one of the goals of your process is to build a more agile organization, you might leverage AI to assess if goals are being adapted to the changing needs of the work. When a strategic business shift happens, what percentage of aligned goals also changes?

Measure Employee Development and Career Progression

As we discussed in the case in Chapter 12, when Dean Carter was at Guild, they measured employee development and career progression through multiple perspectives:

- **Mobility**: We can measure mobility in two important ways: (1) What percentage of employees is moving into new roles that are better aligned with their skills, passions, or interests, and (2) what percentage of employees is getting promoted?
- **Ability**: The extent to which an assessment of employees' skills has moved in a positive direction. A company could also identify the most critical skills for the organization today, as well as the emerging skills that are of growing importance to the future of the business. Then, the company targets a specific amount of growth in those core capabilities.
- **Agility**: This can be assessed in two different ways depending on the company. It could be an assessment of how quickly a company is able to staff and execute a new project of importance to the company. Alternatively, or in addition, it can be measured by the skill growth in new capabilities important for the future of the organization.

Review Process Efficiency and Overall Impact

Finally, we come to the idea that this new PE process should be both more efficient and effective for the organization. In our research study, we asked HR leaders, "What is the Return On Investment (ROI) of your PM Process?" We asked them to consider what their organization invests in PM in terms of time/effort, money, resources, dollar value of rewards, etc., relative to the value their organization sees in terms of engagement, motivation, and performance. It was disappointing (but not surprising) that only 22.8% of respondents thought there was a high or very high ROI. By leveraging technology and implementing a PE solution, we believe that companies can increase the ROI of their process.

Take Steps to Improve the Fairness of the Process

Even if employees don't like the outcome from PM (e.g., their rating), they are more likely to accept it if they feel the process used to determine the outcome is fair and if they were treated fairly during the process. This is at the heart of employee litigation. While PM litigation does happen, the courts favor processes that are clear, fair, and employ due process. There are several steps companies can take from a due process perspective to improve fairness in the design, implementation, training, and communication aspects of PE, many of which we have discussed in prior chapters as a part of the move to this new model:[6]

- Clarify what's expected of employees (job descriptions, goals, and objectives) and discuss those expectations with employees.
- Clarify what is expected of managers as it relates to PE and train them well to carry it out.
- Employees should receive feedback and coaching throughout the year from multiple sources. This feedback should be as accurate and free from bias as possible.
- Employees should be informed if their performance is unsatisfactory in a timely way and made aware of specific deficiencies so they can improve them.
- Employees and managers should discuss performance and any final write-ups face-to-face (when possible). Employees should always be able to provide their input.
- There should be a formal appeal mechanism for employees if they feel their evaluation or pay isn't fair or if they feel they have been treated unfairly.
- The PM process should also be audited periodically to check consistency, bias, and quality of practices.

Research by McKinsey shows that when PM processes incorporated three things, they were far more likely to be seen as fair and effective by employees:[7]

- Transparently link employees' goals to business priorities and maintain a strong element of flexibility.
- Invest in the coaching skills of managers to help them become better arbiters of day-to-day fairness.
- Reward standout performance for some roles, while also managing converging performance for others. Differentiate star performers,

but don't try to create differentiation on a team where everyone is performing similarly.

By focusing on people, not just process, and ensuring alignment with business goals, organizations can build and implement a PE process that is a strategic enabler of growth, agility, and employee success.

Key Takeaways

- Prioritize change management over technology implementation. Invest as much time and effort in implementation as in design, ensuring that the new approach is fully integrated into the company culture.
- Leverage Design Thinking to better achieve a human-centered design that is user-friendly, drives performance, and aligns with business needs.
- Manager and employee training are both essential. Training for managers must include skill development in coaching, feedforward, and goal alignment to drive meaningful performance conversations. But don't leave employees out of training. They need to understand the intent of your process and how to set goals and provide feedback to others.
- Leadership support is necessary but not sufficient. Leaders must actively role model desired behaviors, integrate PE into business conversations, and advocate for its importance.
- Companies must establish clear objectives and success metrics (e.g., engagement, productivity, retention, goal achievement, and skill development) to evaluate whether the new system is achieving its intended outcomes.

17
Flipping the Script from Performance Management to Performance Enablement

In this closing chapter, we want to help you think about where you are as an organization and what you might need to do to "flip the script" from Performance Management (PM) to Performance Enablement (PE). We have created an assessment for you to evaluate how your current approach aligns with these two very different models. Most importantly, we want you to begin by thinking about the Paradigm and the Purpose of your current process. Principles and Practices are easy to follow if you are clear on paradigms and purpose. We want you to start with the philosophical question: What are the beliefs and assumptions underlying your process, and why do you do it in the first place? How do you think about managing talent within your organization? We believe that this root level is where we need to begin. It's a fundamentally different mindset.

Use the assessment in Table 17.1 to think about where you are today compared to the Paradigm, Purpose, Principles, and Practices that will drive your success in the future. On the left side of the assessment, we describe the Paradigm, Purpose, Principles, and Practices of Traditional PM. On the right, we have statements that illustrate how PE differs. The middle option, "we are moving toward the future," should be used when you are doing a little of both PM and PE. For example, maybe your company is still focused on differentiation and pay for performance (P4P), but you have recently focused more on providing context for employees and coaching employees on progress toward goals.

Where Do We Begin?

Moving from PM to PE is a major transformational shift. To use a poker phrase, it requires that you "go all in," meaning you push all of your money

Performance Enablement. Edie Goldberg and Alan Colquitt, Oxford University Press. © Oxford University Press (2026).
DOI: 10.1093/9780197830642.003.0017

Traditional Performance Management	We have a traditional process	We are doing some of both	We flipped the script to PE	Performance Enablement (PE)
PARADIGM				
Motivate employees by coercing them and forcing compliance with policies and practices (e.g., performance monitoring, evaluation, P4P).	☐	☐	☐	Motivate employees by enabling them through alignment, commitment, coaching, support, and development.
PURPOSE				
The purpose of our process is to evaluate and differentiate employees to P4P.	☐	☐	☐	The purpose of our process is to enable individual and organizational progress and performance.
PRINCIPLES				
We cascade goals to create alignment at each level.	☐	☐	☐	Company goals provide general direction to help employees set goals.
Alignment is created by tying ratings and rewards to goal achievement.	☐	☐	☐	Alignment is created by helping employees understand the broader context for their goals.
PM is a calendar-driven process. Goals set at the beginning and evaluated at the end of year.	☐	☐	☐	Goals are flexible and agile, allowing priorities to shift as circumstances change.
We set individual goals, and reward individual performance.	☐	☐	☐	Goals and rewards focus not just on individuals but also on collective accomplishments.
Focused on monitoring performance, ensuring that employees don't get off course.	☐	☐	☐	Positive, enabling, and supportive approach.
Feedback is focused on weaknesses and gaps to improve performance.	☐	☐	☐	Feedback is focused on strengths and progress to drive engagement and support.
The process is complex because we need to justify and defend personnel decisions.	☐	☐	☐	The process is simple and occurs in the flow of work to drive performance.

PRACTICES				
Goals specify what is expected.	☐	☐	☐	Goals reflect stretch achievements meant to energize and challenge employees.
Feedback looks backward to keep score and justify ratings and rewards.	☐	☐	☐	Feedforward and coaching is provided to optimize future performance.
Feedback is provided during periodic, scheduled reviews.	☐	☐	☐	Feedback is always on; provided during regular 1:1s, team meetings, and through other means.
Feedback only comes from the manager.	☐	☐	☐	Feedback may come from your manager, peers, other managers, or customers.
Development is not a central part of the process.	☐	☐	☐	Development is an integral part of the process.
We believe manager ratings are accurate and unbiased (the best measure).	☐	☐	☐	We realize that manager ratings are flawed and we take extra steps to maximize accuracy (e.g., training, calibration, clearly defined anchors).
Strong individual P4P program (e.g., focus on differentiation, variable pay).	☐	☐	☐	Focus is on paying fairly, leveraging team rewards, and rewarding exceptional performance.
We believe in P4P and put more money in variable pay components; reward differentiation at all levels.	☐	☐	☐	We put more money in base pay and ensure that top talent is paid exceptionally well.
We focus heavily on cash rewards.	☐	☐	☐	We use other, noncash rewards to recognize talent.

into the pot—you are betting everything you have. If you want to enable performance (and not coerce it), you need to go all in. It requires a fundamental shift in the paradigms and mental models you use in thinking about how to motivate and direct the work of employees to achieve high performance. It also requires a shift in the purpose and principles that govern this process. Companies should "go all in" if they are serious about driving individual and organizational performance. In the sections below, we will tell you what we think you need to do. However, we aren't naive. We have over 60 years of collective experience working with and in large organizations. We recognize that a big paradigm shift may take your leadership time to digest and commit to a new philosophy. If this is the case, we will also share what you should do if you think you can only go partway.

Many of the case examples we discussed in this book were from organizations that only went partway (However, MidPen Housing was an example of a company that went all in). In many ways, going partway typically shifts an organization's focus to reducing the burden and pain of their current process—creating less of a "headwind." Having worked with many organizations to improve these processes, this is certainly a legitimate goal of your PM or PE process. At this same time, companies need to be realistic about the outcomes they will achieve going partway; they will dampen the likelihood of turning this process into a "tailwind."

Goal-Setting

In Chapter 10, we shared research that the goal-setting process is critical to focusing employees on the right actions and motivating performance. If you want to go all in, make this process the centerpiece of your process. Even if you can't go all in, we strongly recommend you make goal-setting central. Invest more time discussing the strategy and priorities of the organization so employees understand the broader goals, the meaning behind them, and how their work and goals need to align. Make goals more directional in nature so they are more flexible, so you spend less time on detailed "contractual" documentation and more time on creating line of sight for employees and conveying the purpose and meaning in employee's work.

Where it makes sense, set team goals to create alignment and meaning for the team and to connect the individual goals to team success. Spend time throughout the year in 1:1 and team meetings discussing goals, reinforcing the context and meaning. Help employees understand the context of their work and how their work fits into what the company or team is trying to achieve (the Edward Jones example in Chapter 7 is a good place to start). Goals create clarity for employees regarding what is important.

Set stretch goals. We encourage you to set ambitious, achievable targets that inspire and drive performance. Stretch goals create momentum, push people beyond their comfort zones, and lead to innovation.

We also recommend organizations adopt the Objective and Key Result (OKR) framework which Arcesium used to anchor their PM transformation. Reviewing and updating goals frequently (either on a project basis or quarterly) helps a company to remain agile and ensure that employees are focused on the right actions that drive results for the company's most important business priorities. We believe that OKRs have become popular because of their simplified format, focus on stretch, and more frequent reviews, which make them ideally suited to today's constantly changing business environment. Our case study from Arcesium reinforced this point.

If you implement these practices, then evaluating performance using ratings and connecting individual rewards to ratings becomes more challenging (mostly because goals may change during the year, and detailed performance targets will have more stretch, meaning goals will be less likely to be fully achieved). If you must evaluate and differentiate individual performance based on goal achievement, you will need to create more detailed documentation of goals, metrics, and targets and maintain and update that documentation throughout the year. Under these circumstances, we suggest you conduct calibration sessions to ensure that employee goals are clear, specific, and have equivalent amounts of stretch. While calibration sessions make the process more complex, they can make evaluation and feedback more accurate and robust. We would be remiss, however, if we didn't challenge you to consider how you could do without evaluation and differentiation of individual performance. How important are they and are they worth the challenges they pose? Perhaps shifting rewards to company or team achievements makes more sense for your business. Create a goal-setting process that aligns to your business and is not designed just to evaluate and differentiate the performance of employees and distribute rewards.

Creating a Feedback and Coaching Culture

In Chapter 11, we discussed the new expectations that employees have regarding regular feedback. We also shared the data from the i4cp case showing how a performance feedback culture drives business results. Use this data to make the case to your senior leadership team that you need to shift your culture to one where employees and managers view feedback as a gift. We need it to improve. Making progress toward goals is motivating, and employees need feedback to know if they are making progress. Companies should leverage tools that make giving and gathering feedback easy. There are dozens of tools available today (discussed in Chapter 15) that make it easy to gather feedback.

The best organizations don't restrict feedback to a once-a-year performance discussion or annual review. Nor do they restrict feedback to only come from one's manager. Instead, they weave it into daily interactions and capture it in the flow of work. Leaders must model the behavior and reinforce the importance of feedback. You need to set expectations for managers that on-going feedback (or ideally feedforward and coaching) is a critical element of their role. You need to train them on this skill to be successful. Recognize and reward managers who provide frequent, impactful feedback to reinforce this behavior for those managers and their peers. Employees should be encouraged to ask for feedback and to share feedback with their peers. Make it as easy as possible to ask for feedback using new technology available.

Train your managers on how to coach their employees for future performance. Coaching isn't about reliving past mistakes but unlocking future potential. It focuses more on feedforward than feedback (because you can't change the past, but you can learn from your experiences and use them to think through new behaviors or actions that will lead to improved outcomes). Managers who practice *feedforward* coaching help employees grow and stay engaged. As we shared in Chapter 11, managers who use the feedforward approach to feedback significantly outperformed their peers who relied on feedback only.

Leveraging 1:1s and Team Meetings as Part of the Performance Enablement Process

In Chapter 9, we shared the importance of making your PE process a continuous one vs. an annual step back to review performance for the year. Although employees, especially knowledge workers, don't need micromanagement, they need coaching, support, and feedback on progress toward goals. Consider individual one-on-ones and regular team meetings as a core part of the PE process. These conversations should be spaces for growth, problem-solving, and alignment—not opportunities to make judgments or keep score.

What should managers talk about in these regular meetings with employees and teams? Our colleague Steven Rogelberg has identified six categories of questions that have emerged from his research on one-on-ones:[1]

- Productivity/Challenges: His category for addressing roadblocks or concerns about what is getting in the way of performance.
- Giving/Receiving Feedback
- Development, Growth, and Career
- Check-in
- Relationship-Building
- Engagement

Rogelberg suggests that managers can rotate the categories of questions they ask so these frequent meetings do not become stale. These meetings should be specifically focused on current work activities and providing updates. Most importantly, he recognizes the importance of using these meetings to ensure alignment on priorities between the employee and the manager. His book is filled with a variety of questions you could ask your direct reports during regular one-on-ones (or check-ins). We don't disagree with any of his ideas, but we wanted to provide a tool that was focused specifically on PE.

Whether you ask individuals or teams to share one thing you did well and one way you could improve, or if you are using the old "Start, Stop, Continue" framework for feedback, providing regular feedback is critical to driving performance.

Here are some categories and questions that align with our PE model, which we recommend you rotate through during the year.

Direction and Priorities

Purpose: To ensure that the employee has the context they need to align their behavior with the current needs and direction of the organization. This may be the meeting where goals are set or when goals need to be revised.

Sample Questions:

- What goals should we set to align with the company's goals?
- Has the business landscape changed that requires a reprioritization on our part?
- Have any goals or priorities shifted?

continued

continued

Progress on Goals

Purpose: To understand how the employee is progressing against goals and what adjustments need to be made to ensure success.

Sample Questions:

- What progress have you made on your goals since our last check-in?
- Are there any obstacles preventing you from achieving your goals? What support can I provide?

Coaching/Feedback

Purpose: To exchange feedback and coaching to ensure two-way communication.

Sample Questions:

- How might you run that meeting differently next time to get a better outcome?
- Is there feedback you would like for me to share with you on any particular issue?
- Are there any changes or suggestions you would like to see in how we work together?
- How did that interaction go? What might you do next time to achieve a better outcome?

Support and Resources

Purpose: Identify resources or help the employee needs to be successful.

Sample Questions:

- Do you have everything you need to do your job effectively right now?
- Are there any tools, processes, or support that would make your work easier?
- Is there anything you need from me or the team to achieve your objectives?

Well-Being and Personal Connection

Purpose: Build trust and ensure the employee's overall well-being by fostering a supportive relationship.

Sample Questions:

- How have you been feeling about your work and workload lately?
- How do you like and dislike being managed?

- Is there anything you think I should know about in your life outside of work that might impact your performance?
- What type of work do you love to do? What is your passion?

Development

Purpose: Focus on the employee's skill development, career aspirations, and growth opportunities.

Sample Questions:

- What skills are you working to develop, and how can I support you?
- Are there any projects or experiences you would like to explore for your own career growth?
- Are you getting the development you need to achieve your personal goals?
- Is there anything getting in your way of personal growth? How can I help?

Recognition and Celebrations

Purpose: Celebrate achievements and acknowledge contributions.

Sample Questions:

- What accomplishment are you most proud of since we met last?
- How would you like to celebrate your recent success?
- You did a great job on X. How did that make you feel?

Our PE model emphasizes the importance of development in improving individual and company performance. Here, both Rogelberg's research and our proposed 1:1 questions include focusing on development, personal growth, and career. In Chapter 12, Dean Carter shared an example of how he has focused more on skill-building in the PE process. Because skills are shifting quickly in today's organizations, keeping a focus on development will be essential.

Evaluation

If your company is not ready to abandon ratings just yet, there are several steps you can take. However, you need to be aware that keeping ratings means keeping other practices that maximize the quality of ratings (reliability, accuracy, and validity), even if those practices only make minor improvements in their quality. These practices include more detailed goals, metrics, and targets, clearly defining all points on the rating scale, calibration, and roll-up meetings to examine rating distributions, rigorous training of managers, more detailed documentation to support decisions, and other steps to improve the legal defensibility of ratings (e.g., providing due process). It is important to understand that maintaining ratings and the practices that support them, by definition, make the process more complex and time-consuming for both employees and managers. As we discussed in Chapter 13, there are significant limits to how fair and effective you can make this process.

As a first step, we strongly recommend that your process focuses on the groups that are the easiest to differentiate: top performers, poorer performers, and everyone else. As the research by David Futrell, PhD and Walmart in Chapter 13 showed, a three-point rating scale has a lot of advantages and fewer disadvantages over the more popular five-point scale.

Another approach to take is what Deloitte did, and we shared in Chapter 13. Rather than rating employees on performance against goals or behaviors, develop a set of questions that reflect the actions you would be willing to take with an employee if they were a top performer (e.g., "*award this person the highest possible compensation increase and bonus,*" or "*give this person a promotion*").

Linking Rewards to Performance

If you are not ready to abandon more coercive PM practices (individual evaluation, differentiation, and P4P), you must realize that there are limits to what you can do to significantly improve your process since much of the administrative burden is driven by these practices and these practices tend to create a competitive zero-sum culture that may conflict with your attempts to create a more collaborative and team-based culture. If simplicity is one of your design criteria, retaining these practices will make it difficult for you to maximize this objective.

However, there are several things we would recommend to improve the quality and fairness of your process, even if you maintain these more coercive practices. First, base a larger percentage of employee rewards (e.g., bonus) on organizational and/or team performance and a smaller percentage on individual performance. This facilitates collaboration and reduces competitive behaviors that get in the way of maximizing company performance. As we have previously discussed, outcomes are rarely determined by the efforts of one individual. We all work in an ecosystem.

Second, use factors other than individual performance to adjust base pay (market adjustments or cost of living adjustments). Most of you are doing this already but not making it transparent to the employee or marketing the benefits of these practices. Finally, make liberal use of noncash options to recognize employee efforts and accomplishments (e.g., special recognition programs, informal recognition). Spot recognition is helpful as the reward is tied more closely in time to the behavior or outcome being recognized.

Reduce Your Administrative Burden

From reducing documentation requirements to simplifying the calibration process, there are numerous ways to reduce the administrative burden of the process. Technology can really help with this objective. Review Chapter 15 and identify how to leverage technology to improve your process. For example, some technology applications have AI capabilities and can create an initial draft of a review or a development plan for managers and employees.

If you encourage your employees to be brief in their documentation and focus on the conversation, you will get a different outcome. You want to create a record that you can refer to but not to document every action the employee took during the year. Adobe provided a great example of how one organization balances the need for documentation with the need to keep things simple.

Senior Leadership Support Is Critical

As we shared in Chapter 16, our study and our experience show that having senior leadership sponsorship is the most critical factor in driving the success of any significant PM effort, especially a PE transformation effort. Leadership buy-in is the secret sauce. Organizations with senior leaders who actively champion PE and role model desired behaviors are far more likely to achieve their intended outcomes. To be frank, if your leadership does not buy into the changes you want to make (e.g., a more continuous, coaching, and development-oriented approach), and they are not willing to walk the walk, then just stop. You will never be successful in changing behavior and mindsets in the company. But if they do get fully on board, your success will be rewarded with improved individual and organizational performance.

Conclusion

PE is an important management process for companies, "steering" the organization toward high performance. It should not be blown up or eliminated as many have suggested. It needs to be refocused and designed explicitly around these important management functions and it needs to be designed based on more contemporary principles of motivation and control.

At the time of this writing, there are few strong exemplars of PE. As we have shown, however, many companies are experimenting with more progressive practices (e.g., removing ratings, continuous feedback, use of OKRs, organization-based incentive programs). We will continue to monitor the success of these experiments and see if others follow their lead. We think we are in the very early days of transforming to PE. Companies are still coming to grips with how to adapt to the forces disrupting their companies, as discussed in Chapter 4. We think these forces will require a move to PE, and companies would be wise to begin experimenting aggressively.

HR needs to take a strong leadership role in this transformation. As we discussed, traditional PM processes are held in place by a complex system of institutionalized practices and entrenched beliefs and assumptions reinforced by widely available information from dominant external players validating those beliefs. We have shown that the research simply does not support these practices.

The journey to PE won't be easy. HR leaders and outside experts need to have open, frank conversations about the purpose of PM and their underlying assumptions and beliefs, and the research evidence that supports or disputes these assumptions. They see the topics of motivation and rewards through a lens that has been narrowed by their paradigms (economics, reinforcement theory) and their culture (individualistic). There are other ways of looking at the world that reveal new ideas for motivating employees and ensuring that employees and organizations enjoy the rewards they deserve. Our model for PE has a very intentional design element. The ribbon that holds the three important building blocks for PE (Guidance, Direction, and Goals; Coaching, Feedforward, and Support; and Development) is displayed in an upward spiral that creates energy and success within the organization. Organizations that leverage the PE model will find it much easier to focus on the things that really matter, driving individual and organizational performance.

Notes

Chapter 1

1. WorldatWork (2017). *Performance management and rewards.* WorldatWork research report.
2. McGregor, D. (1957). An uneasy look at performance appraisal. *Harvard Business Review*, May–June, 89–94.
3. Agovino, T. (2023). The performance review problem. *SHRM on-line.* March 14. https://www.shrm.org/topics-tools/news/hr-magazine/performance-review-problem
4. For example, see:
   Colquitt, A. L. (2017). *Next generation performance management: The triumph of science over myth and superstition.* Charlotte: Information Age Publishing.
   Effron, M. (2023). *Global performance management report.* Talent Strategy Group.
5. WTW (2016). Getting pay for performance right. Webinar, 2016.
6. Miller, S. (2016). Employers seek better approaches to pay for performance. *SHRM*, February 8. https://www.shrm.org/topics-tools/news/benefits-compensation/employers-seek-better-approaches-to-pay-performance.
7. WorldatWork, 2017, Op. cit.
8. Colquitt, A. L., & Goldberg, E. L. (December, 2020). *Designing performance management for impact: Practices that make a difference.* Unpublished Participant Research Report.
   Effron, 2023, op. cit.
9. Wilkie, D. (2015). Is the annual performance review dead? *SHRM on-line*, August 19. *https://www.shrm.org/topics-tools/news/employee-relations/annual-performance-review-dead.*
10. CEB. (2012). *Driving breakthrough performance in the new work environment.* Arlington, VA.
11. Interaction Design Foundation—IxDF. (2016). *What are wicked problems?* Interaction Design Foundation—IxDF, June 4. https://www.interaction-design.org/literature/topics/wicked-problems.
12. Aguinis, H. (2013). *Performance management.* Upper Saddle River: Pearson.
13. Black, J. S., & Gregersen, H. B. (2002). *Leading strategic change: Breaking through the brain barrier.* New York: Prentice Hall.
14. Argyris, C., & Schon, D. A. (1974). *Theory in practice: Increasing professional effectiveness.* San Francisco: Jossey-Bass.
15. Colquitt & Goldberg, 2020, op. cit.

Chapter 2

1. For example, see:
   Cappelli, P., & Tavis, A. (2016). The performance management revolution. *Harvard Business Review*, 94, 58–67.

Colquitt, A. L. (2017). *Next generation performance management: The triumph of science over myth and superstition*. Charlotte: Information Age Publishing.
Pulakos, E., D. & Battista, M. (2020). *Performance management transformation: Lessons learned and next steps*. New York: Oxford University Press.
Agovino, T. (2023). The performance review problem. *SHRM*. March 14.

2. Brandon Hall Group (2020). Understanding the challenges of reinventing performance management: Research highlights survey report.
3. Shaw, J. D., & Mitra, A. (2017). The science of pay-for-performance systems: Six facts that all managers should know. *WorldatWork Journal*, Q3, 19–27.
4. For example, see:
   Murphy, K. R., & Cleveland, J. N. (1995). *Understanding performance appraisal*. Thousand Oaks, CA: Sage Publications.
5. Colquitt, A. L., & Goldberg, E. L. (December 2020). *Designing performance management for impact: Practices that make a difference*. Unpublished Participant Research Report.
6. Carroll, S. J., & Tosi, H. L. (1973). *Management by objectives*. New York: Macmillan.
7. Colquitt & Goldberg, 2021, op. cit.
8. Maier, N. R. F. (1958). *The appraisal interview*. Hoboken, NJ: Wiley.
9. Colquitt, 2017, op. cit.
10. Colquitt, A. L. (2021). Performance management as organizational control: Breaking free from the ghost of PM's past. Blog Post.
11. Mintzberg, H. (1994). *The rise and fall of strategic planning*. New York: Simon & Schuster.
12. Hollander, S. (1987). *Classical economics*. Oxford: Blackwell.
13. Eisenhardt, K. M. (1989). Agency theory: An assessment and review. *Academy of Management Review*, 14, 57–74.
14. Connelly, B. L., Tihanyi, L., Crook, T. R., & Gangloff, K. A. (2014). Tournament theory: Thirty years of contests and competition. *Journal of Management*, 40, 1, 16–47.
15. Thorndike, E. L. (1898). Animal intelligence: An experimental study of the associative processes in animals. *Psychological Monographs: General and Applied*, 2, 1–109.
16. Luthans, F., & Kreitner, R. (1975). *Organizational behavior modification*. Glenview, IL: Scott, Foresman.
17. Vroom, V. H. (1964). *Work and motivation*. New York: McGraw Hill.
18. For example, see:
   Carver, C. S., & Scheier, M. F. (1982). Control theory: A useful conceptual framework for personality-social, clinical, and health psychology. *Psychological Bulletin*, 92, 111–135.
   Mansel, W. (2020). Changing behavior using control theory. In Hagger, M. S., Cameron, L. D., Hamilton, K., Hankonen, N., & Lintunen, T. (Eds.), *The handbook of behavior change*. Cambridge: Cambridge University Press.
19. Ryan, T. A. (1958). Drives, tasks, and the initiation of behavior. *American Journal of Psychology*, 71, 74–93.
20. Locke, E. A. (1968). Toward a theory of task motivation and incentives. *Organizational Behavior and Human Performance*, 3, 157–189.
21. Thaler, R. (2015). *Misbehaving: A history of behavioral economics*. New York: W.W. Norton & Company.
22. Simon, H. A. (1957). *Models of man, social and rational: Mathematical essays on rational human behavior in a social setting*. New York: John Wiley and Sons.

23. Kahneman, D. (2012). *Thinking, fast and slow.* New York: Farrar, Strauss and Giroux.
24. Black, J. S., & Gregersen, H. B. (2002). *Leading strategic change: Breaking through the brain barrier.* New York: Prentice Hall.
25. Ulrich, D. (2021). HR's reinvention: Moving from benchmarking and best practices to guidance. The RBL Group Post, March 10.
26. Pfeffer, J., & Sutton, R. I. (2006). *Hard facts, dangerous half-truths and total nonsense: Profiting from evidence-based management.* Boston: Harvard Business School Press.
27. For example, see:
    Scott, W. R. (1995). *Institutions and organizations.* Thousand Oaks: Sage.
    Pfeffer & Sutton, 2006, op. cit.

Chapter 3

1. Aguinis, H. (2012). *Performance management.* Pearson: Upper Saddle River, NJ.
2. Colquitt, A. L., & Goldberg, E. L. (2020). *Designing performance management for impact: Practices that make a difference.* Unpublished Participant Research Report, December.
3. WorldatWork (2017). *Performance management and rewards.* WorldatWork research report.
4. Goler, L., Gale, J., & Grant, A. (2016). Let's not kill performance evaluations yet. *Harvard Business Review*, November, 90–94.
5. McKinsey (2018). Straight talk about employee evaluation and performance management. McKinsey Quarterly podcast, October.
6. Hunt, S. (2016). Rating performance may be difficult, but it is also necessary. *Industrial and Organizational Psychology*, 9(2), 296–304.
   Varma, A., Budhwar, P., & DeNisi, A. (Eds.) (2008). *Performance management systems: A global perspective.* Global HRM Series, London: Routledge.
7. Rose, N. L., & Wolfram, C. (2002). Regulating executive pay: Using the tax code to influence chief executive officer compensation. *Journal of Labor Economics, 20*, 138–175.
8. Hall, B. J., & Murphy, K. J. (2003). The trouble with stock options. *Journal of Economic Perspectives, 17*, 3, 49–70.
9. Payscale (2018). *Variable pay trends into 2018: Who gets it, what types and why*? White paper, April 30.
10. For example, see:
    Cohen, P. (2018). Where did your pay raise go? It may have become a bonus. *The New York Times*, February 10.
    Hudner, J., & Oliver, K. (2013). *Current trends and new directions in variable pay.* Working Report, Pearl Meyer & Partners, 2013.
11. WorldatWork (2018). *Inventory of total rewards programs and practices.* Research Report.
12. For example, see:
    Colquitt & Goldberg, op. cit.
    Dominick, P. G. (2009). Forced rankings: Pros, cons, and practices. In J. W. Smither & M. London (Eds.). *Performance management: Putting research into practice.* San Francisco: Jossey-Bass (pp. 411–443).
13. For example, see:
    Caruso, K. N. (2013). *A practical guide to performance calibration: A step-by-step guide to increasing the fairness and accuracy of performance appraisal.* White paper.

Speer, A. B., Tenbrink, A. P., & Schwendeman, M. G. (2019). Let's talk it out: The effects of calibration meetings on performance ratings. *Human Performance*, 32, 107–128.

14. Effron, M. (2020). *We love ratings.* White Paper, Talent Strategy Group.
15. Coens, T., & Jenkins, M. (2002). *Abolishing performance appraisals: Why they backfire and what to do instead.* San Francisco: Berrett-Kohler.
16. Colquitt, A. L. (2018). *The world's worst disease: Is your company infected with it.* White paper.
17. For example, see:
    Ghoshal, S. (2005). Bad management theories are destroying good management practices. *Academy of Management Learning and Education, 4*, 75–91.
    Heath, J. (2009). The uses and abuses of agency theory. *Business Ethics Quarterly, 19*, 497–529.
    Jensen, M., Murphy, K., & Wruck, E. (2004). Remuneration: Where we've been, how we got to here, what are the problems, and how to fix them. *European Corporate Governance Institute—Finance Working Paper, no.44 (July)*, via SSRN.
    Pfeffer, J., & Sutton, R. I. (2006). *Hard facts, dangerous half-truths and total nonsense: Profiting from evidence-based management.* Boston: Harvard Business School Press.
18. For example, see:
    Cable, D., & Vermeulen, F. (2016). Stop paying executives for performance. *Harvard Business Review*, February 23.
    Cohan, P. S., & Cohan, W. D. (2018). Executive compensation and the ethics of misguided incentives. Invited lecture, Bentley University, Center for Business Ethics.
    Dorff, M. B. (2014). *Indispensable and other myths: Why the CEO pay experiment failed and how to fix it.* Los Angeles: University of California Press.
    Lorsch, J., & Khurana, R. (2010). The pay problem. *Harvard magazine*, May–June.
    Samuelson, J. (2018). Overpaying ceos is a terrible way to motivate them. *Quartz*, August 13.
19. For example, see:
    Cooper, M., Gulen, H., & Rau, P. R. (2016). Performance for pay? The relation between CEO incentive compensation and future stock price performance. SSRN article.
    Marshall, R. (2017). *Out of whack: US CEO pay and long-term investment returns.* MSCI White Paper.
20. WorldatWork, op. cit.
21. Jesuthasan, R. (2013). Performance management as business discipline: Why mastery goes beyond the transactional. *People & Strategy, 36*, 58–71.
22. Fayol, H. (1949). *General and industrial management.* London, UK: Pitman.
    Weber, M. (1946). *From Max Weber: Essays in Sociology.* In H. H. Gerth & C.W. Mills (Eds.). New York: Oxford University Press.
23. Mastenbroek, W. (2002). Norbert Elias as organizational sociologist. In, van Iterson, A., Mastenbroek, W., Newton, T., & Smith, D. (Eds), *The civilized organization: Norbert Elias and the future of organization studies.* Amsterdam: The John Benjamin Publishing Company.
24. Cardinal, L. B., Kreutzer, M., & Miller, C. C. (2017). An aspirational view of organizational control research: Re-invigorating empirical work to better meet the challenges of 21st century organizations. *Academy of Management Annals, 11*, 559–592.
25. Adler, P. S., & Borys, B. (1996). Two types of bureaucracy: Enabling and coercive. *Administrative Science Quarterly, 41*, 61–89.

26. Cardinal, Kreutzer, & Miller, 2017, op. cit.
27. Cardinal, Kreutzer, & Miller, 2017, op. cit.
28. Ouchi, W. G. (1979). A conceptual framework for the design of organizational control mechanisms. *Management Science*, 25, 833–848.
29. Carenys, J. (2010). Management control systems: A historical perspective. *International Journal of Economy, Management, and Social Sciences*, 1, 1–18.
30. Mastenbroek, 2002, op. cit.
31. The power of these needs to motivate individuals is well-established. Research on these needs spanning decades has been conducted by some of the most prominent psychologists in the field. For further reading, see the following:
Baumeister, R. F., & Leary, M. R. (1995). The need to belong: Desire for interpersonal attachments as a fundamental human motivation. *Psychological Bulletin*, 117, 497–529.
Deci, E. L. (1971). Effects of externally mediated rewards on intrinsic motivation. *Journal of Personality and Social Psychology*, 18, 105–115.
Herzberg, F., Mausner, B., & Snyderman, B. (1959). *The motivation to work*. Wiley. New York.
Lawler, E. E. (1969). Job design and employee motivation. *Personnel Psychology*, 22, 426–435.
Maslow, A. H. (1943). A theory of human motivation. *Psychological Reviews*, 50, 370–396.
Porter, L. W., Lawler, E. E., & Hackman, J. R. (1975). *Behavior in Organizations*. New York: McGraw Hill.
McGregor, D. (1960). *The human side of enterprise*. New York: McGraw-Hill.
32. Slemp, G. R., Fields, J. G., Ryan, R. M., Forner, V. W., Van den Broeck, A., &. Lewis, K. J. (2024). Interpersonal support for basic psychological needs and their relations with motivation, well-being, and performance: A meta-analysis. *Journal of Personality and Social Psychology*, 127, 1012–1037.
33. For example, see:
Argryis, C. (1964). *Integrating the individual and the organization*. New York: Wiley.
Hackman, J. R., & Oldham, G. R. (1980). *Work redesign*. Addison-Wesley: Reading, MA.
Herzberg, et al., 1959 op. cit.
Lawler, 1969, op. cit.
34. Ouchi, 1979, op. cit.
35. For example, see:
Achor, S., Reece, A., Kellerman, G. R., & Robichaux, A. (2018). 9 out of 10 people are willing to earn less money to do more meaningful work. *Harvard Business Review*, November 6.
Bower, T. (2022). The power of purpose and why it matters now. *Forbes*, January 12.
Kikrschner, P., Kwok, A., Schrimper, M., & Weddle, B. (2022). Your office needs a purpose. *McKinsey Insights*, December 12.
Palmer, R., & Schaninger, B. (2018). The link between meaning and organizational health. *McKinsey Quarterly*, October 26.
Van Ingen, R., Peters, P., De Ruiter, M., & Robben, H. (2021). Exploring the meaning of organizational purpose: The development of a conceptual model through expert interviews. *Frontiers in Psychology*, 12:675543.
Martel, F., Gomez, M., Unanue, W., Araya, S., Bravo, D., & Espejo, A. (2021). What makes work meaningful? Longitudinal evidence for the important of autonomy and beneficence for meaningful work. *Journal of Vocational Behavior*, 131, 103631.

36. Baumeister & Leary, 1995, op. cit.
37. For example, see:
Courtright, S. H., Thurgood, G. R., Stewart, G. L., & Pierotti, A. J. (2015). Structural interdependence in teams: An integrative framework and meta-analysis. *Journal of Applied Psychology*, 100, 1825–1846.
Hu, J., & Liden, R. C. (2011). Antecedents of team potency and team effectiveness: An examination of goal and process clarity and servant leadership. *Journal of Applied Psychology*, 96, 851–862.
Weldon, E., Jehn, K. A., & Pradhan, P. (1991). Processes that mediate the relationship between a group goal and improved group performance. *Journal of Personality and Social Psychology*, 61, 555–569.
Weldon, E., & Weingart, L. R. (1993). Group goals and group performance. *British Journal of Social Psychology*, 32, 307–334.
38. For example, see:
Edmondson, A. C. (2012). *Teaming: How organizations learn, innovate, and compete in the knowledge economy.* San Francisco: Jossey-Bass.
Deloitte (2016). *The new organization: Different by design.* Global Human Capital Trends Report, Deloitte University Press.
Fernandez, J., Landis, K., & Lee, J. (2024). Why collaboration is critical in uncertain times. *Harvard Business Review*, February.
Gaskell, A. (2021). New study finds that collaboration drives workplace performance. *Forbes*, December 10.
Mashek, D. (2022). Collaboration is a key skill. So why aren't we teaching it? *MIT Sloan Management Review*, June 23.
39. Deci, 1971, op. cit.
Deci, E. L., & Ryan, R. M. (2013). The importance of autonomy for development and well-being. In B. W. Sokol, F. M. E. Grouzet, & Muller, U. (Eds.), *Dialectic between organismic and social processes.* London: Cambridge University Press.
Hackman, J. R., & Lawler, E. E. (1971). Employee reactions to job characteristics. *Journal of Applied Psychology Monograph*, 55, 259–296.
40. Elias, N. (1939, 1997). *The civilizing process: The history of manners and state formation and civilization.* Oxford: Blackwell.
Vogt, O. (2024). Autonomy: The misunderstood ideal of self-management. LinkedIn post, December 23.
41. Adler & Borys, 1991, op. cit.
42. Ouchi, 1979, op. cit.
43. Carenys, 2010, op. cit.
44. Hall, Edward T. (1989). *Beyond culture.* New York: Doubleday.
Ramos, D. C. (2014). High context. In S. Thompson (Ed.), *Encyclopedia of diversity and social justice.* Lanham: Rowman & Littlefield Publishers.
45. Chun, Y. H., & Rainey, H. G. (2005). Goal ambiguity and organizational performance in U.S. federal agencies. *Journal of Public Administration Research and Theory*, 15, 529–557.
Wright, B. E. (2004). The role of work context in work motivation: A public sector application of goal and social cognitive theories. *Journal of Public Administration Research and Theory*, 14, 59–78.

Chapter 4

1. Schwab, K. (2017). *The fourth industrial revolution.* New York: Crown Business.
2. Business Roundtable (2019). *Business roundtable redefines the purpose of a corporation to promote "an economy that serves all Americans."* August 19. https://www.businessroundtable.org/business-roundtable-redefines-the-purpose-of-a-corporation-to-promote-an-economy-that-serves-all-americans.
While there has been considerable discussion about the proposed shift in the purpose of a corporation, it is worth noting that this new concept has not been applied uniformly. Shareholder interest still carries the day for publicly traded companies, and some companies (e.g., Unilever) are better at applying this new purpose than others.
3. Bhave, D.P. (2014). The invisible eye? Electronic performance monitoring and employee job performance. *Personnel Psychology*, 67(3), 605–635. DOI: 10.1111/peps.12046.
4. While some may question whether globalization will change given the recent hostile rhetoric on immigration globally, but especially from the current United States administration, and their recent aggressive actions on tariffs, we believe that this is a temporary issue and globalization is here to stay. That is not to say that the influx of people fleeing their home countries does not put a burden on the receiving countries, but we don't believe that there will be a fundamental change in economic globalization. A large number of companies are globally distributed to capitalize on different markets and labor pools. There is no going back. Human resources must continually develop new talent management strategies to address the current challenges in a highly competitive labor and economic market.
5. Woetzel, J., Madgavkar, A., Seong, J., Manyika, J., Sneader, K., Tonby, O., Cadena, A., Gupta, R., Leke, A., Kim, H., & Gupta, S., (2018). *Outperformers: High—growth emerging economies and the companies that propel them.* McKinsey Global Institute Report, September 11.
6. McDowell, T., Agarwal, D., Miller, D., Okamoto, T., & Page, T. (2016). *Global human capital trends 2016: The new organization: Different by design*, 17–25. New York: Deloitte University Press. https://tinyurl.com/fj2yykzn.
7. Cross, R., Rebele, R., & Grant, A. (2016). Collaborative overload. *Harvard Business Review*, 94(1/2), 74–79.
8. Colquitt & Goldberg, 2020, op. cit.
9. Boudreau, J. (2020). Jobs are melting into fluid work. Blog post. USC Center for Effective Organizations. https://ceo.usc.edu/2020/09/29/jobs-are-melting-jobs-into-fluid-work/.
10. Barrero, Jose Maria, Nicholas Bloom, and Steven J. Davis. (2021). Why working from home will stick. *National Bureau of Economic Research Working Paper 28731.* Survey of Working Arrangements and Attitudes, June 2025 update. www.wfhresearch.com.
11. Wong, M. (2025). *Return to office? Not everybody is doing it.* Stanford Institute for Economic Policy Research. March 6. https://siepr.stanford.edu/news/return-office-not-everybody-doing-it.
12. Drucker, P. F. (2001). *Management challenges for the 21st century.* New York: Harper Business.
Pink, D. (2011). *Drive: The surprising truth about what motivates us.* New York: Riverhead Books.

Ryan, R. M., & Deci, E. L. (2000). Self-determination theory and the facilitation of intrinsic motivation, social development, and well-being. *American Psychologist*, 55(1), 68–78.

13. Kyle DeMaria (ed.), Ian Page, Kevin Reuss, and Zoë Zemper (2024). Changes in the U.S. labor supply. *Trendlines*, U.S. Department of Labor Employment and Training Administration, August. https://www.dol.gov/sites/dolgov/files/ETA/opder/DASP/Trendlines/posts/2024_08/Trendlines_August_2024.html.
14. Dhingra, N., Samo, A., Schaninger, B., & Schrimper, M. (2021). Help your employees find purpose—or watch them leave. *McKinsey & Company*. April 5. https://www.mckinsey.com/capabilities/people-and-organizational-performance/our-insights/help-your-employees-find-purpose-or-watch-them-leave.
    Amire, A. & Great Place to Work (2022). The best workplaces for Millennials offer meaning and purpose. *Fortune*, July 18.
15. Dua, A., Ellingrud, K., Hancock, B., Luby, R., Madgavkar, A., & Pemberton, S. (2022). *Freelance, side hustles, and gigs: Many more Americans have become independent workers.* August 23. https://www.mckinsey.com/featured-insights/sustainable-inclusive-growth/future-of-america/freelance-side-hustles-and-gigs-many-more-americans-have-become-independent-workers#/.
16. Gherson, D., & Gratton, L. (2024). Highly skilled professionals want your work but not your job. *Harvard Business Review*, 102(3), 76–85. https://hbr.org/2024/05/highly-skilled-professionals-want-your-work-but-not-your-job.
17. Upwork (2017). *Upwork summit.* San Francisco, CA.
    Upwork (2024). *How Microsoft's teams are increasing their agility.* https://www.upwork.com/success-stories/microsoft-teams-are-increasing-agility.

Chapter 5

1. Goldberg, E. & Steven-Waiss, K. (2020). *The inside gig: How sharing untapped talent across boundaries unleashes organizational capacity*. Los Angeles: Lifetree Media.
2. Cappelli, P., & Tavis, A. (2018). HR goes agile. *Harvard Business Review*, Vol 96(2), 47–52.
3. Beck, K., Beedle, M., van Bennekum, A., Cockburn, A., Cunningham, W., Fowler, M., Grenning, J., Highsmith, J., Hunt, A., Jeffries, R., Kern, J., Marick, B., Martin, R. C., Mellor, S., Schwaber, K., Sutherland, J., & Thomas, D. *Manifesto for Agile software development.* https://agilemanifesto.org/.
4. This is a prime example of where the legal world has not kept up how businesses operate today. Our practices are being driven by old legal precedents that we need to challenge given that technology has changed how companies access temporary talent with the skills and expertise needed to execute on projects of importance.

Chapter 6

1. Latham, G.P., Borgogni, L., & Petitta, L. (2011). Goal setting and performance in the public sector. *International Public Management Journal*, 11(4), 385–403.

Wright, B. E. (2007). Public service and motivation: Does mission matter? *Public Administration Review*, January/February, 54–64.
Locke, E. A., & Latham, G. P. (2002). Building a practically useful theory of goal setting and task motivation: A 35-year odyssey. *American Psychologist*, 57, 705–717.
Achor, S., Reece, A., Kellerman, G. R., & Robichaux, A. (2018). 9 out of 10 people are willing to earn less money to do more meaningful work. *Harvard Business Review online*, November 6. https://hbr.org/2018/11/9-out-of-10-people-are-willing-to-earn-less-money-to-do-more-meaningful-work.
Bower, T. (2022). The power of purpose and why it matters now. *Forbes*, January 12.

2. Hrebiniak, L. G. (2005). *Making strategy work: Leading effective execution and change.* Upper Saddle River: Pearson Education and Wharton School Publishing.
3. Kaplan, R. S., & Norton, D. P. (2004). Measuring the strategic readiness of intangible assets. *Harvard Business Review*, 82(1), 52–63.
4. Cecchi-Dimeglio, P. (2023). How leaders use the power of goal alignment. *Forbes*, September 29. https://www.forbes.com/sites/paolacecchi-dimeglio/2023/09/29/how-leaders-use-the-power-of-goal-alignment/.
5. Locke & Latham, 2002, Op. cit.
6. Rock, D. (2006). *Quiet leadership.* New York: HarperCollins.
7. Kluger, A. N., & DeNisi, A. (1996). The effects of feedback interventions on performance: A historical review, a meta-analysis, and a preliminary feedback intervention theory. *Psychological Bulletin*, 119, 254–284.
8. Amabile, T., & Kramer, S. (2009). *The progress principle: Using small wins to ignite joy, engagement and creativity at work.* Boston: Harvard Business School Press.

Chapter 7

1. Colvin, A. J. S. & Boswell, W. R. (2007). The problem of action and interest alignment: Beyond job requirements and incentive compensation. *Human Resources Management Review, 17*, 38–51.
2. Herway, J. (2021). To get your people's best performance, start with purpose. May 21. https://www.gallup.com/workplace/350060/people-best-performance-start-purpose.aspx.
3. Sull, D., Homkes, R., & Sull, C. (2015). Why strategy execution unravels—and what to do about it. *Harvard Business Review, 93(3)*, 58–66.
4. Sisodia, R., Wolfe, D., & Sheth, J. (2014). *Firms of endearment: How world-class companies profit from passion and purpose.* Upper Saddle River: Pearson FT Press.
5. Dik, B. J., Byrne, Z. S., & Steger, M. F. (2013*). Purpose and meaning in the workplace.* New York: American Psychological Association.
Leider, R. J. (1997). *The power of purpose: Creating meaning in your life and work.* San Francisco: Berrett-Koehler.
Rosso, B. D., Dekas, K. H., & Wrzesniewski, A. (2010). On the meaning of work: A theoretical integration and review. *Research in Organizational Behavior, 30*, 91–127.
6. Allan, B. A., Batz-Barbarich, C., Sterling, H. M., & Tay, L. (2019). Outcomes of meaningful work: A meta-analysis. *Journal of Management Studies, 56*(3), 500–528.
This study revealed a very large correlation (r = .70+) between meaningful work and positive work outcomes. Correlations range from 0.0 (no relationship between two variables)

to 1.0 (a perfect relationship; as one increases, so does the other). Most studies in the psychological literature show correlations between 0.3 and 0.5. This appears to be a strong relationship.

7. Pink, D. H. (2011). *Drive: The surprising truth about what motivates us.* New York: Riverhead Books.
8. Arnold, K. A., Turner, N., Barling, J., Kelloway, E. K., & McKee, M. C. (2007). Transformational leadership and psychological well-being: The mediating role of meaningful work. *Journal of Occupational Psychology, 12*(3), 193–203.
9. Achor, S., Reece, A., Kellerman, G. R., & Robichaux, A. (2018). 9 out of 10 people are willing to earn less money to do more meaningful work. *Harvard Business Review on-line, November 6. https://hbr.org/2018/11/9-out-of-10-people-are-willing-to-earn-less-money-to-do-more-meaningful-work.*
10. Rogers, B. (2013). "Culture of Purpose" is key to success according to new research from Deloitte. *Forbes*, May 21. Interview with Deloitte Chairman Punit Renjen.
11. Simon, H. (1991). Organizations and markets. *Journal of Economic Perspectives, 5*(2), 25–44.
12. Boswell, W. R., Bingham, J. B., & Colvin, A. J. S. (2006). Aligning employees through "line of sight." *Business Horizons, 49*, 499–509.
    Byrne, J. A. (2004). Why JetBlue is a fast company. *Fast Company, 82*, 16–17.
13. Jacobsen, D. (2024). How bad performance management killed Microsoft's edge. September 5. https://www.workhuman.com/blog/how-bad-performance-management-killed-microsoft-s-edge/.
14. Somasegar, S. (2014). Microsoft's resurgence: Reflecting on Satya Nadella's leadership, a decade after he became CEO. February 1. https://www.geekwire.com/2024/microsofts-resurgence-reflecting-on-satya-nadellas-leadership-a-decade-after-he-became-ceo/.
15. Ferrazzi, K. (2022). A new social contract for teams. *Harvard Business Review, 100*(5), 88–97.
16. Hu, J., & Liden, R. C. (2011). Antecedents of team potency and team effectiveness: An examination of goal and process clarity and servant leadership. *Journal of Applied Psychology, 96*, 851–862.
17. Baumeister, R. F., & Leary, M. R. (1995). The need to belong: Desire for interpersonal attachments as a fundamental human motivation. *Psychological Bulletin, 117*, 497–529.
    Ryan, R. M., & Deci, E. L. (2000). Self-determination theory and the facilitation of intrinsic motivation, social development, and well-being. *American Psychologist, 55*, 68–78.
18. Gardner, H. K., & Matviak, I. (2022). Performance management shouldn't kill collaboration: How to align goals across functions. *Harvard Business* Review, *100*(5), 118–127.

Chapter 8

1. Carver, C. S., & Scheier, M. F. (1998). *On the self-regulation of behavior.* New York: Cambridge University Press.
2. Chang, C., Johnson, R. E., & Lord, R. G. (2010). Moving beyond discrepancies: The important of velocity as a predictor of satisfaction and motivation. *Human Performance*, 23, 58–80.
3. Hawk, R. (2015). Daniel Pink—The science of motivation. The Learning Leader Podcast. Episode 82.

4. Amabile, T., & Kramer, S. (2009). *The progress principle.* Boston: Harvard Business Review Press.
5. Franklin, B. (2023). *Autobiography of Benjamin Franklin.* Sea Wolf Press Illustrated Classic.
Vozza, S. (2019). What happened when I followed Ben Franklin's schedule for a month? *Fast Company*, January 15.
6. Klug, H. J., & Maier, G. W. (2015). Linking goal progress and subjective wellbeing: A meta-analysis. *Journal of Happiness Studies*, 16, 37–65.
7. Oettingen, G. (2014). *Rethinking positive thinking: Inside the new science of motivation.* New York: Penguin.
8. Amabile & Kramer, 2009, op. cit.
9. Barsade, S. G., & Gibson, D. (2007). Why does affect matter in organizations? *The Academy of Management Perspectives*, 21, 36–59.
10. Killingsworth, M. A., & Gilbert, D. T. (2010). A wandering mind is an unhappy mind. *Science*, 330, 932.
11. Lyubomirsky, S., King, L., & Diener, E. (2005). The benefits of frequent positive affect: Does happiness lead to success? *Psychological Bulletin*, 131, 803–855.
12. Fredrickson, B. L. (2001). The role of positive emotions in positive psychology: The broaden-and-build theory of positive emotions. *American Psychologist*, 56, 218–26.
13. Harkin, B., Webb, T. L., Chang, B. P., Prestwich, A., Conner, M., Kellar, I., Benn, Y., & Sheeran, P. (2016). Does monitoring goal progress promote goal attainment? A meta-analysis of the experimental evidence. *Psychological Bulletin*, 142, 198–229.
14. Fishbach, A., Eyal, T., & Finkelstein, S. R. (2010). How positive and negative feedback motivate goal pursuit. *Social and Personality Psychology Compass*, 4/8, 517–530.
15. Kluger, A. N., & DeNisi, A. (1996). The effects of feedback interventions on performance: A historical review, a meta-analysis, and a preliminary feedback intervention theory. *Psychological Bulletin*, 119, 254–284.
16. Van Dijk, D., & Kluger, A. N. (2004). Feedback sign's effect on motivation: Is it moderated by regulatory focus? *Applied Psychology: An International Review*, 53, 113–135.
Van Dijk, D., & Kluger, A. N. (2011). Task type as a moderator of positive/negative feedback effects on motivation and performance: A regulatory focus perspective. *Journal of Organizational Behavior*, 32, 1084–1105.
17. Zenger, J., & Folkman, J. (2017). Why do so many managers avoid giving praise? *Harvard Business Review Online*, May 2.
18. Buckingham, M., & Goodall, A. (2019). *Nine lies about work: A freethinking leaders' guide to the real world.* Cambridge: Harvard Business Review Press.
19. Aguinis, H., Gottfredson, R. K., & Joo, H. (2012). Delivering effective performance feedback: The strengths-based approach. *Business Horizons*, 55, 105–111.
20. Losada, M., & Heaphy, E. (2004). The role of positivity and connectivity in the performance of business teams: A nonlinear dynamics model. *American Behavioral Scientist*, 47, 740–765.
21. Fredrickson, B. L., & Losada, M. F. (2005). Positive affect and complex dynamics of human flourishing. *American Psychologist*, 60, 678–686.
Full disclosure is in order here; parts of this paper have been discredited and partially withdrawn. The authors ground their findings in some very complex mathematical modeling using differential equations drawn from fluid dynamics, a subfield of physics.

Researchers Nick Brown and Alan Sokal criticize the application and relevance of these equations and point out numerous fundamental conceptual and mathematical errors. The paper's authors retracted the modeling elements, but other elements of the article remain valid and are unaffected by this correction notice, notably (a) the supporting theoretical and empirical literature, (b) the data drawn from two independent samples, and (c) the finding that positivity ratios were significantly higher for individuals identified as flourishing relative to those identified as nonflourishing. The critique can be seen here: Brown, N., Sokal, A. D., & Friedman, H. L. (2013). The complex dynamics of wishful thinking: The critical positivity ratio. *American Psychologist*, 68, 801–813.

22. Seligman, M. E. P., Steen, T. A., Park, N., & Peterson, C. (2005). Positive psychology progress: Empirical validation of interventions. *American Psychologist*, 60, 410–421.
23. Gottman, J. M. (1994). *Why marriages succeed or fail.* New York: Simon and Schuster.
24. Fredrickson & Losada, 2005, op. cit.
25. Baumeister, R. F., Bratslavsky, E., Finkenauer, C., & Vohs, K. D. (2001). Bad is stronger than good. *Review of General Psychology*, 5, 323–370.
26. Amabile & Kramer, 2009, op. cit.
27. Boyatzis, R., & McKee, A. (2005). *Resonant leadership: Renewing yourself and connecting with others through mindfulness, hope, and compassion.* Boston: Harvard Business School Press.
28. Bouskila-Yam, O., & Kluger, A. N. (2011). Strength-based performance appraisal and goal setting. *Human Resource Management Review*, 21, 137–147.
29. Buckingham, M., & Clifton, D. O. (2001). *Now, discover your strengths.* New York, NY: Free Press.
30. Linley, P. A., Woolston, L., & Biswas-Diener, R. (2009). Strengths coaching with leaders. *International Coaching Psychology Review*, 4, 37–48.
    Luthans, F. (2002). The need for and meaning of positive organizational behavior. *Journal of Organizational Behavior*, 23, 695–706.
    Van Woerkom, M., Oerlemans, W., & Bakker, A. B. (2015). Strengths use and work engagement: A weekly diary study. *European Journal of Work and Organizational Psychology*, 25, 384–397.
    Roberts, L. M., Spreitzer, G., Dutton, J., Quinn, R., Heaphy, E., & Barker, B. (2005b). How to play to your strengths. *Harvard Business Review*, 83, 74–80.
31. Ghielen, S. T. S., van Woerkom, M., & Christina Meyers, M. (2017). Promoting positive outcomes through strengths interventions: A literature review. *The Journal of Positive Psychology*, 13, 573–585.
    Quinlan, D., Swain, N., & Vella-Brodrick, D. A. (2012). Character strengths interventions: Building on what we know for improved outcomes. *Journal of Happiness Studies*, 13, 1145–1163.
32. Bouskila-Yam, O., & Kluger, A. N. (2011). Strength-based performance appraisal and goal setting. *Human Resource Management Review*, 21, 137–147.
33. Boyatzis, R. (2012). Neuroscience and the link between inspirational leadership and resonant relationships. *Ivey Business Journal*, January–February.
34. Zenger & Folkman, 2014, op. cit.
35. Bandura, A. (2012). The role of self-efficacy in goal-based motivation. In E. A. Locke and G. P. Latham (Eds), *New developments in goal setting and task performance.* Routledge.
36. Likert, R. (1967). *New patterns of management.* McGraw-Hill, New York.

37. Amabile & Kramer, 2009, op. cit.
38. Slemp, G. R., Fields, J. G., Ryan, R. M., Forner, V. W., Van den Broeck, A., & Lewis, K. J. (2024). Interpersonal support for basic psychological needs and their relations with motivation, well-being, and performance: A meta-analysis. *Journal of Personality and Social Psychology*, 127, 1012–1037.
39. Ryan, R. M., & Deci, E. L. (2017). *Self-determination theory: Basic psychological needs in motivation, development, and wellness.* The Guilford Press.
40. Bindl, U. K., & Parker, S. K. (2011). Proactive work behavior: Forward thinking and change-oriented action in organizations. In S. Zedeck (Ed.), *APA Handbook of Industrial and Organizational Psychology* (pp. 567–598). American Psychological Association.
41. Edmunds, J., Ntoumanis, N., & Duda, J. L. (2008). Testing a self-determination theory-based teaching style intervention in the exercise domain. *European Journal of Social Psychology*, 38, 375–388.
42. Ryan & Deci, 2017, op. cit.
43. Slemp et al., 2024, op.cit.
44. Rhoades, L., & Eisenberger, R. (2002). Perceived organizational support: A review of the literature. *Journal of Applied Psychology*, 87, 698–714.
45. Eisenberger, R., Stinglhamber, F., Vandenberghe, C., Sucharski, I. L., & Rhoades, L. (2002). Perceived supervisor support: Contributions to perceived organizational support and employee retention. *Journal of Applied Psychology*, 87, 565–573.

Chapter 9

1. Wilkie, D. (2015). Is the annual performance review dead? *SHRM On-Line.* August 19. https://www.shrm.org/topics-tools/news/employee-relations/annual-performance-review-dead.
2. Lissitz, R. W., & Green, S. B. (1975). Effect of the number of scale points on reliability: A Monte Carlo approach. *Journal of Applied Psychology*, 60(1), 10–13.
3. SHRM (on-line). Which performance rating scale is best, and what should an employer consider before adopting a performance rating scale? *HR Q&A. https://www.shrm.org/topics-tools/tools/hr-answers/performance-rating-scale-best-employer-consider-adopting-performance-rating-scale.*
4. Aguinis, H., & Bradley, K. J. (2015). The secret sauce for organizational success: Managing and producing star performers. *Organizational Dynamics*, 44, 161–168.
   It is important to note that other researchers disagree that performance best fits a power-law distribution, that this finding is unique to the types of performance measures.
   Beck, J. W., Beatty, A. S., & Sackett, P. R. (2014). On the distribution of job performance: The role of measurement characteristics in observed departures from normality. *Personnel Psychology*, 67(3), 531–566.
5. Sharma, S., Prakash, S., & Devchand (2024). The role of technology in enhancing the effectiveness of integrated performance appraisal frameworks. *Journal of Informatics and Research*, 4(3), 3411–3419.
6. Amabile, T., & Kramer, S. (2009). *The progress principle: Using small wins to ignite joy, engagement and creativity at work.* Boston: Harvard Business School Press.
7. Gherson, D., & Gratton, L. (2022). Managers can't do it all. *Harvard Business Review*, 100(2), 96–105.

8. Petermann, M. K. H., & Zacher, H. (2022). Workforce agility: Development and validation of a multidimensional measure. *Frontiers in Psychology*, 13, 1–15.
9. Sarah Rietze & Hannes Zacher (in press). Relations between daily stand-up meetings, work satisfaction, and team performance perceptions: The role of psychological safety. *European Journal of Work and Organizational Psychology*. https://doi.org/10.1080/1359432X.2025.2508178
10. Darling, M., Parry, C., & Moore, J. (2005). Learning in the thick of it. *Harvard Business Review*, 83, 84–92.
11. CEB (2004). *Driving employee performance and retention through engagement: A quantitative analysis of the effectiveness of employee engagement strategies* (Catalog No. CLC12PV0PD). Author.

Chapter 10

1. Locke, E. A., & Latham, G. P. (2002). Building a practically useful theory of goal setting and task motivation: A 35-Year odyssey. *American Psychologist*, 57, 9, 705–715.
2. Hattie, J. & Timperley, H. (2007). The power of feedback. *Review of Educational Research*, 77, 1, 81–112.
3. For example, see:
   Kleingeld, A., van Mierlo, H., & Arends, L. (2011). The effect of goal setting on group performance: A meta-analysis. *Journal of Applied Psychology*, 96, 6, 1289–1304.
   Locke & Latham, 2002, op. cit.
   Locke, E. A., & Latham, G. P. (2013). *New developments in goal setting and task performance.* East Sussex: Routlege.
4. Klein, H. J., Wesson, M. J., Hollenbeck, J. R., & Alge, B. J. (1999). Goal commitment and the goal-setting process: Conceptual clarification and empirical synthesis. *Journal of Applied Psychology*, 84, 885–896.
5. Locke & Latham, 2013, op. cit.
6. For example, see:
   Locke, E. A., & Latham, G. P. (2015). Breaking the rules: A historical overview of goal-setting theory. In A. J. Elliot (Ed.), *Advances in Motivation Science* (Vol. 2, pp. 99–126). Waltham, MA: Academic Press.
   Locke, E. A., & Latham, G. P. (2019). The development of goal setting theory: A half century retrospective. *Motivation Science*, *5*, 93–105.
7. For example, see:
   Cross, R., Rebele, R., & Grant, A. (2016). Collaborative overload. *Harvard Business Review*, January–February.
   Edmondson, A. C. (2012). *Teaming: How organizations learn, innovate, and compete in the knowledge economy.* San Francisco: Jossey-Bass.
   McDowell, T., Agarwal, D., Miller, D., Okamoto, T., & Page, T. (2016). *Organizational design: The rise of Teams.* White Paper. Deloitte University Press.
8. Kleingeld, et al., 2011, op. cit.
9. Betterworks (2022). When organizational goals don't align with employee goals, productivity flounders. *Betterworks Insights*, September 26.
10. Wigert, B., & Tatel, C. (December 3, 2024). The great detachment: Why employees feel stuck. *Gallup Workplace.*

11. Oracle (2013). Goal setting: A fresh perspective. *White paper*, June.
12. Goodhart, C. (1975). Problems of monetary management: The UK experience. *Papers in Monetary Economics—Sydney Reserve Bank of Australia*, 1, 1–20.
13. Ordonez, L. D., Schweitzer, M. E., Galinsky, A. D., & Bazerman, M. H. (2009). Goals gone wild: The systematic side effects of over-prescribing goal setting. *Harvard Business School working paper, 09-083.*
14. Kleingeld, et al., 2011, op. cit.
15. Latham, G. P., & Wexley, K. N. (1977). Behavioral observation scales for performance appraisal purposes. *Personnel Psychology*, 30(2), 255–268. https://doi.org/10.1111/j.1744-6570.1977.tb02092.x.
16. Kuvaas, B., Buch, R., & Dysvik, A. (2014). Performance management: Perceiving goals as invariable and implications for job autonomy and work performance. *Human Resource Management*, 55, 401–412.
17. Bersin & Associates (2011). *High impact performance management research.*
18. Doerr, J. (2018). *Measure what matters.* London: Penguin.
19. For example, see:
    Doerr, 2018, op. cit.
    Beck, K., Beedle, M., van Bennekum, A., Cockburn, A., Cunningham, W., Fowler, M., Grenning, J., Highsmith, J., Hunt, A., Jeffries, R., et al. (2001). *Manifesto for Agile software development.* Agile Alliance. http://agilemanifesto.org/.
20. Sull, D., & Sull, C. (2019). With goals, FAST beats SMART. *MIT Sloan Management Review*, June 5, 1–14.

Chapter 11

1. Locke, E. A., & Latham, G. P. (1990). *A theory of goal setting and task performance.* Englewood Cliffs: Prentice Hall.
2. Erez, M. (1977). Feedback: A necessary condition for the goal setting-performance relationship. *Journal of Applied Psychology*, 62(5), 624–627.
3. Kluger, A. N., & DeNisi, A. (1996). The effects of feedback interventions on performance: A historical review, a meta-analysis, and preliminary feedback intervention theory. *Psychological Bulletin*, 119(2), 254–284.
4. Wang, M., Burlacu, G., Truxillo, D. M., James, K., & Xiang, Y. (2015). Age differences in feedback reactions: The roles of employee feedback orientation on social awareness and utility. *Journal of Applied Psychology*, 100(4), 1296–1308.
5. Dweck, C. S. (2007). *Mindset: The new psychology of success.* New York: Ballantine Books.
6. Dweck, C. (1986). Motivational processes affecting learning. *American Psychologist*, 41, 1040–1048.
7. Hogan, K. (October 9, 2017). 10 things we have learned about culture. https://www.linkedin.com/pulse/10-things-weve-learned-culture-kathleen-hogan/.
8. Keating, L. A., & Heslin, P.A. (2015). The potential role of mindsets in unleashing employee engagement. *Human Resource Management Review*, 25(4), 329–341.
   Effron, M. (April 22, 2020). Does growth mindset actually work? *Talent Quarterly.* https://tinyurl.com/ndt5sxjm.
9. Heslin, P. A., Latham, G. P., & VandeWalle, D. (2005). The effect of implicit person theory on performance appraisal. *Journal of Applied Psychology*, 90, 842–856.

Heslin, P.A., Vandewalle, D., & Latham, G. P. (2006). Keen to help? Managers' IPT and their subsequent employee coaching. *Personnel Psychology*, 59, 871–902.

10. London, M., & Smither, J. W. (2002). Feedback orientation, feedback culture, and the longitudinal performance management process. *Human Resource Management Review*, 12, 81–100.
11. Deci, E. L., & Ryan, R. M. (2012). Motivation, personality, and development within embedded social contexts: An overview of self-determination theory. In R. M. Ryan (Ed.), *Oxford handbook of human motivation* (pp. 85–107). Oxford: Oxford University Press.
12. Rock, D. (2008). SCARF: A brain-based model for collaborating with and influencing others. *NeuroLeadership Journal*, Issue 1, 1–9.
13. Waldman, D. A., Balthazard, P. S., & Peterson, S. J. (2015). Conclusions and look forward. In Waldman, D. A., & Balthazard, P.A. (Eds.), *Organizational Neuroscience*, 295–306. London: Emerald Books.
14. London and Smither, 2002, op. cit.
15. Gallup (2024). *Leadership & management indicators.* https://www.gallup.com/404252/indicator-leadership-management.aspx.
16. Gallup (2017). *State of the American workplace*, Research Report.
17. Kluger & DiNisi, 1996, op. cit.
18. Ledford, G.E., & Schneider, B. (2018). *Performance feedback culture drives business impact.* Seattle: i4cp.
19. Toegel, G., & Conjer, J.A. (2003). 360-degree assessment: Time for reinvention. *Academy of Management Learning & Educations*, 2, 297–311.
20. Conway, J., & Huffcutt, A. (1997). Psychometric properties of multi-source performance ratings: A meta-analysis of subordinate, supervisor, peer, and self-ratings. *Human Performance*, 10, 331–360.
21. Bracken, D. W., Does, D. S., & Church, A. H. (2016). The evolution and devolution of 360^0 feedback. *Industrial and Organizational Psychology*, 9(4), pp 761–794.
22. Goldberg, E. (2014). Performance management gets social. *HR magazine*, 34–38. July 21. https://www.shrm.org/topics-tools/news/hr-magazine/performance-management-gets-social.
23. Locke & Latham, 1990, op. cit.
24. Hsiang, C., Johnson, R. E., & Lord, R. G. (2009). Moving beyond discrepancies: The importance of velocity as a predictor of satisfaction and motivation. *Human Performance*, 23, 58–80.
25. Van Quaqauebeke, N., & Felps, W. (2018). Respectful inquiry: A motivational account of leading through asking questions. *Academy of Management Review*, 43, 5–27.
26. Edmondson, A. C. (2018). How fearless organizations succeed. *Strategy+Business, a PWC publication.* November 14. https://www.strategy-business.com/article/How-Fearless-Organizations-Succeed.
27. O'Flaherty, S., Sanders, M. T., & Whillans, A. (2021). Research: A little recognition can provide a big morale boost. *Harvard Business Review on-line.* https://hbr.org/2021/03/research-a-little-recognition-can-provide-a-big-morale-boost.
28. Komaki, J., Coombs, T., & Schepman, S. (1996). Motivational implications of reinforcement theory. In Steers, R. M., Porter, L. W., Bigley, G. A. (Eds.), *Motivation and leadership at work*, 34–52. New York: McGraw-Hill.

29. Stajkovic, A. D., & Luthans, F. (1997). A meta-analysis of the effects of organizational behavior modification on task performance, 1975–95. *Academy of Management Journal*, 40(5), 1122–1149.
30. Gallup & Workhuman (2023). *From praise to profits: The business case for recognition at work.* chrome-extension://efaidnbmnnnibpcajpcglclefindmkaj/https://assets.ctfassets.net/hff6luki1ys4/DjH2m0CgenFWSymyjUMWD/363cf879c37af3708fb0f520566aefc0/from-praise-to-profits-the-business-case-for-recognition-at-work__1_.pdf.
31. Glassdoor (2013). Employers to retain half of their employees longer if bosses show more appreciation; Glassdoor survey. November 13. https://www.glassdoor.com/blog/employers-to-retain-half-of-their-employees-longer-if-bosses-showed-more-appreciation-glassdoor-survey/.
32. Guzzo, R. A., Nalbantian, H. R., & Anderson, N. L. (January 24, 2023). Don't underestimate the value of employee tenure. *Harvard Business Review digital article*, https://hbr.org/2023/01/dont-underestimate-the-value-of-employee-tenure.
33. Luthans, F., & Stajkovic, A. D. (Unpublished manuscript). *The impact of recognition on employee performance: Theory, research and practice.* https://tinyurl.com/9zrmmnbk.
34. Bandura, A. (1986). *Social foundations of thought and action: A social cognitive theory.* Englewood Cliffs: Prentice-Hall, Inc.
35. Mercurio, Z. (2025). The power of mattering at work. *Harvard Business Review*, 103(3), p. 100–109.
36. Gallup (2024). *The importance of employee recognition: Low cost, high impact.* https://www.gallup.com/workplace/236441/employee-recognition-low-cost-high-impact.aspx.
37. Clifton, D. O., & Harter, J. K. (2003). Investing in strengths. In Cameron, K. S., Dutton, J. E., & Quinn R. E. (Eds.), *Positive organizational scholarship: Foundations of a new discipline*, 111–121. San Francisco: Berrett-Koehler.
    Aguinis, H., Gottfredson, R. K., & Joo, H. (2012). Delivering effective performance feedback: The strengths-based approach. *Human Performance*, 55, 105–111.
38. Goldsmith, M. (2015). Try feedforward instead of feedback. https://www.marshallgoldsmith.com/post/try-feedforward-instead-of-feedback
39. Kluger, A. N., & Nir, D. (2010). The feedforward interview. *Human Resources Management Review*, 20, 235–246.
    Bouskila-Yam, O., & Kluger, A. N. (2011). Strength-based performance appraisal and goal setting. *Human Resource Management Review*, 21, 137–147.
40. Budworth, M., Lathan, G. P., & Manroop, L. (2015). Looking forward to performance improvement: A field test of the feedforward interview for performance management. *Human Resource Management*, 54(1), 45–54.
41. It is possible that the small number of companies that strictly focused on coaching for future performance made it more difficult to find significant differences due to low statistical power.

Chapter 12

1. Desimone, R. (2024). Improve work performance with a focus on employee development. *Gallup digital article.* January 19. https://www.gallup.com/workplace/269405/high-performance-workplaces-differently.aspx?version=print.

2. Boswell, W. R., & Boudreau, J.W. (2000). Employee satisfaction with performance appraisals and appraisers: The role of perceived appraisal use. *Human Resource Development Quarterly*, 11(3), 283–299.
3. i4cp (2012). *Performance management survey*, 2012. i4cp Proprietary Research.
4. Ledford, G.E., & Schneider, B. (2018). *Performance feedback culture drives business impact.* Seattle: i4cp.
5. Meyer, H. H., Kay, E., & French, J. R. P. (1965). Split roles in performance appraisal, *Harvard Business Review*, 43(1), 123–129.
6. Croswell, L. (2019). *Why you should separate performance measurement and development.* Culture Amp eBook.
   Dysick, C., & Rock, D. (2019). Why performance management needs to become feedback management. Your Brain at Work. Blog Post, NeuroLeadership Institute, January 8. https://neuroleadership.com/your-brain-at-work/performance-management-feedback-management.
   Lee, C. D. (2006). *Performance conversations: An alternative to appraisals.* Tucson: Fenestra Books.
   Raingeard, V. (2024). *Why employers are separating pay and performance conversations.* BuiltIn White Paper.
7. Rock, D. (2014). Webinar on performance management practices. NeuroLeadership Group, March.
8. Linkedin (2025). CHRO case studies: Leading from the front. https://www.linkedin.com/business/talent/blog/talent-acquisition/leading-from-the-front.
9. Clifton, D. O., & Harter, J. K. (2003). Investing in strengths. In Cameron, K. S., Dutton, J. E., & Quinn, R. E. (Eds.), *Positive organizational scholarship: Foundations of a new discipline*, 111–121. San Francisco: Berrett-Koehler.
   Aguinis, H., Gottfredson, R. K., & Joo, H. (2012). Delivering effective performance feedback: The strengths-based approach. *Business Horizons*, 55, 105–111.
10. Glint (2020). The state of employee engagement and experience. chrome-extension://efaidnbmnnnibpcajpcglclefindmkaj/https://info.glintinc.com/rs/586-OTD-288/images/state-of-employee-engagement-2020.pdf.
11. DeSmet, A. D., Dowling, B., Hancock, B., & Schaninger, B. (2022). The Great Attrition is making hiring harder. Are you searching the right talent pools? *McKinsey Quarterly. July.*
12. World Economic Forum (2025). *Future of jobs report.* https://www.weforum.org/reports/the-future-of-jobs-report-2025/.
13. McCall, M. W., Lombardo, M. M., & Morrison, A. (1988). *The lessons of experience.* Free Press, Glencoe, IL.
14. Goldberg, E., & Steven-Waiss, K. (2020). *The inside gig: How sharing untapped talent across boundaries unleashes organizational capacity.* Los Angeles: LifeTree Media.

Chapter 13

1. Colquitt, A. L., & Goldberg, E. L. (December 2020). Designing performance management for impact: Practices that make a difference. *Unpublished Participant Research Report.*
   Mercer (2012). Current trends in performance management. *Survey report*, Mercer Consulting.
2. WTW (2023). *Performance reset survey report*, February 2.

3. For example, see:
Adler, S., Campion, M., Colquitt, A., Grubb, A., Murphy, K. R., Ollander-Krane, R., & Pulakos, E. D. (2016). Getting rid of performance ratings: Genius or folly. *Industrial and Organizational Psychology: Perspectives on Science and Practice*, 9, 219–252.
Buckingham, M., & Goodall, A. (2019). *Nine lies about work: A freethinking guide to the real world.* Cambridge: Harvard Business Review Press.
Colquitt, A. L. (2017). *Next generation performance management: The triumph of science over myth and superstition.* Charlotte: Information Age Publishing.
Murphy, K. R. (2019). Performance evaluation will not die, but it should. *Human Resource Management Journal*, 30, 1–19.
4. For example, see:
Colquitt, 2017, op. cit.
5. For example, see:
Aguinis, H. (2013). *Performance management.* Upper Saddle River: Pearson.
Kahneman, D. (2012). *Thinking, fast and slow.* New York: Farrar, Strauss and Giroux.
6. Bridge, D. J., & Paller, K. A. (2012). Neural correlates of reactivation and retrieval-induced distortion. *The Journal of Neuroscience*, 29, 12144–12151.
7. Deming, W. E. (1994). *The new economics (2nd Edition).* Cambridge: MIT Center for Advanced Engineering Study.
8. For example, see:
Adler, S., Chamorro-Premuzic, T., Colquitt, A. L., Effron, M., & Sacket, P. (2017). Giving top performers the star treatment: Is meritocracy overrated? *Debate at the Annual Meeting of the Society of Industrial and Organizational Psychologists*, Orlando, FL.
Groysberg, B. (2011). *Chasing stars: They myth of talent and the portability of performance.* Princeton: Princeton University Press.
9. For example, see:
Kruger, J., & Dunning, D. (1999). Unskilled and unaware of it: How difficulties in recognizing one's own incompetence lead to inflated self-assessments. *Journal of Personality and Social Psychology*, 77, 1121–1134.
Meyer, H. H. (1980). Self-appraisal of job performance. *Personnel Psychology*, 33, 291–295.
10. Kozlowski, S. W. J., Chao, G. T., & Morrison, R. F. (1998). Games raters play: Politics, strategies, and impression management in performance appraisal. In Smither J. W. (Ed.), *Performance appraisal: State of the art methods for performance appraisal* (pp. 163–205). San Francisco: Jossey-Bass.
11. For example, see:
Murphy, K. R. (2008). Explaining the weak relationship between job performance and ratings of job performance. *Industrial and Organizational Psychology*, 1, 148–160.
Murphy, 2019, op. cit.
O'Neill, T. A., Carswell, J. J., & McLarnon, M. J. W. (2012), Performance ratings have larger rater and small ratee components, usually. *Paper presented at the annual meeting of the Society for Industrial and Organizational Psychology*, San Diego, CA.
12. For example, see:
Adler et al., 2016, op. cit.
Effron, M. (2020). We love ratings. *White paper*, Talent Strategy Group.

Effron, M. (2021). Why you need to fire the next 10 percent. Talent Strategy Group, *Talent Quarterly*, October 15.

13. Murphy, 2019, op. cit.
14. Bureau of Labor Statistics (2025). *Job openings and labor turnover report*, November 2024.
    Coens, T., & Jenkins, M. (2002). *Abolishing performance appraisals: Why they backfire and what to do instead.* San Francisco: Berrett-Kohler.
    EEOC (2023). *Enforcement and litigation statistics report.*
    Mercer (2011). Next generation of pay for performance. *Survey report*, May.
    Trading Economics (2025). *Report: Working age population: Aged 15–64 for the United States.*
15. For example, see:
    Beck-Dudley, C. L., & McEvoy, G. M. (1991). Performance appraisals and discrimination suits: Do courts pay attention to validity? *Employee Responsibilities and Rights Journal*, 4, 149–163.
    Werner, J. M., & Bolino, M. C. (1997). Explaining U.S. courts of appeals decisions involving performance appraisal: Accuracy, fairness, and validation. *Personnel Psychology*, 50, 1–24.
16. Coens & Jenkins, 2002, op. cit.
17. Barankay, I. (2011). Rankings and social tournaments: Evidence from a crowd-sourcing experiment. *University of Pennsylvania working paper.*
    Eriksson, T., Poulsen, A., & Villeval, M. C. (2009). Feedback and incentives: Experimental evidence. *Labour Economics*, 16, 679–688.
    Fehr, E., & Gachter, S. (2000). Fairness and retaliation: The economics of reciprocity. *Journal of Economic Perspectives*, 14, 159–181.
18. Casas-Arce, P., & Martinez-Jerez, F. A. (2009). Relative performance compensation, contests, and dynamic incentives. *Management Science*, 55, 1306–1320.
19. Bandiera, O., Barankay, I., & Rasul, I. (2005). Social preferences and the response to incentives: Evidence from personnel data. *Quarterly Journal of Economics*, 120, 917–962.
    Fehr & Gachter, 2000, op. cit.
20. Rock, D. & Ferrara, M. (2015). Transforming performance management: An Eli Lilly case study. *NeuroLeadership Institute Webinar*, September 21, 2015.
21. For example, see:
    Kruger & Dunning, 1999, op. cit.
    Meyer, 1980, op. cit.
22. Barankay, 2011, op. cit.
23. WorldatWork (2018). Inventory of total rewards programs and practices. *Survey Report.*
24. Landy, F., & Farr, J. L. (1980). Performance rating. *Psychological Bulletin*, 87, 72–107.
25. Futrell, D., Desrosiers, E., and Bryant, D. (2024). *Managing performance management: A practical approach for optimization.* Pre-Conference Workshop, Society for Industrial and Organizational Psychology 2024 Conference Chicago, IL.
    Futrell, D. (2022). *It's about the conversation! Having high quality performance discussions.* Society for Industrial and Organizational Psychology 2022 Conference, Seattle, WA.
26. Botelho, T. L., Jun, S., Humes, D., & DeCelles, K. A. (2025). Scale dichotomization reduces customer racial discrimination and income inequality. *Nature*, February 19.
27. Jacobs, R., Kafry, D., & Zedeck, S. (1980). Expectations of behaviorally anchored rating scales. *Personnel Psychology*, Vol. 33 (3), pp. 595–640.

28. Futrell, 2022, op. cit.
29. Buckingham, M., & Goodall, A. (2015). Reinventing performance management. *Harvard Business Review*, April, 40–50.
30. WTW, 2023, op. cit.
31. For example, see:
Hauenstein, N. M. A. (1999). Training raters to increase the accuracy of appraisals and the usefulness of feedback. In Smithers, J. W. (1998), *Performance management: Putting research into practice.* San Francisco: Jossey-Bass.
Murphy, 2019, op. cit.
Woehr, D. J., & Huffcutt, A. I. (1994). Rater training for performance appraisal: A quantitative review. *Journal of Occupational Psychology*, 67, 189–205.
32. See Colquitt, 2017, op. cit. for a review of this research.
33. Shaw, J. D., & Mitra, A. (2017). The science of pay-for-performance systems: Six facts that all managers should know. *WorldatWork Journal*, Q3, 19–27.
34. Effron, 2020, op. cit.
Effron, 2021, op. cit.
Grote, R.C. (2005). *Forced ranking: Making performance management work.* Cambridge: Harvard Business School Press.
Welch, J., & Byrne, J.A. (2003). *Jack: Straight from the gut.* New York: Warner Books, N.
35. For example, see:
Colquitt, 2017, op. cit.
Dominick, P. G. (2009). Forced rankings: Pros, cons, and practices. In Smither, J. W., & London, M. (2009), *Performance management: Putting research into practice.* San Francisco: Jossey-Bass (pp. 411–443).
Loberg, L., Nüesch, S., & Foege, J. N. (2021). Forced distribution rating systems and team collaboration. *Journal of Economic Behavior & Organization*, 188, 18–35.
Stewart, S. M., Gruys, M. L., & Storm, M. (2010). Forced distribution performance evaluation systems: Advantages, disadvantages and keys to implementation. *Journal of Management and Organization, 16*, 168–179.
36. Colquitt, A. L. (2020). Calibration: What is it good for? *White paper.*
37. Speer, A. B., Tenbrink, A. P., & Schwendeman, M. G. (2019). Let's talk it out: The effects of calibration meetings on performance ratings. *Human Performance*, 32, 1–22.
38. Palmer, J. K., & Loveland, J. M. (2008). The influence of group discussion on performance judgments: Rating accuracy, contrast effects and halo. *The Journal of Psychology*, 142, 117–130.
39. Adler et al., 2016, op. cit.
Goldberg, E. (2014). Performance management gets social. *HR Magazine*, August, 34–38. *SHRM*, Washington, D.C.
40. Conference Executive Board (2016). The real impact of eliminating performance ratings: Insights from employees and managers. *Research report.*
Human Capital Institute (2015). Talent Pulse: No review, no problem. *Research report*, Cincinnati, OH.
Ledford, G. E., & Benson, G. (2019). Ratingless performance reviews: A quasi-experiment. *Center for Effective Organizations Publication G19-04 (695).*
41. Conference Executive Board, 2016, op. cit.
Ledford & Benson, 2019, op. cit.

Chapter 14

1. WorldatWork. (2021). Incentive pay practices: Publicly traded companies. *Survey report*, July.
2. Abosch, K. (2019). With salaries and bonuses projected to increase, U.S. employees can expect a pay hike in 2020. *Aon 2019–2020 US Salary Increase Survey*. September.
3. Manzoni, J. F. (2008). On the folly of hoping for A, simply because you are trying to pay for A. *Studies in Managerial and Financial Accounting*, 18, 19–41.
   Pfeffer, J., & Sutton, R. I. (2006). *Hard facts, dangerous half-truths and total nonsense: Profiting from evidence-based management*. Cambridge: Harvard Business School Press.
4. Mercer (2019). *Global performance management study report*.
5. Shaw, J.D., & Mitra, A. (2017). The science of pay-for-performance systems: Six facts that all managers should know. *WorldatWork Journal*, Q3, 19–27.
6. For a more complete review, see:
   Colquitt, A. L. (2017). *Next generation performance management: The triumph of science over myth and superstition*. Charlotte: Information Age Publishing.
7. For example, see:
   Chen, Y., Zhang, Z., Zhou, J., Liu, C., Zhang, X., & Yu, T. (2023). A cognitive evaluation and equity-based perspective of pay for performance on job performance: A meta-analysis and path model. *Frontiers in Psychology*, 13, 1–26.
   Pfeffer & Sutton, 2006, op. cit.
   Pink, D. H. (2009). *Drive: The surprising truth about what motivates us*. New York: Riverhead Books.
   Manzoni, 2008, op. cit.
   Gneezy, U., Meier, S., & Rey-Biel, P. (2011). When and why incentives (don't) work to modify behavior. *Journal of Economic Perspectives*, 25, 1–21.
8. Mahy, B., Rycx, F., & Volral, M. (2011). Does wage dispersion make all firms productive? *Scottish Journal of Political Economy*, 58, 455–489.
   Shaw, J. D. (2014). Pay dispersion. *Annual Review of Organizational Psychology and Organizational Behavior*, 1, 521–544.
9. Rouen, E. (2017). Rethinking measurement of pay disparity and its relation to firm performance. *Harvard Business School working paper 18-007*.
   Shaw, 2014, op. cit.
10. Rouen, 2017, op. cit.
11. Song, J., Price, D. J., Guvenen, F., Bloom, N., & von Wachter, T. (2016). Firming up inequality. *National Bureau of Economic Research*, working paper No. 21199.
12. Trank, C. Q., Rynes, S. L., & Bretz, R. D. (2002). Attracting applicants in the war for talent: Differences in work preferences among high achievers. *Journal of Business and Psychology*, 16, 331–345.
13. Griffeth, R. W., Hom, P. W., & Gaertner, S. (2000). A meta-analysis of antecedents and correlates of employee turnover: Update, moderator tests, and research implications for the next millennium. *Journal of Management*, 26, 463–488.
14. O'Halloran, P. L. (2009). Do performance-pay workers experience less job turnover and longer tenures? *Paper presented at 9th Global Conference on Business and Economics, Cambridge, UK.*
15. Bloom, M., & Michel, J. G. (2002). The relationships among organizational context, pay dispersion, and managerial turnover. *Academy of Management Journal, 45*, 33–42.

Shaw, J. D., & Gupta, N. (2007). Pay system characteristics and quit patterns of good, average, and poor performers. *Personnel Psychology*, 60, 903–923.

16. Amabile, T. M., Conti, R., Coon, H., Lazenby, J., & Herron, M. (1996). Assessing the work environment for creativity. *The Academy of Management Journal*, 39, 1154–1184.
17. Azoulay, P., Graff Zivin, J. S., & Manso, G. (2011). Incentives and creativity: Evidence from the academic life sciences. *Journal of Economics*, 42, 527–554.
    Cui, V., & Yanadori, Y. (2013). Creating incentives for innovation? The relationship between pay dispersion in R&D groups and firm innovation performance. *Strategic Management Journal*, 34, 1502–1511.
18. Judge, T. A., Piccolo, R., Podsakoff, N. P., Shaw, J. C., & Rich, B. L. (2010). The relationship between pay and job satisfaction: A meta-analysis of the literature. *Journal of Vocational Behavior*, 77, 157–167.
19. Clark, A. E., Frijters, P., & Shields, M. A. (2008). Relative income, happiness, and utility: An explanation for the Easterlin paradox and other puzzles. *Journal of Economic Literature*, 46, 95–144.
20. Kerr, S. (1975). On the folly of rewarding A, while hoping for B. *Academy of Management Journal*, 18, 769–783.
21. See Colquitt, 2017, op. cit. for a more examples of these consequences.
22. Shirom, A., Westman, M., & Melamed, S. (1999). The effects of pay systems on blue-collar employees' emotional distress: The mediating effects of objective and subjective work monotony. *Human Relations*, 52, 1077–1097.
    Dahl, M. S., & Pierce, L. (2020). Pay-for-performance and employee mental health: Large sample evidence using employee prescription drug usage. *Academy of Management Discoveries*, 6, 12–38.
23. Deci, E. L., Ryan, R. M., & Koestner, R. (1999). A meta-analytic review of experiments examining the effects of extrinsic rewards on intrinsic motivation. *Psychological Bulletin*, 125, 627–668.
24. Vohs, K. D. (2015). Money priming can change people's thoughts, feelings, motivations and behaviors: An update on 10 years of experiments. *Journal of Experimental Psychology*, 144, 73–85.
    Burks, S., Carpenter, J., & Goette, L. (2006). Performance pay and the erosion of worker cooperation: Field experimental evidence. *IZA Discussion Paper, 2013.*
    Gneezy et al., 2011, op. cit.
25. Devoe, S. E., Pfeffer, J., & Lee, B. Y. (2013). Why does money make money more important? Survey and experimental evidence. *Industrial Labor Relations Review*, 66, 1078–1096.
    Manzoni, 2008, op. cit.
26. Lea, S. E. G., & Webley, P. (2006). Money as tool, money as drug: The biological psychology of a strong incentive. *Behavioral and Brain Sciences*, 29, 161–209.
    Zhou, X., Vohs, K. D., & Baumeister, R. F. (2009). The symbolic power of money: Reminders of money alter social distress and physical pain. *Psychological Science*, 20, 700–706.
27. Heath, C. (1999). On the social psychology of agency relationships: Lay theories of motivation overemphasize extrinsic incentives. *Organizational Behavior and Human Decision Processes*, 78, 25–62.
    Beer, M., & Katz, N. (2003). Do incentives work? The perceptions of a world-wide sample of senior executives. *Human Resource Planning*, 26, 30–44.

28. Deloitte (2017). Total rewards survey report, Summer.
29. Herzberg, F. (1974). Motivation-hygiene profiles: Pinpointing what ails the organization. *Organizational Dynamics*, 3, 18–29.
30. Pink, 2009, op. cit.
31. Bloom, M., & Milkovich, G. (1998). The relationship between risk, incentive pay, and organizational performance. *CAHRS Working Paper Series. 41.*
32. Cybulski, C. G., Sever, S. C., & Stoskopf, G. A. (2019). The evolution of salary structures: Are broadbands a thing of the past? *Workspan*. May.
33. Cohen, P. (2018). Where did your pay raise go? It may have become a bonus. *The New York Times*, February 10.
34. Bruce, S., & Sykes, T. (2019). The next era of compensation planning: The fate of the merit matrix and pay for performance. *WorldatWork webinar by People Fluent*, September 26.
35. Cybulski et al., 2019, op. cit.
36. Romansky, L. (2019). Ease your talent crunch by building a vibrant internal labor market. *Human Resource Executive*, April 18.
37. Cybulski et al., 2019, op. cit.
38. Kruse, D. L., Freeman, R. B., & Blasi, J. R. (2010). Shared capitalism at work: Employee ownership, profit and gain sharing, and broad-based stock options. *National Bureau of Economic Research conference report*. Chicago: University of Chicago Press.

Chapter 15

1. Colquitt, A. L. (2017). *Next generation performance management: The triumph of science over myth and superstition*. Charlotte: Information Age Publishing.
2. i4cp (2012). *HR technology: The state of software as a service (SaaS). HR Technology: Directions for 2012*. Survey report.
3. Avedon, M. J., & Scholes, G. (2010). Building competitive advantage through integrated talent management. In *Strategy-Driven Talent Management: A Leadership Imperative* (Eds. Silzer, R. & Dowell, B. E.), Chapter 2, 73–118. San Francisco: Jossey Bass.
4. Goldberg, E. L. (2014). Performance management gets social. *SHRM HR Magazine*. July 21. https://www.shrm.org/topics-tools/news/hr-magazine/performance-management-gets-social.
5. Thaler, R. H., & Sunstein, C. R. (2009). *Nudge: Improving decisions about health, wealth and happiness*. New York: Penguin.
6. Schellmann, H. (2024). *The algorithm: How AI decides who gets hired, monitored, promoted, and fired and why we need to fight back now*. p.204., New York: Hachette Books.
7. Kantor, J., & Sundaram, A. (2022). The rise of the worker productivity score. *New York Times*, August 14. https://www.nytimes.com/interactive/2022/08/14/business/worker-productivity-tracking.html.
8. Hernandez, D., & Strong, J. (2018). How computers could make your customer-service calls more human. *Wall Street Journal*, June 14. https://www.wsj.com/articles/call-center-agents-get-a-human-touch-1528984801.
9. Niehoff, B. P., & Moorman, R. H. (1993). Justice as a mediator of the relationship between methods of monitoring and organizational citizenship behavior. *Academy of Management Journal*, 36, 557–556.

10. Bhave, D. P. (2014). The invisible eye? Electronic performance monitoring and employee job performance. *Personnel Psychology*, 67(3), 605–635. DOI: 10.1111/peps.12046
11. Thiel, C. E., McClean, S., Harvey, J., & Prince, N. (2023). Trouble with big brother: Counterproductive consequences of electronic monitoring through the erosion of leader-member social exchange. *Journal of Organizational Behavior*, 44, 1320–1339.
12. Bauer, T. N., & Erdogan, B. (2015). Leader–member exchange (LMX) theory: An introduction and overview. In *Oxford Handbook of Leader-member Exchange*, 3–9.
13. Thiel, McClean, Harvey, & Prince (2023), op. cit.
14. Ravid, D. M., White, J. C., Tomczak, D. L., Miles, A. F., & Behrend, T. S. (2022). A meta-analysis of the effects of electronic performance monitoring on work outcomes. *Personnel Psychology*, 76, 5–40. https://doi.org/10.1111/peps.12514
15. Pentland, A. (2012). The new science of building great teams, *Harvard Business Review*, 90(4), 60–70.
16. Cross, R., & Garau, R. (2018). *The invisible network strategies of successful people.* Connected Commons. https://www.robcross.org/white-paper/the-invisible-network-strategies-of-successful-people-counterintuitive-ways-to-innovate-execute-and-thrive-at-work/.

Chapter 16

1. Design Thinking is mostly credited to Peter Rowe of Harvard from his ground-breaking book *Design Thinking.* It was more recently popularized by the design firm IDEO and Stanford University, where they teach a very popular course on the subject.
   Rowe, P. (1987). *Design thinking.* MIT Press, Boston, MA.
2. Kiron, D., & Spindel, B. (2019). Rebooting work for a digital era: How IBM reimagined talent and performance management, *MIT Sloan Management Review*, February 19. On-line performance management case study. https://sloanreview.mit.edu/case-study/rebooting-work-for-a-digital-era/.
3. Goldberg, E. (2007). *A comparison of effective and ineffective performance management initiatives: Best practices in design and implementation.* E. L. Goldberg & Associates Unpublished Research Report.
4. Goldberg, 2007, op. cit.
5. Woehr, D. J., & Huffcutt, A. I. (1994). Rater training for performance appraisal: A quantitative review. *Journal of Occupational and Organizational Psychology*, 67(3), 189–205. https://doi.org/10.1111/j.2044-8325.1994.tb00562.x
6. See for example:
   Malos, S. (2005). The importance of valid selection and performance appraisal: Do management practices figure in case law? In Landy F. J. (Ed.), *Employment discrimination litigation*, 373–409. San Francisco: Jossey-Bass.
   Martin, D. C., Bartol, K. M., & Kehoe, P. E. (2000). The legal ramifications of performance appraisal: The growing significance. *Public Personnel Management*, 29, 379–406.
   Taylor, M. S., Tracy, K. B., Renard, M. K., Harrison, J. K., & Carroll, S. J. (1995). Due process in performance appraisal: A quasi-experiment in procedural justice. *Administrative Science Quarterly*, 40, 495–523.
   Roehling, M. V. (1993). Extracting policy from judicial opinions: The dangers of policy capturing in a field setting. *Personnel Psychology*, 46, 477–502.

7. Hancock, B., Hioe, E., & Schaninger, B. (2018). The fairness factor in performance management. *McKinsey Quarterly*, April.

Chapter 17

1. Rogelberg, S. G. (2024). *Glad we met: The art and science of 1:1 meetings.* New York: Oxford University Press.

Index

For the benefit of digital users, indexed terms that span two pages (e.g., 52–53) may, on occasion, appear on only one of those pages.

Tables, figures, and boxes are indicated by an italic *t*, *f*, or *b*.

A

AARs (After Action Reviews), 50, 98–99
Accenture, 137–138
accountability
  for employee development, 64, 137
  of executives, 25
  goals and, 109–110
  for individual goals, 39
  of managers, 86*b*
  for performance conversations, 197
  of performance raters, 162
  for team goals, 75–76*b*
action plans, 143, 147
administrative burden, 85*b*, 93, 99, 183, 192, 210–211
Adobe, 98, 99–102*b*, 102, 164, 211
After Action Reviews (AARs), 50, 98–99
Agency Theory, 15–16, 24–25, 186
Agile Manifesto, 48, 77
Agile work methodologies, 48–50, 69, 96–97, 115, 192
agility
  alignment and, 77–78
  continuous improvement and, 63
  continuous support and, 63
  goal-setting and, 59, 112–118, 114*b*, 205
  measurement of, 198
  reward practices and, 175
Agyris, Chris, 5
AI. *See* artificial intelligence
alignment
  agility and, 77–78, 115
  of behavior with evaluation and rewards, 77
  of change management with HR processes, 193–194
  context and, 59, 69–71
  line of sight and, 71–73
  OKRs and, 113*b*, 115*b*
  team-based, 73–75, 75*b*
Amabile, Teresa, 79–81, 84, 87–88
American Opportunity Survey, 43
Arcesium, 114–115*b*, 205
artificial intelligence (AI)
  advancements in, 35–37, 182–183
  coaching tools and, 184–185
  data analytics and, 184
  Generative, 145–146, 184–185
  performance reviews and, 94
  performance tracking and, 184–186
  real-time feedback and, 182–183, 186
  for streamlining, 183
  for tracking progress toward goals, 184–185
automation, 180, 183–184
autonomy
  employees need for, 87–88, 130
  as enabling control mechanism, 29
  EPM and loss of, 187
  knowledge workers and, 41
  organizational control and, 26–28

B

Balanced Scorecard approach, 59
base pay, 25, 37–38, 140, 141*b*, 174, 177*b*, 210–211
behavioral economics, 19
behavioral expectations, 59–60, 108–110, 144–145
behaviorally anchored rating scales (BARS), 158, 195
behaviorism, 16–17, 19
belonging, 28–29, 74–75, 164–165, 170–171
benchmarking, 4–5, 20, 108–109, 171
bias
  feedback and, 83–84, 199
  illusory superiority, 157
  leniency, 162

bias (*Continued*)
motivation and, 171
performance evaluations and, 53–54
performance reviews and, 94
purpose of PM and, 23
racial, 157–158
ratings and, 53–54, 91, 92–93, 153–154, 157–158, 162–163
training for managers on, 195
biotech industry, 38, 118*b*
Black, Stewart, 5
bonuses
budgets for, 10, 12
failure to drive performance, 3
manager decisions on, 164
performance ratings and, 161
performance ratings tied to, 1–2
skills-based, 141*b*
spot bonuses, 172
bounded rationality, 19
Brees, Drew, 79–80
budgets
for bonuses, 10, 12
for merit pay, 10, 12, 54–55, 168, 172, 174
for rewards, 24–25, 54–55, 154, 172, 175
for variable pay, 172
business context
Agile work methodologies in, 48–50
continuous and crowdsourced feedback in, 50–51
cost pressures changing reward structures in, 54–55
employee development in, 53
inclusion of external partners in, 52–53
mismatch of PM practices with, 47, 47*t*
rethinking role and value of evaluations in, 53–54
team *vs.* individual performance management in, 51–52
VUCA environment and, 46–47, 50

C

calendar-driven PM, 94–95, 95*f*
calibration process, 24–25, 92–93, 160*b*, 162–163, 205, 209–211
call centers, 183, 185–187
career management, 43, 53–54, 143–145, 144*f*
Carter, Dean, 140–142, 140–142*b*, 198, 209
Center for Effective Organizations (CEO), 127*b*
change management
alignment with HR processes, 193–194
Design Thinking and, 191–192, 196, 237 n.1
evaluation of effectiveness, 196–198
fairness improvement and, 199–200
investment of time in, 190
key message communication and, 192–194
senior leadership's role in, 194*f*, 194, 211
stakeholder engagement and, 190–191
training for managers on, 194–196
check-ins. *See also* one-on-one meetings
Adobe's process for, 99–102*b*, 102
benefits of, 51, 130, 132
event-driven, 98
mid-year, 94–95, 98
OKRs and, 112
pandemic-era shifts in, 50
performance documentation and, 100*b*, 101*b*
quarterly, 85–86*b*, 99–100*b*, 101*b*, 102, 115*b*
recognizing progress at, 97–98
training for managers on, 86–86*b*
weekly and biweekly, 115–116
classical economics, 14–16, 19, 24
coaching
AI tools for, 184–185
collaboration and, 73–74
continuous support through, 60–61, 62–63
culture of, 85–86*b*
in deficit-focused cultures, 84
employee development and, 63, 140
formal and informal, 29–30
for future performance, 133–135, 206, 229 n.41
micro-coaching, 37
in one-on-one meetings, 96, 115
in team meetings, 96
training for managers on, 206
coercive control
abandonment of, 164–165
goal-setting and, 109–110
internalization of, 27–28
mechanisms of, 26–27, 37–38, 41
performance evaluations and, 153

problems involving, 26–27
securing compliance through, 7
Cognitive Revolution, 19, 36
collaboration. *See also* teamwork
in Agile work methodologies, 48–50, 115
cross-functional, 114–115*b*
culture of, 162, 169, 193
discouragement of, 73
in Fifth Industrial Revolution, 36
goal-setting and, 59
growing complexity of work and increase in, 38–40
joint ventures and, 44*b*
knowledge workers and, 41–42
as organizational capability, 28–29
promotion of, 73–74, 88, 117
team goals and, 77
technology for, 40, 43, 188–189
compensation. *See also* base pay; bonuses; merit pay; pay for performance; variable pay
differentiation of, 54–55, 160*b*, 170–171, 175
for executives, 24–25
increases over time, 174
inequality in, 169–170
market rates and, 174, 177*b*
performance ratings and, 1–2, 175*b*
skills-based, 141*b*
Tournament Theory on, 16
transparency of, 172, 210–211
competition, 16, 24–25, 37–38, 110, 156, 161, 170
context. *See also* business context
alignment and, 59, 69–71
autonomy as governance process and, 29
in clarifying behavioral expectations, 59–60
as enabling control mechanism, 30
goal-setting and, 72, 110–111, 117
high-context environments, 30, 107
line of sight and, 71–72
PE and, 8, 58–60
purpose and, 8, 30, 70–71
continuous process, 57, 82, 94–102, 95*f*, 99*b*
continuous support, 60–64
contract workers, 43–44, 52–53, 220 n.4
control processes. *See* coercive control; enabling control
Control Theory, 16–17, 79
conversations. *See* development conversations; performance conversations
COVID-19 pandemic, 39–40, 49–50, 187–188
Cross, Rob, 39
culture
of coaching, 85–86*b*
of collaboration, 162, 169, 193
of continuous improvement, 51, 62–64, 99, 101*b*
deficit-focused, 84
as enabling control mechanism, 29–30
feedback, 125–127, 127*t*, 127*b*, 129–130, 138, 205–206
growth-mindset, 124
of know-it-alls *vs.* learn-it-alls, 123–124
of resilience and high performance, 60
shifting, 73–74, 114*b*
telling *vs.* asking, 85–87*b*
toxic, 73
of trust, 85–86*b*

D

daily stand-up meetings (DSMs), 96–97
data analytics, 37, 184, 188
Deloitte, 38, 71, 161, 210
Deming, Edward, 154
Design Thinking, 191–192, 196, 237 n.1
development. *See* employee development
development conversations, 139–140, 142*b*, 145
differentiation
of compensation, 54–55, 160*b*, 170–171, 175
of rewards, 16, 24–25, 53–54, 137, 167, 168–170, 172–173
digital transformation, 37, 165
documentation of performance. *See* performance documentation
double-loop learning, 5
Doyle, Lauren, 100–101*b*, 101*b*
DSMs (daily stand-up meetings), 96–97
Dweck, Carol, 122–124

E

EBP (evidence-based practice), 9, 20, 57–58
economics, 14–16, 19, 24
Edward Jones, 75–76*b*

Electronic Performance Monitoring (EPM), 185–187
Elias, Norbert, 29
Eli Lilly and Company, 137–138, 156*b*, 164
employee development. *See also* talent management
  accountability for, 64, 137
  benefits of, 63–64, 137–138
  in business context, 53
  career management and, 43, 53–54, 143–145, 144*f*
  Carter on, 140–142, 140–142*b*
  check-ins and, 100*b*
  coaching and, 63, 140
  continuous support and, 63
  conversations on, 139–140, 142*b*, 145
  effectiveness of, 146–147, 147*f*
  feedforward and, 63, 140
  goal-setting and, 138, 143, 147
  history of, 138–139
  IDPs and, 7, 143–145, 147
  measurement of, 198
  PM and, 13, 53, 138–140
  prioritization of, 53
  skill development, 63, 142*b*, 142
  technology and, 184–185, 211
  training for managers on, 64, 177*b*
  transparency of, 142*b*
employee stock ownership programs, 174–175
enabling control
  advantages of, 27–28
  continuous support and, 63
  goal-setting and, 110–118
  investment in practices of, 164–165
  reward practices and, 173
  securing commitment through, 7
  social and psychological mechanisms of, 28–29
endowment effect, 19
EPM (Electronic Performance Monitoring), 185–187
evaluation of performance. *See* performance evaluations
event-driven PM, 94–95, 95*f*, 98
evidence-based practice (EBP), 9, 20, 57–58
executives. *See also* leadership
  accountability of, 25
  compensation for, 24–25
  development of, 146
  on purpose and meaning, 71
Expectancy Theory, 16–17

F

fairness, 12, 162–163, 199, 210
Farr, James, 157–158
fatalism, 21
Fayol, Henri, 26
feedback. *See also* coaching
  Agency Theory on, 15
  bias and, 83–84, 199
  change management and, 197
  constructive, 61, 125
  continuous, 48, 50–51, 64, 73–74, 164–165, 212
  for contract workers, 52–53
  Control Theory on, 17, 79
  crowdsourced, 51, 129–130, 147, 163, 182
  in deficit-focused cultures, 84
  emphasizing importance of, 126
  enabling performance through, 28
  enhancing quality of, 125–126
  feedforward *vs.*, 61, 133–134, 134*t*
  formal and informal, 1, 117, 126
  frequency of, 121
  globalization and, 38
  growth mindset and, 122–124
  ineffectiveness of, 121
  for Millennial and Gen Z workers, 42–43
  motivation and, 121, 122*f*
  negative, 17, 82–84, 123
  NeuroLeadership and, 124–125
  positive, 76*b*, 79, 82–84, 87, 133
  on progress toward goals, 28, 64, 79–80, 107, 121, 125, 130
  providing support for using, 126–127
  real-time, 37, 51, 77, 99, 182–183, 185–186
  received by managers, 86*b*
  recognition as, 131–133
  research driving today's practices, 122–127
  strategies for effectiveness, 61
  strengths-based, 133
  task-based, 122
  360-degree, 83, 128–129, 163
  Tournament Theory on, 16
  in traditional PM model, 26
  training for managers on, 87, 126–127, 130, 195–196

transparency of, 16, 182–183
feedback culture, 125–127, 127*t*, 127*b*, 129–130, 138, 205–206
feedforward
continuous support through, 61–63
employee development and, 63, 140
feedback *vs.*, 61, 133–134, 134*t*
training for managers on, 195–196, 206
Fifth Industrial Revolution (5IR), 36–37
FifthThird Bank, 85
First Industrial Revolution, 35
fixed mindset, 122–123
forced distribution, 20, 24–25, 73, 92–93, 110, 162
forced ranking, 24–25
Fourth Industrial Revolution (4IR), 35–37
Frame of Reference Training, 195
Franklin, Benjamin, 80, 81*f*
freelancers. *See* contract workers
Futrell, David A., 157–158, 158*b*, 210

G

gainsharing, 174–175
Gap Inc., 98, 123–124, 137–139
General Electric (GE), 20, 24–25, 98, 138, 162
Generative AI (GenAI), 145–146, 184–185
Gen X workers, 42
Gen Z workers, 42–43, 71
globalization, 37–38, 219 n.4
goals. *See also* goal-setting; objectives; organizational goals; progress toward goals; team goals; individual goals
accountability and, 109–110
adjusting, 36–37, 72, 77–78, 99, 110, 112, 115
Agency Theory on, 15
in Agile work methodologies, 48, 50
career-related, 64, 184–185
cascading, 36–37, 75*b*, 77, 90, 94, 110
commitment to, 58–59, 70, 72, 87, 107–108, 112
continuous conversations about, 111–112
development, 138, 140, 144–145, 147, 195–196
directional, 90–91, 204
FAST, 116
instrumental role of, 109–110
performance, 53, 71, 140, 142, 147, 195–196
SMART, 3–5, 112, 114*b*, 177*b*
stretch, 205
transparency of, 110, 114–115*b*, 115–117, 199
goal-setting. *See also* Objectives and Key Results
Agency Theory on, 15
agility and flexibility of, 59, 112–118, 114*b*, 205
annual, 36–37, 47, 77, 112
coercive control and, 109–110
collaboration and, 59
context and, 72, 110–111, 117
effectiveness of, 107–110
employee development and, 138, 143, 147
enabling control and, 110–118
failure of, 108–110
in Management by Objectives, 12–13
motivation and, 107–109, 121
at planning meetings, 1
simplification of, 90–91
team-based approach to, 76*b*, 108
theory of, 59, 121
training for managers on, 115*b*
training on, 115*b*
Goldsmith, Marshall, 133–134
Goodhart's law, 109–110
Google, 112
Gopalakrishnan, Bhavya, 114*b*, 115*b*
Gregersen, Hal, 5
growth mindset, 122–124, 138, 177*b*, 192
guided distribution, 162

H

Hawk, Ryan, 79–80
Honda, joint venture with LG, 44*b*
human-centered design, 192, 196
Human Resources Information Systems (HRIS), 181
hybrid workers, 40

I

IBM, 44, 75*b*, 142, 192
IDPs. *See* Individual Development Plans
i4cp. *See* Institute for Corporate Productivity
Implicit Person Theory, 124
incentives
Agency Theory on, 15, 24
failure to drive performance, 3
team and organizational, 52, 167–168

income. *See* compensation
Individual Development Plans (IDPs), 7, 143–145, 147
individual goals
  accountability for, 39
  alignment and, 59, 70, 74–75, 197–198
  in biotech industry, 118*b*
  context and, 117
  continuous support and, 62–63
  focusing on, 110
  line of sight and, 110
  nature of work and, 39, 52
Industrial/Organizational Psychology, 91, 122, 181, 195
Industrial Revolutions, 35–37
Institute for Corporate Productivity (i4cp), 127*b*, 138, 181, 205–206
institutional envy, 20, 171
institutionalization, 1, 4–5, 10, 21, 23–24, 212
Intel, 112

J
JetBlue, 72, 110
joint ventures, 44*b*

K
Kahneman, Daniel, 19
Kaplan, R. S., 59
Kelly Services, 164
Kerr, Steve, 170–171
key messages, 192–194
Killingsworth, Matthew, 82
knowledge workers, 41–42, 54, 133, 186, 187–188, 206
Kozlowski, Steve, 154

L
labor economics, 14–16
Landy, Frank, 157–158
Latham, Garry, 107–108
law of effect, 16–17, 24
leader–member social exchange theory (LMSX), 187
leadership. *See also* executives; managers
  in Agile work methodologies, 49
  in change management, 194*f*, 194, 211
  Gen X workers and, 42
  goal-setting by, 90–91
  NeuroLeadership, 124–125, 139
  resonant *vs.* dissonant, 84
  succession planning by, 144–145
  transformational, 71
LG, joint venture with Honda, 44*b*
Likert, Rensis, 87
line of sight (LOS), 28, 71–73, 94, 110–111, 204
LMSX (leader–member social exchange theory), 187
Locke, Edwin, 19

M
Maier, Norman R. F., 13
Management by Objectives (MBO), 12–13
management control. *See* coercive control; enabling control
management of performance. *See* performance management
managers. *See also* coaching; feedback; leadership; one-on-one meetings; team meetings; training for managers
  accountability of, 86*b*
  in Agile work methodologies, 49
  continuous support by, 60–64
  enabling and supporting, 87–89
  feedback received by, 86*b*
  hours per year spent on PM, 4, 90
  mental models of, 5, 14, 18, 194–195, 201–204
  micromanagement, 49, 73, 107, 206
  ratings by, 24–25, 141*b*, 153–155, 165, 169, 185
  role in PE, 58, 60–63
MBO (Management by Objectives), 12–13
McDaniel, Suzan, 75*b*
McGregor, Douglas, 2
McKinsey, 43, 143, 199
meaning. *See* purpose and meaning
meetings. *See* one-on-one meetings; team meetings
mental models, 5, 14, 18, 194–195, 201–204
merit pay
  budgets for, 10, 12, 54–55, 168, 172, 174
  failure to drive performance, 3
  manager decisions on, 164
  performance ratings and, 161
  shift to variable pay from, 172
  skills-based, 141*b*
MetLife Inc., 186
micromanagement, 49, 73, 107, 206

Microsoft, 44, 73–74, 110, 123–124, 137–138, 143, 164
MidPen Housing, 175–178*b*, 178*t*
Millennial workers, 42–43, 71
Mintzberg, Henry, 14
moments that matter, 97
monitoring performance. *See* performance monitoring
motivation
as benefit of PE, 58, 64
bias associated with, 171
classical economics on, 14–15
enhanced, 64
Expectancy Theory on, 17
extrinsic, 133
feedback and, 121, 122*f*
goal-setting and, 107–109, 121
intrinsic, 27–28, 64, 133, 139, 170–171
of knowledge workers, 41, 133
of Millennial and Gen Z workers, 42–43
performance ratings and, 156
progress toward goals and, 79–81
purpose/meaning and, 28, 71
recognition and, 132–133
social and psychological mechanisms of, 28, 217 n.31
Social Cognitive Theory on, 132
supportive behaviors and, 88
Tournament Theory on, 16, 156
Murphy, Kevin, 155

N
Nadella, Satya, 73–74, 123–124
NeuroLeadership, 124–125, 139
normal distribution curve, 91, 92*f*, 157–158
Norton, D. P., 59
nudge technology, 37, 184

O
objectives. *See also* goals
achievement of, 26, 51
in change management, 196
individual, 12–13, 58–59
Management by Objectives, 12–13
organizational, 12–13, 26, 28, 59, 64, 147
strategic, 26, 52, 59, 72, 115
Objectives and Key Results (OKRs)
alignment and, 113*b*, 115*b*
Arcesium and, 114–115*b*, 205
description of, 112–113, 113*f*
examples of, 114, 114*t*
performance evaluations and, 113*b*, 115*b*
OCBs (organizational citizenship behaviors), 186–187
ONA (organization network analysis), 188–189
one-on-one (1:1) meetings. *See also* check-ins
benefits of, 96, 206
coaching during, 96, 115
continuous feedback and, 50
continuous support and, 60
data gathered from, 94
discussion topics at, 111, 204–205, 207*b*, 207–209
identification of underperformance in, 93
improvement of, 130
open talent marketplace, 44
operant conditioning, 16–17, 24
organizational citizenship behaviors (OCBs), 186–187
organizational control, 25–27. *See also* coercive control; enabling control
organizational goals
alignment and, 48, 51, 57, 61, 70, 74, 197–198, 204
context and, 72, 117
continuous support and, 62–63
contract workers and, 52
feedback and, 15
line of sight and, 110
organizational support theory, 88
organization network analysis (ONA), 188–189
Ouchi, William, 27–29

P
pay. *See* compensation
pay for performance (P4P). *See also* merit pay; rewards; variable pay
abandonment of, 164–165
effectiveness of, 168–170
expansion of, 24–25, 167–168
failure of, 3, 55, 168
performance evaluations and, 153
separation of performance and development conversations in, 139
in traditional PM model, 1–2, 13, 137, 167–168
unintended consequences of, 170–171

PE. *See* Performance Enablement
Pepsi Co., 128
Perceived Organizational Support (POS), 88–89
Perceived Supervisor Support (PSS), 89
performance appraisals, 2, 12–13, 35, 38, 85, 138
performance coaching. *See* coaching
performance conversations
  accountability for, 197
  documentation and, 93–94
  looking forward to, 192
  NeuroLeadership and, 124–125, 139
  separation from development conversations, 139–140, 142*b*
  supporting and enabling, 94
  training for managers on, 101*b*, 195
performance documentation
  as administrative burden, 93
  Agile Manifesto on, 48
  check-ins and, 100*b*, 101*b*
  legal considerations, 13, 93, 155
  simplification of, 93–94, 211
Performance Enablement (PE). *See also* alignment; employee development; goal-setting
  benefits of, 58, 64–65, 212
  coaching for future performance and, 133–135, 206, 229 n.41
  context and, 8, 58–60
  as continuous process, 57, 82, 94–102, 95*f*, 99*b*
  designing and implementing, 190–200
  feedback culture and, 125–127, 127*t*, 127*b*, 129–130, 138, 205–206
  flipping the script from PM to, 201–212
  managers, role in, 58, 60–63
  overview, 7*f*, 7–8
  paradigm of, 58*f*, 58
  positivity and, 82–84
  progress and, 57–58, 79–82
  purpose of, 57–58
  simplicity of, 90–94, 99
  strengths and, 64, 79, 84–87
  supportive behaviors within, 87–89
  technology in support of, 182–189
performance evaluations. *See also* performance ratings
  alignment of behavior with, 77
  bias associated with, 53–54
  globalization and, 38
  objective, 165
  OKRs and, 113*b*, 115*b*
  pay for performance and, 153
  rethinking role and value of, 53–54
  in traditional PM model, 1
performance feedback. *See* feedback
performance feedback culture (PFC), 127*b*, 138, 205–206
Performance Improvement Plans (PIPs), 93, 157–158
performance management (PM)
  administrative burden of, 85*b*, 93, 99, 183, 192, 210–211
  barriers to change, 4–5, 18, 20–22
  business context and implications for, 46–55
  calendar-driven, 94–95, 95*f*
  economic foundations of, 14–16
  employee development and, 13, 53, 138
  event-driven, 94–95, 95*f*, 98
  external partners included in, 44, 52–53
  failure of, 2–4, 57
  flipping the script to PE from, 201–212
  frequency of modifications to, 190
  history and evolution of, 12–13
  hours per year spent on, 4, 90
  as organizational control, 25–27
  psychological foundations of, 16–17
  purpose of, 23–30, 57–58, 212
  survey research on, 6–7, 23
  traditional model of, 1, 2*f*
  as wicked problem, 4–5
performance monitoring
  Agency Theory on, 15
  electronic, 185–187
  technology for, 37, 185–188
  in traditional PM model, 26
  transparency of, 187
performance ratings. *See also* rating scales
  abandonment of, 156*b*, 164–165, 178*b*
  alternative ratings, 161, 210
  bias and, 53–54, 91, 92–93, 153–154, 157–158, 162–163
  calibration process, 24–25, 92–93, 160*b*, 162–163, 205, 209–211
  compensation and, 1–2, 175*b*
  extraneous factors affecting, 154
  forced and guided distribution processes, 24–25, 92–93, 110, 162

improvement strategies, 157–163, 210–211
by managers, 24–25, 141*b*, 153–155, 165, 169, 185
motivation and, 156
nonperformance factors impacting, 154–155
persistence of, 155–157, 209–210
rewards based on, 1, 167–168, 210–211
simplification of, 91–93, 158*b*
training for managers on, 161
performance reviews
After Action Reviews, 50, 98–99
annual, 36–37, 50, 60, 98, 99–100*b*, 139–140, 206
bias associated with, 94
employee engagement following, 156*b*, 156*f*
event-driven, 98
technology for improvement of, 94
in traditional PM model, 1, 13, 51
performance tracking, 43, 70, 94, 97–98, 184–188
PFC (performance feedback culture), 127*b*, 138, 205–206
P4P. *See* pay for performance
Pink, Dan, 71, 79–80, 174
PIPs (Performance Improvement Plans), 93, 157–158
PM. *See* performance management
POS (Perceived Organizational Support), 88–89
Positive Psychology, 64, 83–84, 96
power-law distribution curve, 91, 92*f*, 225 n.4
Procter & Gamble, 44
profit-sharing, 174–175
progress toward goals
discussions regarding, 53–54, 93–94, 96, 111
feedback on, 28, 64, 79–80, 107, 121, 125, 130
feedforward and, 61
motivation and, 79–81
PE and, 57–58, 79–82
recognizing, 97–98
tracking, 115–116, 130, 147, 183, 184–185
promotions, 12, 16, 140, 174, 188–189, 196
prospect theory, 19
PSS (Perceived Supervisor Support), 89
psychology
enabling control and, 28–29
foundations of PM and, 16–17
Industrial/Organizational, 91, 122, 181, 195
motivation and, 28, 217 n.31
operant conditioning and, 16–17, 24
Positive, 64, 83–84, 96
purpose and meaning
context and, 8, 30, 70–71
of corporations, 36, 219 n.2
as enabling control mechanism, 28
institutionalized, 23–24
for knowledge workers, 41
line of sight to, 28, 71–73
for Millennial and Gen Z workers, 42–43, 71
motivation and, 28, 71
of Performance Enablement, 57–58
of performance management, 23–30, 57–58, 212
purpose-driven companies, 70, 76*b*

R

rating scales. *See also* performance ratings
behaviorally anchored, 158, 195
five-point, 91–93, 153, 157–158, 158–159*b*, 210
improvement strategies, 157–158
simplification of, 91, 94
three-point, 91, 157–158, 158–159*b*, 160*b*, 210
two-point, 91, 157–158
rationalization, 21
Reinforcement Theory, 16–17, 19, 131
remote workers, 40
return on investment (ROI), 2–3, 36, 127*b*, 198
reviews. *See* performance reviews
rewards. *See also* bonuses; pay for performance; promotions
Agency Theory on, 15
alignment of behavior with, 77
allocation of, 23–25, 155
budgets for, 24–25, 54–55, 154, 172, 175
classical economics on, 14–15
as coercive control mechanism, 26, 41
cost pressures impacting, 54–55
differentiation of, 16, 24–25, 53–54, 137, 167, 168–170, 172–173

rewards (*Continued*)
extrinsic, 17, 29, 83, 170–171
individual, 3, 14–15, 53–54, 167, 205
nonfinancial, 172, 175
organization-based, 14–15, 174–175
performance ratings as basis for, 1, 167–168, 210–211
strategic changes related to, 173–175
tactical changes related to, 172
Tournament Theory on, 16
in traditional PM model, 1, 3, 13
Rock, David, 61, 124–125, 141*b*
Rogelberg, Steven, 207, 209
ROI. *See* return on investment
Rouen, Ethan, 169–170
Rowe, Peter, 237 n.1

S
salary. *See* compensation
Schon, Donald, 5
Schwab, Klaus, 35
scientific management approach, 24
Second Industrial Revolution, 35
Self-Determination Theory, 88, 124
self-efficacy, 8, 87–88, 107–108, 132
self-esteem, 87, 132
70-20-10 rule, 146
Shell Oil Company, 14
SHRM (Society for Human Resource Management), 3, 36
Simon, Herbert, 19
single-loop learning, 5
skill development, 63, 142*b*, 142
skills-based talent management, 145–146
Skinner, B. F., 16–17
Social Cognitive Theory, 132
social performance management (SPM) systems, 182
Society for Human Resource Management (SHRM), 3, 36
sociometric badges, 188
Soda Stream, 85
spot bonuses, 172
streamlining, 40, 62, 99, 158*b*, 183
strengths
individual, 62
leveraging, 49, 53–54, 75*b*, 79, 85, 89, 143
PE and, 64, 79, 84–87
succession planning, 144–145
surveillance. *See* performance monitoring
Synaptics, 98

T
talent management. *See also* employee development
financial rewards and, 167–168
freelance workers and, 43–44
globalization and, 37–38, 219 n.4
integrated systems of, 181
processes of, 144*f*, 144–145
skills-based, 145–146
unified strategy for, 193
Taylor, Fredrick, 24
team alignment, 73–75, 75*b*
team goals
accountability for, 75–76*b*
agility and flexibility of, 49, 117–118
alignment and, 57, 59, 74–77, 75*b*, 197–198, 204–205
in biotech industry, 118*b*
collaboration and, 77
context and, 117
IDPs and, 147
line of sight and, 110
nature of work and, 39
setting, 108
team meetings
benefits of, 206
coaching during, 96
continuous feedback and, 50
continuous support and, 60
daily stand-up meetings, 96–97
discussion topics at, 111, 207*b*, 207–209
improvement of, 130
recognizing progress during, 97–98
teamwork. *See also* collaboration
in Agile work methodologies, 49–50
cross-functional, 38, 49, 118*b*
globalization and, 38
by Millennial and Gen Z workers, 42
as organizational capability, 28–29
technology. *See also* artificial intelligence
advantages and disadvantages, 180–181
for automation, 180, 183–184
as barrier to change, 4–5, 21–22
for collaboration, 40, 43, 188–189
digital transformation and, 37, 165
employee development and, 184–185, 211

Industrial Revolutions and, 35–37
nudge technology, 37, 184
organization network analysis, 188–189
for performance monitoring, 37, 185–188
for performance tracking, 43, 94, 184–188
PE supported through, 182–189
sociometric badges, 188
for streamlining, 183
tailoring to specific purposes, 181–182
talent management systems and, 181
Thaler, Richard, 19
Third Industrial Revolution, 35
Thorndike's law of effect, 16–17
360-degree feedback, 83, 128–129, 163
top performers, 54–55, 142, 167, 172, 210
Tournament Theory, 16, 156
tracking
compliance, 180
employee behavior, 156*b*, 188
performance, 43, 70, 94, 97–98, 184–188
progress toward goals, 115–116, 130, 147, 183, 184–185
verbal communication among team members, 83
training for managers
on bias, 195
on change management, 194–196
on check-ins, 86*b*
on coaching for future performance, 206
on employee development, 64, 177*b*
on feedback, 87, 126–127, 130, 195–196
on feedforward, 195–196, 206
Frame of Reference Training, 195
on goal-setting, 115*b*
on performance conversations, 101*b*, 195
on performance ratings, 161
transparency
coercive control's lack of, 26
of compensation, 172, 210–211
daily stand-up meetings and, 96–97
of employee development, 142*b*
enabling control and, 27–29
of feedback, 16, 182–183
of goals, 110, 114–115*b*, 115–117, 199
Millennial and Gen Z workers on, 43
of performance monitoring, 187
Tversky, Amos, 19

V

variable pay. *See also* bonuses
budgets for, 172
executive compensation and, 24–25
expansion of, 24–25, 167–168
shift from merit pay to, 172
unfair programs of, 169–170
Vogt, Otti, 29
Volatility, Uncertainty, Complexity, and Ambiguity (VUCA), 46–47, 50

W

wages. *See* compensation
Walmart, 158–160*b*, 160*f*, 210
Waters, Shonna, 85*b*
Weber, Max, 26
Welch, Jack, 24–25, 162
wicked problems, 4–5
workforce transformation
alternative employment arrangements, 43–44
digital transformation, 37, 165
globalization and increased competition, 37–38
growing complexity and increase in collaboration, 38–40
hybrid and remote workers, 40
Industrial Revolutions and, 35–37
knowledge workers, 41–42
Millennial and Gen Z workers, 42–43
work-planning-and review (WP&R), 138